MACHADO DE ASSIS, THE BRAZILIAN PYRRHONIAN

Purdue Studies in Romance Literatures

MACHADO DE ASSIS, THE BRAZILIAN PYRRHONIAN

José Raimundo Maia Neto

Purdue University Press
West Lafayette, Indiana

98 97 96 95 94   5 4 3 2 1

The paper used in this book meets the minimum requirements of
American National Standard for Information Sciences—Permanence of
Paper for Printed Library Materials, ANSI Z39.48-1984.

Printed in the United States of America
Design by Anita Noble

Library of Congress Cataloging-in-Publication Data
Maia Neto, José Raimundo, 1959–
      Machado de Assis, the Brazilian Pyrrhonian / José Raimundo Maia
Neto
        p.   cm.   — (Purdue studies in Romance literatures ; v. 5)
      Includes bibliographical references and index.
      ISBN 1-55753-051-3 (alk. paper)
      1. Machado de Assis, 1839–1908—Philosophy. 2. Skepticism in
literature. I. Title. II. Series.
PQ9697.M18Z7153 1994
869.3—dc20   94–3008
                                                          CIP

**To my parents,
Célia e Américo**

In Memoriam
Professor José Raimundo Neto

Un philosophe digne de ce nom n'a jamais dit qu'une seule chose: encore a-t-il plutôt cherché à la dire qu'il ne l'a dite véritablement.

—Bergson

Contents

Contents

List of Abbreviations

The following abbreviations have been used to refer to the works of Machado de Assis:

CAM
Counselor Ayres' Memorial, trans. Helen Caldwell (Berkeley and Los Angeles: U of California P, 1972).

DC
Dom Casmurro, trans. Helen Caldwell (Berkeley and Los Angeles: U of California P, 1966).

DV
The Devil's Church and Other Stories, trans. Jack Schmitt and Lorie Ishimatsu (Austin: U of Texas P, 1977; Manchester: Carcanet, 1985).

E
Epitaph of a Small Winner, trans. William L. Grossman (New York: Noonday, 1952).

EJ
Esau and Jacob, trans. Helen Caldwell (Berkeley and Los Angeles: U of California P, 1965).

HG
The Hand and the Glove, trans. Albert I. Bagby, Jr. (Lexington: UP of Kentucky, 1970).

IG
Iaiá Garcia, trans. Albert I. Bagby, Jr. (Lexington: UP of Kentucky, 1977).

MJ I
Contos esparsos, org. R. Magalhães Júnior (Rio de Janeiro: Edições de Ouro, 1966).

MJ II
Contos esquecidos, org. R. Magalhães Júnior (Rio de Janeiro: Edições de Ouro, 1966).

MJ III
Contos recolhidos, org. R. Magalhães Júnior (Rio de Janeiro: Edições de Ouro, 1966).

OC
Obra completa, org. Afrânio Coutinho, 3 vols. (Rio de Janeiro: Editora José Aguilar, 1962).

OC-1937
Obras completas, 31 vols. (Rio de Janeiro and São Paulo: W. M. Jackson, 1937–58).

The following abbreviations have been used to refer to these works by others:

La
　Blaise Pascal, *Pensées,* trans. A. J. Krailsheimer, Lafuma ed. (London and New York: Penguin, 1988).

M
　Sextus Empiricus, *Against the Mathematicians,* trans. R. G. Bury, Loeb Classical Library (London: Heinemann; Cambridge: Harvard UP, 1933–49).

PH
　Sextus Empiricus, *Outlines of Pyrrhonism,* trans. R. G. Bury, Loeb Classical Library (London: Heinemann; Cambridge: Harvard UP, 1933–49).

Preface

Joaquim Maria Machado de Assis (1839–1908) wrote novels and short stories which—once philosophically analyzed—reveal a remarkable and original skeptical perspective. This perspective makes Machado the only Brazilian author who deserves a place in the history of the skeptical tradition. The defense of Machado's right to be included among the great modern skeptics is the main ambition of this book. For this reason, Machado's novels and short stories are here viewed as works written by a skeptical thinker rather than a literary author. Accordingly, the analytic position here assumed and the critical vocabulary and method employed are those of a philosopher, not of a literary critic. However, insofar as some basic literary techniques used by Machado are crucial to the skeptical position he develops, these techniques are taken into account in all chapters of this book.

I am grateful to CNPq (Conselho Nacional de Desenvolvimento Científico e Tecnológico) for the fellowship that made the research possible and to Capes (Coordenação de Aperfeiçoamento de Pessoal de Nível Superior) for the fellowship which enabled me to revise and develop further my work on Machado. I thank Eduardo Jardim de Moraes, Danilo Marcondes de Souza Filho, Vera Cristina Bueno, and Kátia Muricy from the Philosophy Department of the Catholic University in Rio de Janeiro for their help with this project in its early stages. I also thank Luiz Fernando Carvalho, Oswaldo Porchat Pereira, Ezequiel de Olaso, and the referees from Purdue Studies in Romance Literatures for their continuous support. Special thanks go to Richard A. Watson for many helpful suggestions.

I have modernized the Portuguese in all quotations from Machado. The basic edition used is the *Obra completa* organized by Afrânio Coutinho (1962), but the older 1937 Jackson edition was also used, for it contains some short stories not included in the 1962 edition. Except when referenced, the English translations are mine. Longer translations are found in the Appendix, keyed by the number following the reference for the Portuguese quotation.

Introduction

This is not the first study to examine the skepticism exhibited in the fiction of Machado de Assis.[1] It is, however, the first in which Machado's skepticism is identified as belonging to the Pyrrhonian tradition. This tradition originates with Pyrrho of Elis (from around 365 to 275 BC), flourishes from the first century BC to the third AD, and revives in the Renaissance, having become since then a major intellectual challenge to modern and contemporary philosophy.

Sextus Empiricus's writings are the only surviving primary source of information about ancient skeptical thought. In his *Outlines of Pyrrhonism,* Sextus provides a comprehensive characterization of ancient Pyrrhonism. He defines it as

> an ability, or mental attitude, which opposes appearances to judgements in any way whatsoever, with the result that, owing to the equipollence of the objects and reasons thus opposed, we are brought firstly to a state of mental suspense and next to a state of "unperturbedness" or quietude. (PH 1.8)

Sextus carefully indicates that Pyrrhonism is not a philosophical system in the sense of an interrelated body of doctrines. He calls it, instead, an ability. The Pyrrhonian does not hold the position that knowledge cannot be achieved, nor is he committed to any of the arguments he uses to attack dogmatism. He has no doctrine about the possibility of attaining knowledge. All he has is an ability to examine any piece of knowledge held by dogmatic thinkers (defined by Sextus as those who hold doctrines about the nature of things) in order to check its cogency. The arguments the Pyrrhonian uses in this examination are eliminated as soon as they do the job of refuting the doctrine under consideration in the same way that purgatives are expelled together with the humors they are intended to remove (PH 1.206 and M 8.479–81). This elimination is brought about by the equipollence established by the Pyrrhonian: since the counter-arguments he brings forth against a doctrine are as persuasive as the doctrine they contradict, both are discarded. The Pyrrhonian reports that because he has not found any conclusive evidence either that there is some criterion for truth or that there is no such criterion, he continues his examination (PH 1.3).

1

Sextus's definition alludes to what can be described as the Pyrrhonian's journey. The Pyrrhonian-to-be begins like any "man of talent" disturbed by conflicting appearances (PH 1.12). For example, honey appears sweet at one moment and sour at another. These conflicting appearances create a mental disturbance. The Pyrrhonian-to-be then begins an inquiry (*zetesis*), hoping to attain tranquility (*ataraxia*) by ascertaining the true nature of honey. According to Sextus, this initial stage of the Pyrrhonian-to-be's journey is one that the dogmatist also experiences. The dogmatic philosopher, however, finds tranquility by discovering (what he thinks is) the true nature of the thing. For instance, he postulates a theory of what honey really is that explains to his satisfaction the conflicting appearances, thereby resolving his internal confusion. The Pyrrhonian-to-be holds that dogmatic tranquility is only attained through rash or precipitate judgment. More rigorous inquiry shows either that the explanation of the conflicting appearance is not satisfactory (it may have some logical flaw, for example), that there are other theories inconsistent with the one in question that also explain the appearances, or that there are other appearances or arguments—overlooked by dogmatists—that invalidate the explanation. Dogmatic tranquility is not solid after all, because none of the doctrines the Pyrrhonian has examined have resisted a more rigorous inquiry.

Thus the Pyrrhonian's journey differs from the dogmatist's in that instead of arriving at a doctrine, his inquiry (*zetesis*) leads him to equipollence. Unable to choose one doctrine or its contrary, he suspends judgment (*epoche*) and unexpectedly attains the tranquility (*ataraxia*) he initially hoped to achieve by finding the truth (PH 1.29). While one can understand why dogmatic tranquility may be fragile, Sextus does not explain why *ataraxia* follows from *epoche*. Some explanations of this psychological outcome of suspension of judgment as well as criticisms and solutions to problems in the Pyrrhonian's journey will be discussed in connection with Machado's text in the body of this study.

Sextus reports that the main arguments the Pyrrhonians use in their inquiry about philosophical dogmas were classified by earlier Pyrrhonians in various numbers of *tropoi* or modes. Sextus lists one set of *tropoi* supposedly collected by the

Pyrrhonian Aenesidemus (first century BC) and another systematized by a second follower of Pyrrho, Agrippa (first century AD).

Aenesidemus lists ten modes. The first mode is based on the variety observed in animals. Since different animal species have different sense organs, each processes different information about the reality of things. It is therefore an unjustified presumption to assume that humans are the only beings capable of grasping the true nature of things. The second derives from the variety in human beings: people have different sense organs because of differing natural (genetic) characteristics, and "[w]hen the Dogmatists—a self-loving class of men—assert that in judging things they ought to prefer themselves to other people, we know that their claim is absurd; for they themselves are a party to the controversy" (PH 1.90). The third comes from the difference among the senses. Two sense organs may give contradictory information about the same external object, leading to opposing conclusions. How, then, does one decide which conclusion is correct? The fourth appeals to the different circumstances that are always biasing perceptions and conceptions—either dispositions of mood or bodily conditions (such as age) or mental states (such as sleeping or waking). The fifth is based on positions, distances, and locations:

> all apparent objects are viewed in a certain place (the light of a lamp appears dim in the sun but bright in the dark [PH 1.119]), and from a certain distance (the same tower from a distance appears round but from a near point quadrangular [PH 1.118]), or in a certain position. (PH 1.121)

One cannot, therefore, make assertions about the external nature of the object because objects are always located in a particular place and position. The sixth derives from the fact that objects are never perceived all by themselves but through some media or blended with some other object (one cannot therefore know whether what one perceives is the particular object or its admixture with something else). The seventh is based "on the quantity and constitution of the underlying object" (PH 1.129). For example, "food exhibits different effects according to the quantity consumed" (PH 1.131); therefore, one cannot claim to have knowledge of the nature of food, since such knowledge requires knowledge of its effects. The eighth "is that based on relativity; and by it we conclude that, since all things are relative, we shall suspend judgement as to what things are absolutely and really existent" (PH 1.135). The ninth is based on constancy or rarity of occurrence. For example, "if we should imagine gold to be simply scattered in quantities over the earth like stones, to whom do we suppose it would then be precious and worth hoarding?" (PH 1.143). Or, to cite an early precursor of Machado's skeptics, Captain Mendonça:

> —Aos olhos do mundo o diamante é a riqueza, bem sei; mas é a riqueza relativa. Suponha . . . que as minas de carvão do mundo inteiro . . . se transformam em diamante. De um dia para outro o mundo caía na miséria. O carvão é a riqueza; o diamante é o supérfluo. (MJ III 174; see Appendix 1)

Finally, the tenth concerns customs, laws, and opinions: because they vary and conflict in time and space, one cannot judge which is true absolutely.

Agrippa describes five modes based on, first, relativity; second, conflict of opinions (to take a position is to be trapped in the conflict, so unable to judge); third, circular reasoning (in order to prove a proposition one appeals to another, which in turn, in order to be proved, must rely on the first); fourth, infinite regress (if one tries to avoid circular reasoning by appealing to a third proposition, the latter must be proved by appeal to a fourth, and so forth *ad infinitum*); and fifth, hypothesis (the only way to avoid both circular reasoning and infinite regress is to leave a proposition ungrounded, which is arbitrary) (PH 1.164–77). We shall see that Machado's skeptics—who are not strictly philosophers—employ Aenesidemus's *tropoi* rather than Agrippa's.

Two final points about ancient Pyrrhonism must be stated briefly. The first is that the Pyrrhonian does not suspend judgment about the appearances that strike either his senses or his intellect. He does not deny that he tastes the sweetness of honey, for example, but instead suspends judgment as to whether or not honey is sweet. The Pyrrhonian's acknowledgment of appearances is crucial for his practical life, for these appearances (among which he includes the laws and customs of the place where he lives; natural instincts, such as thirst [which leads him to drink] and hunger [which leads him to eat]; and natural intellectual and bodily functions, such as thinking, perceiving, etc.) are the criteria according to which he lives (PH 1.22). The point is that the Pyrrhonian never assents to anything voluntarily. He "assents" to appearances because such assent, being compulsory, does not depend on his will. Accordingly, all his statements are mere descriptions of the appearances that strike him. The Pyrrhonian does not have any epistemic commitment to his utterances (M 7.159–60 and 8.443–44).

The second point concerns the limits of Pyrrhonian therapy, which is effective only when beliefs are involved. The disquiet caused by pain, for example, cannot be avoided by Pyrrhonian *zetesis,* but Pyrrhonism can mitigate the accompanying passions insofar as they are strengthened by beliefs. Sextus claims that besides the pain caused by some external object, for example, one feels the extra disturbance of believing that the pain being felt is an evil. The Pyrrhonian is able to quell this extra disturbance by suspending judgment about the nature of good and evil (PH 1.29–30 and M 11.110–67). We shall see that these two points are crucial for consideration of the skepticism present in Machado's fiction.

There were two skeptical traditions in antiquity, the Pyrrhonian just described and the Academic (by Pyrrho's time, Plato's Academy had become skeptic, remaining so until 200–100 BC). Because Machado's skepticism is closer to Pyrrhonism, the exposition of this type suffices as background for the analysis that follows. However, Machado's connection with the skeptical tradition was not directly with ancient Pyrrhonism. Machado's library did not contain a copy of any of Sextus's works nor of any ancient source of skepticism (Massa). Besides, Sextus was probably very little known in Brazil at the time. However, Machado did know the ancient skeptical tradition, because he possessed early modern works that dealt extensively with ancient Pyrrhonism. Both his library and his writings show that Montaigne—and above all, Pascal—are his main sources of Pyrrhonism.[2] It is therefore necessary to extend this brief review of the history of skepticism up to the early modern period.

After the decline of ancient skepticism, skeptical *tropoi* were again used by some church fathers—Lactantius, in particular. The church fathers employed the *tropoi* not to attain tranquility (as the Pyrrhonians did) nor out of intellectual integrity (the Academic skeptics' supreme commitment) but to show the inability of unaided reason to attain truth and goodness, thereby justifying the need for revelation. Skepticism almost disappeared during the Middle Ages and revived in the late Renaissance, mainly as a weapon used by Catholic fideists in the theological controversies of the Counter-Reformation. Catholics claimed that only by sticking to the tradition of the Roman Catholic church could one avoid skepticism about religious knowledge. Richard H. Popkin (*History of Scepticism*) describes this revival and the spread of a debate that was initially about the rule of faith to the philosophical problem of the criterion of truth. Popkin shows that this debate culminated in Descartes's monumental effort to overcome the skeptical challenge. Not only Descartes but also philosophers such as Sanchez, Gassendi, and Mersenne used skeptical arguments to defeat Aristotelian philosophy, thereby paving the way to the New Science.

Even more than as a means to build a new science, skepticism was used by Renaissance authors (Agrippa von Nettesheim, Pico della Mirandola, Michel de Montaigne, and Pierre Charron) to show the vanity of human knowledge in general and the need to embrace the Christian religion on the basis of faith alone (Popkin, *History of Scepticism*). Montaigne was the most influential among these authors and a most valuable modern source of ancient Pyrrhonism given that, particularly in his "Apology for Raymond Sebond," he reproduces and develops the main Pyrrhonian modes as well as the Pyrrhonian's goal of tranquility and rules of life. Montaigne thought that the Pyrrhonian sage—tranquil, following the customs of his country, rejecting the proud and vain speculation of philosophy, and accepting Christian faith as the supernatural solution to human natural ignorance—was the best alternative both to the too rigorous Stoic sage and to the too lax Epicurean moralist.

In the seventeenth century, skeptically inclined thinkers were divided into two groups. La Mothe le Vayer, Simon Foucher, Pierre-Daniel Huet, and Pierre Bayle were full supporters of the skeptical tradition. They employed skeptical arguments against both Scholastic and modern philosophies and claimed that skepticism is the ancient philosophy most consistent with Christianity, since it teaches humility by pointing to the frailty of human reason and senses. The second group was composed of Augustinians, who believed in the doctrine of human depravity. They accepted epistemological skepticism but qualified it as the punishment for Original Sin. The main representative of this group is Blaise Pascal.

Pascal radically modifies the skeptical tradition by qualifying skepticism as the epistemological result of the Fall of Man. This implies a rupture with the ancient skeptics' commitment to *ataraxia* (ignorance is not a tranquil state, but a miserable one, for humans were created capable of an intuitive knowledge that they actually and fully enjoyed in the state of innocence) and to intellectual integrity (for humans are presently morally *and intellectually* corrupt). Philosophical solutions to skepticism are, according to Pascal, impossible. On the other hand, skepticism as suspension of judgment is equally rejected. Human beings are either frustrated dogmatic thinkers (for Pascal agrees with the skeptic that doubt can always be raised against claims of knowledge) or frustrated skeptics (for he argues that nature and ordinary life oblige one to believe, despite the lack of epistemological ground). This tragic human condition is only overcome by Christian faith, to which reason must submit.

Pascal was a sharp critic of (pagan) philosophy in general and, in particular, of Stoicism. According to Pascal, Stoicism is the philosophical doctrine that most emphasizes what he considers the major aim of most philosophical inquiries, viz., an attempt at divinization or—in the case of the Christian philosophers—redemption of humankind, through human knowledge. The Jansenists are well known for denouncing as Pelagianism (the heresy of denying or mitigating Original Sin) any position according to which the natural reason of humans can conduct them to truth and virtue without the assistance of divine grace. Whereas Pascal sees in Epictetus the paradigm of Pelagianism, we shall see that Brás Cubas sees it in Quincas Borba's "Humanitism." The analysis of *Memórias póstumas de Brás Cubas (Epitaph of a Small Winner)* provided in Chapter Five shows that divinization of humankind is the basic feature of Humanitism and the main target of the narrator Brás Cubas.

7

Pascal is the main influence on Machado's skepticism. Pascal's Christianized form of ancient skepticism is identifiable in the skeptical crisis presented in *Epitaph*. In his subsequent novels, Machado moves away from Pascal, getting closer to ancient Pyrrhonism. By refusing Pascal's leap of faith and by pursuing *ataraxia* in authorship and in an aesthetic-cognitive stance in life, Machado "dechristianizes" the skepticism that Pascal had Christianized.

Skepticism as an intellectual movement becomes less relevant during the eighteenth and nineteenth centuries. "Skepticism" becomes associated with skepticism about religion, whereas epistemological skepticism is by-and-large absorbed by philosophers who no longer hope to attain absolute, certain knowledge, contenting themselves with probable and hypothetical science. This is the position of Auguste Comte, who, by Machado's time, was very influential in Brazil. Some of Comte's enthusiastic Brazilian followers believed that the development of the sciences—in particular of the positive science of society—would lead to the solution of all human problems (cognitive, moral, political, etc.). It was in reacting against this excessive optimism that Machado turned to the skeptical authors of the seventeenth century, finding in them inspiration to develop his own—unique—skeptical position.

Although the skepticism in Machado's fiction is quite consistent with Pyrrhonism, it is framed in terms of specific Machadian themes dealt with throughout his fiction. Most of these themes concern social life in one way or another. This fact shows Machado's immersion in the Brazilian intellectual milieu of his time, a milieu that exalted not only Comte's positive sociology but also Spencer's social evolutionism. Nonetheless, Machado's interest in social life is not sociological but philosophical. He is concerned with philosophical anthropology (What meaning and function does social life have in human life?), ontology (What is the status of social reality?), and ethics (What is the value of social life? Is it good or evil?). As noted by Raimundo Faoro in *A pirâmide e o trapézio*, Machado de Assis sees social life from the point of view of the so-called French moralists of the seventeenth century such as Pascal, La Bruyère, La Fontaine, and La Rochefoucauld.

Machado de Assis is not a philosopher *stricto sensu*. The aforementioned philosophical questions are embodied in fictional situations, motifs, characters, life-views, and other elements proper to fictional literature. In order to capture the uniqueness of the skepticism and its resolution, which Machado carefully constructs throughout his fiction, basic categories that appear, above all, in Machado's first phase are employed in this study. When these categories are rendered problematic at the end of his first phase and during his second, the skeptical life-view becomes possible.[3] The main categories are the following:

1. *vida exterior* ("outward life"): social life as viewed by Blaise Pascal, *locus* of *divertissement* and of precarious beliefs, of duality, strategy, and hypocrisy;

2. *paz doméstica* ("domestic peace"): the environment associated with marriage, set apart from the outward life, *locus* of truth, transparency, and morality;

3. *homem de espírito* ("spiritual man"): ethical character, indifferent and/or hostile to the outward life; and

4. *tolo* ("vulgar man"): immoral character, well adjusted to the outward life.[4]

Putting it briefly, the hypothesis presented in this study is that Machado develops the skeptical life-view as the theoretical and practical alternative available to the *homem de espírito* when outward life becomes hegemonic, that is, when the alternative of truth and morality in the domestic peace of marriage is no longer available (this is the occasion of the characters' skeptical crisis). The uniqueness of Machadian skepticism within the skeptical tradition lies, above all, in the solution he presents: to assume the stance of spectator and become an author of memoirs.

In Machado de Assis, the disturbance of conflicting appearances arises from social life and women. Women are the main objects of perplexity and the main source of disturbance for *homens de espírito*—Machado's equivalent to Sextus's "man of talent" (PH 1.12). The characters that most clearly exhibit the skeptical life-view—Brás Cubas, Dom Casmurro, and Aires—go through *zetesis, epoche,* and *ataraxia*. These three stages are not completely defined at the outset of Machado's second phase. The development of the skeptical life-view is exhibited in the progressive and increasing definition and elaboration of each stage: *zetesis* with Brás Cubas, *epoche* with Dom Casmurro, and *ataraxia* with Aires (although Brás Cubas exhibits embryonic *epoche* and *ataraxia* and Dom Casmurro an embryonic *ataraxia*).

The skepticism in Machado's fiction is here considered to be not just one of its features but its foundation. The thesis presented in this study is that the totality of Machado's fiction can be organically and chronologically understood in terms of first a gestation and then an evolution of a skeptical life-view. The gestation occurs during Machado's first phase, the evolution during the second. The gestation and development are structured on two levels: there is, first, an increasing elaboration of the characterization of the outsider and, second, an adjustment of the literary forms of the novels and short stories to the skeptical life-view that these outsiders exhibit. Machado's main skeptical characters are the fictional authors of his novels, but the skeptical life-view can also be attributed to the fictional authors of the short stories of his second phase. Some of these authors are discussed in Chapter Three. However, examination of Brás Cubas, Dom Casmurro, and Counselor Aires suffices to delineate the skeptical character and the development of his life-view.

In the first four chapters of this study, I examine a sample of Machado's work belonging to his first phase and identify the predecessors of his skeptical characters. These predecessors suffer from a problematic condition that is resolved in the second phase by their adoption of a skeptical life-view.

In the last three chapters, I present detailed analyses of the skeptical narrators and their narratives, focusing on the constitution of each character, the kind of skepticism exhibited, and the relevance of the literary form of each narrative in the context of the developing skeptical life-view. This development has three stages: the first corresponds to Brás Cubas, the second to Dom Casmurro, and the third and final one to Counselor Aires. Because I identify Machado's literary development with the chronological development of the skeptical life-view, I compare each work with preceding and succeeding short stories and novels.

My assessment of the skeptical life-view in Machado's fiction is enhanced by references to three other life-views that are counterpoints to the skeptical one. The first, peculiar to Machado's first phase, is not exactly a life-view, but rather a predicament that I call "problematic." In this predicament one is divorced from (social) life. It is a pre-reflective, unstable state exhibited by the *homens de espírito* who do not get married or who marry but do not find domestic peace in marriage. Before suffering the skeptical crisis, the *homem de espírito* holds beliefs (*dogmas* in Sextus Empiricus's sense of the term) concerning the possibility of living an ethical life and the existence of truth alternative to the false appearances of social life. I thus call "naive" the nonreflective life-view exhibited by the *homem de espírito* before his skeptical crisis. Finally, I call "strategic" the life-view exhibited by the *tolos* of the first phase, by their successors (the "stuffed shirts" and the bonze's disciples) of Machado's second phase, and by the majority of Machado's female characters. These characters exhibit an intuitive knowledge of social life. Their life-view is opposed to the skeptical life-view in that their "knowledge" is pragmatic instead of theoretical, and their action is unethical. The characters that exhibit the strategic life-view manipulate social appearances in order to attain social, economic, political, and sentimental success. The strategic life-view is explicitly elaborated in the short story "Teoria do medalhão" ("Education of a stuffed shirt").

Quincas Borba (Philosopher or Dog?) is not discussed in this study. Although it is regarded as one of Machado's best novels, it is, nevertheless, not a first-person novel and so does not provide a narrator-character. For this reason, I have not considered it in this analysis.

All of Machado's novels and most of his short stories are structured by a sentimental triangle: a woman and two men who exhibit opposing life-views. On the one hand there is the *tolo* (first phase) or "stuffed shirt" (second phase), who exhibits the strategic life-view. On the other there is the *homem de espírito,* who exhibits the naive life-view. Because the woman usually prefers the *tolo* or "stuffed shirt" (see Chapter One), the *homem de espírito* becomes either a problematic character (first phase) or a skeptical one (second phase). The main difference between the two phases is that in the first phase the *homem de espírito*'s experience of separation from woman (active life) makes him a problematic (mad, suicidal, displaced) character (see Chapter Three), while in the second he becomes a reflective character who is also a narrator. Authorship is an alternative stance that allows the expression of the skeptical life-view.

Philosopher or Dog?, a second-phase work, is not an exception as far as the sentimental triangle goes. The difference is that the *homem de espírito* in the novel (Rubião), unlike Brás

Cubas and Dom Casmurro, does not adopt the skeptical life-view. The naive man's failure to establish a satisfactory relationship with Sofia (that is, his failure to engage with the world) instead makes him a problematic character. In place of becoming a writer of memoirs and expressing a reflective view, he goes mad. Accordingly, the narrator of *Philosopher or Dog?* is omniscient. The situation in the novel is then equivalent to that of Machado's first phase, discussed in Chapter Three. The presence of a skeptical life-view requires first-person narration by the character divorced from the world (woman). Although *Philosopher or Dog?* is an interruption in the development toward Pyrrhonism that underlies Machado's second phase, I do not think that the novel is inferior to the others nor am I suggesting that it adds nothing to the short stories and novels of Machado's first phase. The skeptical life-view, the main novelty in the second phase, is omitted, but *Philosopher or Dog?* does show a remarkable development of the other two life-views. The problematic condition of Rubião is far more complex, subtle, and interesting than that of the problematic characters of the first phase discussed in Chapter Three. In *Philosopher or Dog?* Machado interrupts his development of the skeptical life-view to explore the problematic condition in a context in which the strategic life-view (Palha and Carlos Maria) and the characterization of woman (Sofia) are far more sophisticated than they are in the first phase. However, since this does not advance the skeptical life-view, I do not discuss the novel here.

The protagonists I will study are Machado's narrator-characters Brás Cubas, Dom Casmurro, and Aires. Because their reliability has been under attack by critics of the last two decades, I shall explain why I depart from the mainstream of Machado's contemporary scholarship. The attack begins on Dom Casmurro (Caldwell; Ellis; and Gledson, *Deceptive Realism*), then envelopes Brás Cubas (Kinnear; Nunes, *Craft;* and Schwarz), and has also touched Aires (Gledson, "Last Betrayal").

J. C. Kinnear argues that the problem of reliability "sums up one of the major differences between the novels of Machado's two periods: in the first, the narrator is to be believed, in the second he is to be doubted at every turn" (Kinnear 54). A point generally agreed upon by Machado scholars is that the shift from the omniscient to the restricted first-person narrator is the determining factor of the transformation that occurs in Machado's fiction with *Epitaph*. This transformation marks the beginning of Machado's second phase, during which he wrote his best novels and short stories. One of my main points in this study is that the appearance of first-person narration made possible the expression of the skeptical life-view. I agree with Kinnear and others that unlike the narrators of the first phase, those of the second have a problematic relation with truth. The omniscient narrators of the first phase have nonproblematic access to the truth; the restricted narrators of the second have views conditioned and limited by their positions in the plot.

My disagreement with the critics begins when they claim that Brás Cubas's, Dom Casmurro's, and Aires's views are either false or partial in the sense that they do not present the whole truth that is present in the novel. This implies that it is then the job of the critic to uncover the true picture (or the whole truth) that is assumed to be implicit or hidden in the novel. My disagreement increases when the critics claim, as Kinnear's statement quoted above suggests, that the narrators are unreliable in the sense that they deliberately misrepresent the story. Given that every single word in the novels is written by the *fictional* authors, how do the critics circumvent the views of these designated authors to reach the views of the "real" author (Machado)? I have identified three major strategies used to transcend the narrator's discourse in order to disclose a "real" or "implied" author's view. In what follows, I summarize these strategies and criticize some examples. Criticism of some examples, of course, does not invalidate the strategies *per se*. My purpose is to show what kind of problems can be avoided by pursuing another line of critical inquiry.

A first strategy employed by the critics to reveal Machado's views is to pick an event in the plot, usually one not directly related to the narrator's experience, and interpret it as an "authorial statement." Anne-Marie Gill pursues this approach with respect to *Dom Casmurro*.

> The opera [a theory about creation developed by a secondary character] has the effect of a metafictional reflection on the way in which reading *Dom Casmurro* provides a more satisfactory run of the "opera." It is an authorial statement

> on the unity of the novel, on the control which the "real au-
> thor" exerts over his narrative persona's apparent narration.
> (Gill 24)

I do not see why "the opera" should be an authorial statement
rather than a statement made by the narrator, nor how it can
show the "real author's" control over the narrative and not Dom
Casmurro's. It is Dom Casmurro who notices and points out
this relation between his life (the plot) and the theory of "the
opera." Indeed, his recognition of the connection is the reason
for presenting the theory in his memoirs. The reader has no
access to the "opera theory" other than Dom Casmurro's report
of it. If he is unreliable, so is the theory as described in the novel.

A second critical strategy for revealing Machado's views is
to identify ambiguity in the narration, described by Kinnear as
"one set of words with different meanings for narrator and author" (Kinnear 65). Helen Caldwell and Keith Ellis use this
strategy to analyze *Dom Casmurro;* Kinnear for *Epitaph, Philosopher or Dog?,* and *Dom Casmurro;* Maria Luisa Nunes for
Epitaph and *Dom Casmurro;* and Roberto Schwarz for *Epitaph.*
Since I contend with Schwarz and Caldwell, respectively, in my
chapters on *Epitaph* and *Dom Casmurro,* I limit myself here
first to an example of this procedure by Kinnear on *Epitaph,*
and then another by Nunes on *Dom Casmurro.* I have selected
these two examples because they deal with philosophers belonging to the skeptical tradition.

Kinnear makes the following assertions:

> Machado, like his model [Erasmus], criticizes through
> sustained irony all that his character praises. . . . in the chap-
> ter in which Quincas Borba, a madman, puts forward his
> *teoria do benefício,* which is that the donor receives more
> pleasure than the recipient. Quincas assumes that Erasmus
> and not Folly spoke the *Praise* and uses it to support his
> argument. It is not difficult to see Machado using Quincas
> in the way that Erasmus uses Folly, namely to highlight cer-
> tain features which the narrator praises and the author criti-
> cizes. (62)

This example shows that a distinction more fruitful than the one
between narrator and author in *Epitaph* and *Dom Casmurro* is
that between the active characters Bento and Brás Cubas and

the withdrawn authors Dom Casmurro and the deceased Brás Cubas. Going back to Gill's approach, I grant that Bento is certainly unaware that he is performing in "the opera." This occurs to him only later, when he withdraws from active life and becomes an author (Dom Casmurro). In the same way, I will show in Chapter Five that if the living Brás Cubas praises Quincas Borba's values, Brás Cubas, the deceased writer, is a bitter critic of them. If Brás Cubas, the live character, holds Folly's view, Brás Cubas, the deceased writer, holds Erasmus's.

Nunes makes the following statement:

> In Chapter LXVIII, Casmurro's reference to Montaigne's autobiography is a clear indication of the ambiguity of first-person narratives. Like Montaigne, Casmurro knows that confessional literature can never achieve truth. (*Craft* 176)

Neither Montaigne nor Dom Casmurro claims to have achieved truth. In the passage referred to by Nunes, all Dom Casmurro says is that he is not hiding anything about himself, that "he tell[s] it all, the good and the bad" (DC 138). He tells exactly—and nothing more—what he is in a position to tell: his impressions of himself and of the external world. Instead of inviting the reader to rely on the "implied author" for the objective, true story of the plot, the comparison with Montaigne suggests that there is no access to an objective truth independent of a first-person narrator's impression of it.

Most cases of ambiguity can be resolved without appealing to an "implied author" once the views held by the withdrawn narrator and the active character are distinguished. I give examples of this resolution in my chapters on *Epitaph* and *Dom Casmurro*. However, regardless of whether or not such resolution is possible, why should we suppose that the *narrator* does not intend to create ambiguity? Statement of contrary views to force the suspension of judgment (not to uncover some hidden truth) is, after all, the Pyrrhonian's characteristic procedure.

The third main strategy used by critics to go beyond the narrators' discourse consists in providing metaphorical or, as John Gledson puts it, "allegorical," interpretations of events in the plot that reveal their true, hidden meanings, which supposedly differ from, or even contradict, the narrator's view of the facts.

The problem with this approach is that the scope of possible interpretations is infinite. Allegorical or metaphorical interpretations tend to be speculative. A case in point is Gledson's interpretation of *Counselor Ayres' Memorial*. From the name Tristão and the fact that Tristão once plays Wagner on the piano, Gledson deduces the character's relation to Tristan of Wagner's *Tristan und Isolde*. He then takes this as evidence for his reconstruction of the plot. Fidélia met Tristão in Portugal "just as Tristan and Isolde met before in Ireland" (Gledson, "Last Betrayal" 143), and their marriage represents Portugal's (Tristão's) seizure of Brazilian wealth (Fidélia). "This Tristan and Isolde," concludes Gledson, "are not joined by a magic potion, but by 300 *contos,* and their love affair is not tragic, but scandalously successful" ("Last Betrayal" 144). This interpretation is so speculative that it is no wonder it is "secreted from the other characters, from the narrator, perhaps even from the author" (Gledson, "Last Betrayal" 150).

My reliance on Machado's narrators and my objections to both the "ambiguity" and the "allegorical" approaches can be justified fully only if I succeed in persuading the reader that Machado deals with epistemological problems throughout his fiction and develops a skeptical resolution of them. The restricted, conditioned, and subjective view of the narrators is a statement about the limits of knowledge that obtain in the world. Many of the often-mentioned "gaps" the reader finds in Machado's second-phase novels can be "filled" by the critic only at the cost of disregarding Machado's skepticism. The scholar interested in capturing Machado's skeptical position must tolerate and accept as definitive—as all that can ever be known or as all there is—the limited, subjective, biased view exhibited by the narrators. To suggest that an independent, objective, complete, or even certain truth is hidden in the plot or not revealed by the narrator—be it "love," "quest myth," criticism of nineteenth-century Brazilian liberal ideology, or whatever—is to abandon the Pyrrhonian framework within which these narrators are located and to adopt the very dogmatic framework (in Sextus Empiricus's sense of the term) from which Machado distances himself. Such a procedure therefore falsifies Machado's own development from the dogmatic-omniscient narrators of the first phase to the skeptical-restricted narrators of the second.

Among the critics who have dealt with the problem of the reliability of Machado's narrators, Paul B. Dixon is probably the most sensitive to the epistemological import of the narrator's stance. Although he sees a criticism of the quest myth behind the surface of *Dom Casmurro,* he is reluctant to attribute this "skeptical perspective" to the "implied author." In *Dom Casmurro,* he claims,

> there is very little space in which an "implied author" can operate. Implying something requires not saying it explicitly. The ironic implied author functions best when the narrator is limited in understanding or intelligence. . . . The fascinating problem with *Dom Casmurro* is that its narrator is highly intelligent, critical, and self-conscious. Rather than leaving room for that other, implied author to provide an ironic critique of his attitudes, he does so himself. . . . While I recognize that *Dom Casmurro* is ultimately Machado's creation, it is more to the point to show how the *narrator* displays a mythic mentality in this book. (11–12)

Leaving the question of what Dom Casmurro displays to Chapter Six, I am in complete agreement with Dixon's methodological point. What he says of Dom Casmurro is equally applicable to Brás Cubas and Aires. If there are hidden meanings in *Epitaph, Dom Casmurro, Esau and Jacob,* and *Counselor Ayres' Memorial,* to find them I refer the reader to the variety of suggestions made by contemporary critics mentioned above. The contribution I offer in this book is more modest and preliminary. Because Machado's narrators are "highly intelligent, critical, and self-conscious," I find it worthwhile to focus on the life-view they exhibit. I first point to its roots in Machado's early fiction. Then I analyze the turns and developments from Brás Cubas to Dom Casmurro to Aires, indicate their relevance to the history of skepticism and of modern philosophy in general, and show how they reveal the architectonic character of Machado's fiction.

Part 1
Machado's First Phase
(1861 to 1878)

Chapter One

An Essay of 1861 and
the Short Stories from 1862 to 1871

In his first published work, Machado de Assis introduces two life-views in rudimentary form: the naive and the strategic. "Queda que as mulheres têm para os tolos" ("Women's preference for *tolos*") is an essay, not a novel. The essay form allows Machado to characterize these two life-views directly and explicitly, and this is the only occasion on which he does so.

Three types of people are defined in "Women's preference": the woman, the *tolo* ("vulgar man"), and the *homem de espírito* ("spiritual man"). Machado describes the relationships that obtain among them, asserting, as the title suggests, that the essence of these relationships lies in women's preference for *tolos* over *homens de espírito*. "A conclusão final," concludes a resigned author, "é, que os tolos triunfam, e os homens de espírito falham [nos seus projetos afetivos]" (OC 3: 972) ("The final conclusion is that the *tolos* succeed and the *homens de espírito* fail [in their sentimental aspirations]").

Women's partiality for *tolos* is attributed to the differing personalities of *tolos* and *homens de espírito*. The *tolo* is self-assured, determined, and stubborn in his approach to women. He does not hesitate to simulate qualities and to feign passionate feelings whenever these attributes and appearances are instrumental in accomplishing his projects. The *homem de espírito*, however,

> [deixa-se] embalar por estranhas ilusões. . . . Imagina que para agradar-lhes [as mulheres] é preciso ter qualidades acima do vulgar. Naturalmente tímido, exagera mais ao pé delas a sua insuficiência. (OC 3: 967; see Appendix 2)

The two types also differ in the manner in which each type experiences love.

> [C]omo nos tolos tudo é superficial e exterior, não é o amor um acontecimento que lhes mude a vida: continuam como antes a dissipá-la nos jogos, nos salões e nos passeios. (OC 3: 967; see Appendix 3)

The *homem de espírito,* on the contrary,

> vê no amor um grande e sério negócio, ocupa-se dele como do mais grave interesse de sua vida, sem distração, nem reserva. (OC 3: 968; see Appendix 4)

The personal trait that enables the *tolo* to undertake the strategy of seduction successfully is his inward distance from affections.

> Como não é ele quem ama, é ele quem domina. Para vencer uma mulher finge por alguns momentos o excesso de desespero e de paixão; mas isso não passa de um meio de guerra, tática de cerco para enganar e seduzir o inimigo. (OC 3: 969; see Appendix 5)

Another component of the *tolo*'s strategy is love letters. They are merely rhetorical and although they impress the woman, they tell nothing of his true feelings and dispositions. His discourse is merely instrumental. He has "uma coleção de cartas prontas para todos os graus de paixão" ("a collection of ready-made letters for all degrees of love"), in which he claims "em linguagem brusca" ("in a grotesque language") "*o ardor de sua chama*" ("*the heat of his flame*"). His romantic rhetoric is "emphatic" and "boring," "nada que indique uma personalidade" ("nothing that might indicate a personality"). His lack of originality is crucial for his success: "é medíocre e ridículo, tanto melhor. . . . [N]a mocidade o pai da menina escrevia assim; a própria menina não esperava outra coisa" (OC 3: 971) ("He is mediocre and ridiculous, but so much the better. . . . During his youth the girl's father wrote in the same fashion; she herself did not expect anything different").

The *tolo*—the type that adopts the first version of the strategic life-view—appears very frequently in Machado's short stories of his early period. These characters are "libertines," "harebrains," or "dandies" whose essential and common characteristics are lack of morality and uniqueness. They perform instrumental actions that reveal the disparity between a very impersonal social appearance (external behavior) and hidden and perverse subjective dispositions (feelings and intentions). Their speech is full of romantic rhetoric and their actions conform to conventional social attitudes and behavior. They are, therefore, according to the narrator, vulgar people, "short of anything that might indicate a personality." In other words, the *tolo* has his singularity compromised by his social being. The actor is corrupted by the role.

In Machado's short stories belonging to this early period, the female characters more often than not explicitly prefer the *tolo,* for

> o homem de espírito, em vista do que é, inspira às mulheres uma secreta repulsa. Elas se admiram com o ver tímido, acanham-se com o ver delicado, humilham-se com vê-lo distinto, . . . o tolo não atrapalha, nem ofusca as mulheres. Desde a primeira entrevista, ele as anima e fraterniza-se com elas. Eleva-se sem acanhamento nas conversas mais insulsas, palra e requebra-se como elas. Compreende-as e elas o compreendem. Longe de se sentirem deslocadas na sua companhia, elas a procuram, porque brilham nela. Podem diante dele absorver todos os assuntos e conversar sobre tudo, inocentemente, sem consequência. (OC 3: 971; see Appendix 6)

The *homem de espírito* fails because he does not compromise with the patterns of social interest and conversation valued by women—the social "diversions" denounced by Pascal (La 132–39) for distracting man's attention from his miserable condition. He fails because he refuses to play society's game either for ethical reasons or from mere incompetence. For, "[p]ara conquistar esses entes frágeis e ligeiros, é preciso atordoá-los pelo rumor dos vossos louvores, pelo fasto de vosso vestuário, pela publicidade das vossas homenagens" (OC 3: 972) ("in order to conquer those fragile and fleeting beings, it is necessary to stun them with the wildness of your flatteries, with the extravagance of your clothes, with the publicity of your praises").

This description discloses a dramatic view of social life in which immoral roles are performed by mediocre actors. Exaggerated flattery, modern elegance, the public and social (instead of private and reserved) nature of sentimental interactions, in a word, the primacy and efficacy of public appearances frame the social scenario in which women are brought together with *tolos,* and *homens de espírito* are excluded.

Thus there can be found in one of Machado's first writings the elements that underlie social life, determining its negative meaning from the *homem de espírito*'s point of view. The *homem de espírito* himself, however, is almost completely devoid of such reflection. In this early work, his critical life-view is only alluded to by the author. The *homem de espírito* believes in the possibility of a moral life beyond the false appearances of strategic games. Because of these views, we say that he adopts the "naive life-view." His failures and exclusion, outcomes of his naïveté, render the type a problematic character during Machado's first phase. In a play written in this period— *Desencantos (Disenchantments)*—a *tolo* anticipates the disappearance of the *homem de espírito* that takes place in Machado's fiction between 1872 and 1878.

> Pedro Alves [the *tolo*]: —A corda em que acaba de tocar está desafinada há muito tempo e não dá som. O amor, o respeito, e a dedicação! Se o não conhecesse, diria que o senhor acaba de chegar do outro mundo.
> Luiz [the *homem de espírito*]: —Com efeito, pertenço a um mundo que não é absolutamente o seu. . . .
> Pedro Alves: —Já sei; pertence à esfera dos sonhadores e dos visionários. . . . É uma tribo que se não acaba, pelo que vejo?
> Luiz: —Ao que parece, não?
> Pedro Alves: —Mas é evidente que perecerá. (OC-1937 28: 40; see Appendix 7)

The *homem de espírito* gradually vanishes as Machado works out a solution to the predicament of his problematic character. This solution, which begins to take form in the 1879 novel *Memórias póstumas de Brás Cubas (Epitaph of a Small Winner),* is twofold. The practical solution is to take the stance of an observer. The theoretical solution is the adoption of a skeptical life-view. Some features of the *homem de espírito* anticipate this future solution. He wonders at, and becomes disturbed by, the rapid variations of mood and disposition in women:

> É possível que ela tenha mudado tão de repente? Pois não
> foi ainda ontem que . . . lhe enxugou o suor da testa? . . .
> Hoje, nem mais doçuras, nem mais apertos de mão. (OC
> 3: 970; see Appendix 8)

We shall see that as early as the short stories written in the 1872–78 period, but in particular in female characters of the second phase—Virgília, Capitu, and even Fidélia—the problem of life's finitude and precariousness is metaphorically expressed in the variable and uncertain behavior of women. This condition disturbs the observer. It is Machado's equivalent to fleeting and uncertain appearances that, according to Sextus, disturb the philosopher who pursues unchangeable truths behind conflicting appearances (PH 1.12).

The frequent emotional failures experienced by the *homem de espírito* occasion in him a shift of life-view that the *tolo* does not experience. Failures teach the *homem de espírito* that this world is far from being the kingdom of ethics he hopes for. This leads him to adopt a theoretical point of view and, insofar as this supports skepticism about the possibility of a moral life, it leads him also to inward detachment. This attitude provides some protection from emotional disappointment and mental disturbance, as the pragmatic stance is replaced by a contemplative one. The *homem de espírito* attempts to establish a new relationship with women that prefigures the aesthetic-cognitive solution to be embodied in Machado's last protagonist, Counselor Aires. The narrator of "Women's preference" says that the *homem de espírito* may acquire "uma certa dureza" ("a kind of hardness") after repeated experiences of deception, which enables him "aproximar-se sem perigo das mais belas e sedutoras" ("to get safely closer to the most beautiful and seductive women"). The narrator makes it clear that such an approach is not a pragmatic but an aesthetic one ("uma admiração de artista" ["an artist's kind of admiration"]). He adds that the *homem de espírito* also "ganha . . . uma penetração cruel para ver, através de todos os artifícios de casquilha, o que vale a submissão que elas ostentam, a doçura que afetam, a ignorância que fingem" (OC 3: 970) ("acquires a cruel sensibility to perceive behind all the superficial artifices, what worth there is in the submission they show, the sweetness they pretend, the ignorance they feign").

Note that a "cruel sensibility" makes it possible to unmask false social appearances, and that such appearances are, above all, associated with women who show themselves, who preen and pretend. Woman is the observer's main preoccupation and the cause of his disturbance throughout Machado's fiction. The skeptical life-view arises and unfolds during Machado's second phase (1879–1908) as a result of his reflections on woman. Woman stands for reality in Machado de Assis.[1] Reality is thus seen as essentially precarious, for it is identified with highly volatile social life.

The observer's stance is at this early period of Machado's work, however, far from being developed. Deception in love does not here lead the *homem de espírito* to the observer's stance, as it does later with Brás Cubas and Dom Casmurro. This alternative is not yet available for the character. The *homem de espírito* easily falls back on his previous problematic stance. It remains possible that he

> venha a sentir um amor tão puro, tão fervente, tão *ingênuo* como nos frescos anos da adolescência; *longe de ter perdido as perturbações* [emphasis added], . . . [ei-lo] obrigado a ajoelhar-se aos pés de uma mulher. (OC 3: 970; see Appendix 9)

Because the failures of the naive life-view do not yet lead to the solution provided by the skeptical life-view (which, according to Sextus, alone affords *ataraxia* or tranquility [M 11: 111–18]), these failures leave the character in a problematic situation. Refusing to be vulgar, manipulative, and duplicitous, and having to "fall on his knees," the *homem de espírito* is defeated by the very social life he rejects. The absence of the observer's alternative poses the question of what solution can be found for, as Machado puts it, "a disgraça dos homens de espírito" ("the *homem de espírito*'s disgrace"). Ironically, the narrator wonders why the *homem de espírito* does not study the *tolo*'s behavior in order to imitate him. "Há de custar-vos muito fazer um tal papel: mas há proveito sem desar?" (OC 3: 972) ("It must be hard to perform such a role: yet, is there profit without 'costs'?").

We shall see in Chapter Five that Brás Cubas attempts precisely this solution, paying all the costs of "performing such a role." Facing human misery in repeated instances, he ends up failing completely, as Machado anticipates in his 1861 essay. Machado's pessimism with respect to women's instability, that is, with respect to the human condition, is also already in place in the essay.

> [V]isto como não vos dão outro meio de solução, querer subtrair o belo sexo a império dos tolos, descortinando-lhe a perversidade do seu gosto, é coisa em que ninguém deve pensar, é uma loucura; fora o mesmo que querer mudar a natureza, ou contrariar a fatalidade. (OC 3: 972; see Appendix 10)

We thereby place Machado's second phase in a frame presented in his first work: the skeptical life-view will be the solution for the *homem de espírito* who is unable to lower himself to the level of the *tolo* or to change the nature of woman, that is, who is equally unable either to transform the immoral nature of social life or to compromise with it.

Such pessimism, however, although alluded to in "Women's preference," is fully present in Machado's fiction only after 1871. Between 1861 and 1871, as we will see in what follows, there are nevertheless female characters who deplore the frivolity of the *tolo,* preferring the *homem de espírito.* Thus the *homem de espírito* maintains his naive life-view during the 1861–71 period through marriage with one of these female characters, although these "mulheres de espírito" ("spiritual women") are not the majority even in this period. Marriage is the alternative to the immoral, impersonal, public social life. This picture precludes the development of the skeptical life-view. The so frequently mentioned and exalted "domestic peace" of marriage is the *locus* of truth, of transparency and morality, being the alternative to the "outward life": *locus* of false appearances, duplicity, and strategies. The preconditions for the occurrence of the skeptical crisis that inaugurates Machado's second phase first appear in Machado's fiction in the short stories written from 1872 onward. At this point, female characters having a strategic stance largely outnumber "spiritual women," and marriage becomes part of the very negative social life to which it was hitherto an alternative. In this way, that which was domestic peace becomes part of the outward life. The false appearances characteristic of outward life now corrupt the morality of marriage. Appearances corrupt the truth. Once the truth is no longer available for the *homens de espírito,* they become problematic characters.

***

The first short story to be examined is entitled "Confissões de uma viúva moça" ("Confessions of a young widow"). It was first published in a newspaper in 1865. Five years later, Machado included the story in his volume *Contos fluminenses (Short stories from Rio de Janeiro).* In the story, the widow "confesses" her regret for having let herself fall in love with a *tolo.* The short story illuminates some interesting features and thus throws light on Machado's future development.

"Confessions" is structured in epistolary form. From a withdrawn point of view, the widow writes letters to her friend Carlota. Petrópolis, where the writer resides, is located far from the agitated court of Rio. The distance is both spatial and temporal, for the reported events happened long ago. The widow's explicit goal is to warn her friend of the danger of being attracted by the passionate appearance of a "sedutor vulgar [que] só se diferençava dos outros em ter um pouco mais de habilidade que eles" (OC 2: 117) ("*tolo* seducer [who] differs from other [seducers] only in being a bit more skillful than they").

Although the widow was not happy with her husband, her mistake was to despise domestic peace and thus to be caught by the outward delights of social life. In the letters, the reader is told how this happened. The circumstance under which she first met the seducer points to the dramatic nature of social life: he looks at her with staring eyes in a theater. His second step is secretly to mail love letters to her in which he emphatically states his intense passion for her. Those letters are written in the romantic rhetorical style used strategically by the *tolo.* Although flattered, she at first resists. In reporting this period to her friend, she says that her self-love was instrumental in his success. The seducer's third step is Machiavellian. He develops a friendship with her husband, becoming his confidant and a frequent guest at their house. At the same time, he secretly keeps telling his new friend's wife how desperately in love with her he is. In response to her resistance, he feigns tears and despair and even hints at the possibility of committing suicide. In the narrator's household, he proves to be a perfect guest.

[O]lhar profundo e magnético, maneiras elegantes e deli-
cadas, certo ar distinto e próprio que fazia contraste com o
ar afetado e prosaicamente medido dos outros rapazes. . . .
[M]ostrava-se tão apreciador do gosto como era conversador
discreto e pertinente.
No fim da noite tinha cativado a todos. (OC 2: 105–06;
see Appendix 11)

Acting strategically, "sabia apresentar-se no momento mais
próprio a ocupar-me a imaginação como uma figura poética e
imponente" (OC 2: 106–07) ("he knew how to introduce himself at the most opportune moment and how to fill my imagination with his imposing and poetical image").

The seducer's success can be traced to his ability to present
himself as the "romantic-in-love" type of person, known by
women through the European romantic literature of the time,
and as a "social man," a caricature of the worldly gentleman
that Pascal tries to bring back to Christianity. This image causes
such an impression because it contrasts with the prosaic,
"down-to-earth" figure of Brazilian husbands of the day. The
narrator's husband, "apesar de franco cavalheiro . . . , não tinha
o dom particular de um conviva para tais reuniões" (OC 2: 105)
("although a frank gentleman . . . , did not have the [social] gifts
of a guest at these parties"). Unlike her husband, "[a]quele
homem parecia-me realizar o amor que eu sonhara e vira
descrito" (OC 2: 110) ("that man appeared to me as the fulfillment of the love I had dreamed of and had seen described").

But all were false appearances. Accidentally the narrator
becomes a widow, and so available for marriage. The libertine
then shows his true face. He writes to her that he is "homem de
hábitos opostos ao casamento" (OC 2: 117) ("a man of habits
contrary to marriage") and announces that he is leaving forever.

The libertine's presence in her domestic life meant the
intrusion of the immoral social life (outward life) into domestic peace. The conclusion is that the realm of the outward life
is a realm of false appearances. Marriage—the realm of morality
and truth—is the alternative recommended by the widow to her
friend in her last letter.

***

The corrupting power of social life is again the main theme of
Machado's 1866 short story "Fernando e Fernanda" ("Fernando

and Fernanda"). Characters who were once ethical and in love with each other while still living in the countryside, Fernando and Fernanda adopt contrary life-views when the first enrolls in a European university and the second moves to Rio de Janeiro. The diversion and hustle and bustle (Pascal, La 132–39) characteristic of court life bring about the moral corruption of the woman. "Para não ficar atrás das suas companheiras" (MJ III 83) ("In order not to get behind her girlfriends"), Fernanda falls in love with a "simpleton." Putting it in terms of the categorical framework of early Machado: the female character adjusts herself to the impersonal social life by substituting a *tolo* for the *homem de espírito*.

The *tolo* holds the first version of the strategic life-view (later to be developed and conceptualized by Machado in his short story "Education of a stuffed shirt"). Soares, the *tolo* in question,

> [n]ão tendo consciência da nulidade do seu espírito, obrara como se fosse um espírito eminente, de modo que conseguia aquilo que nenhum homem avisado fora capaz de conseguir. . . . sabia entremear uma declaração com três períodos e dois tropos, destes que já cheiram mal, por andarem em tantas bocas, mas que Fernanda ouvia com encanto porque era uma linguagem nova para ela. (MJ III 83–84; see Appendix 12)

Rhetoric, elegance, and other social appearances seduce and corrupt the woman, causing a deep disillusion in Fernando, once back from Europe. Yet, at this point Machado still conceives of the alternative of ethics and truth. Not all women prefer the *tolos*. Fernando finds a woman who, like him, was once despised for not compromising with the vanity of social life. They marry, thereby typifying domestic peace as an alternative to outward life.

The triangular structure of "Fernando and Fernanda" exemplifies the view Machado develops in "Women's preference" and is characteristic of the majority of his short stories and of the totality of his novels. Here, given that the skeptical life-view is not yet in place, the main opposition is between the naive and strategic life-views. Woman and *tolo* are united in the strategic life-view. The *homem de espírito*'s sentimental aspirations fail, given his incompatibility with the pragmatism of social life. In these early short stories, however, the failure is frequent but still not definitive or exclusive. The *homem de espírito,* therefore, continues believing in a truth lying beyond false appearances. Like the dogmatic philosophers described by Sextus Empiricus, he eases his disturbance—caused by the contradictory nature of social appearances—by finding an essence: the domestic peace of marriage. This means that the naive life-view prevails, there being no transition to the skeptical life-view.

***

The third short story to be examined is also from 1866. Its title, "Felicidade pelo casamento" ("Happiness through marriage"), indicates the alternative to the outward life. Marriage is—as it is in *Epitaph, Dom Casmurro,* and *Counselor Ayres' Memorial*—the condition under which happiness would be possible, where truth would be achieved by overcoming the disturbance caused by the conflicting appearances of social life. In "Happiness through marriage," this result is actually and fully achieved. The transformation that takes place later is radical. *Dom Casmurro* could be subtitled "*Un*happiness through marriage," for it is as a husband that the protagonist is most entangled in the immoral net of social acting. In *Epitaph,* Brás Cubas makes several attempts to get married. His repeated failures are among the factors that lead him to deceased authorship. In this novel and in the following one—*Philosopher or Dog?*—marriage is the very core of the outward life, with no trace at all of some domestic peace distant from and alternative to social life.

Comparison of "Happiness through marriage" with *Epitaph* and *Dom Casmurro* sheds light on Machado's development. Like the two novels, the short story is autobiographical, and the narrative—which tells the main events in the narrator's life—provides an explanation for the present authorship. Furthermore, the anonymous author of "Happiness through marriage" makes references to Pascal and to the book of Ecclesiastes, in which he notes an affinity between Ecclesiastes and his spiritual condition before marriage. The crucial difference is that Brás Cubas's and Dom Casmurro's authorships are definitive.

Their positions are theoretical and distant whereas that of the anonymous author of "Happiness through marriage" is circumstantial and nonessentially theoretical. In sum, there is no skeptical life-view in the short story. Unlike Brás Cubas and Dom Casmurro, the narrator of "Happiness through marriage" does not introduce himself as an author. He takes the pen motivated by the single and objective goal of telling others the way to happiness. As soon as he finds domestic peace—i.e., truth and the ethical life—both his authorship and his pessimistic philosophy vanish.[2] He claims that by marrying, "todo o sentimento de reserva e de misantropia que caracterizava os primeiros anos da minha mocidade desaparecia" (MJ I 260–61) ("all the misanthropy and reserve that characterized the first years of my youth disappeared").

Notice that his trajectory is contrary to that of Brás Cubas. Compare Brás Cubas's last chapter, "Das negativas" ("Negatives"),[3] with our happy author's conclusion:

> Há cinco anos que tenho a felicidade de possuir Angela por mulher; e cada dia descubro-lhe mais suas qualidades. . . .
> Procurei por tanto tempo a felicidade na solidão; é errado; achei-a no casamento, no ajuntamento moral de duas vontades, dois pensamentos e dois corações. (MJ I 261; see Appendix 13)

The beginning of their relationship is worth mentioning. Like the *homem de espírito* matured by his emotional failures, the narrator's initial interest in Angela is supposedly merely cognitive: he wants to know if she is going to marry a *tolo* who approaches her. He eventually becomes jealous, proposes marriage, and is immediately accepted. Comparison with *Counselor Ayres' Memorial* is of help here. Aires's initial interest in Fidélia is also cognitive: he wants to know if she, a widow devoted to the memory of her deceased husband, will marry again. Unlike the narrator of the short story, Aires does remain in this withdrawn position to the end. Machado's observer-character is by then already constituted. One can thus conclude that the presence of the character of the observer (developed only during Machado's second phase) is a precondition for securing the theoretical stance.

In order for their happiness to be complete, the couple leave the pernicious capital, returning to the narrator's backward hometown. Here we notice another contrast with *Counselor Ayres' Memorial*. Aires and the Aguiar couple—who act as parents to Fidélia and Tristão—melancholically witness the departure of the younger couple for Portugal (Tristão's country). In the short story under examination, Angela's father and uncle share the couple's happiness by joining them on their return to the countryside. The destinies of the two sets of characters are also contrary. Fidélia and Tristão go back to the Portuguese capital, where there is an amusing and intense outward life waiting for them (Tristão is a politician). The characters of the short story leave the Brazilian city for the countryside, where there is a tranquil, intimate domestic life to be lived. Still another difference is that the narrator of the short story concludes his tale with the birth of his child, welcomed as the "completion of his happiness." As we shall see in the second part of this study, the desire for fatherhood is a basic problem common to Brás Cubas, Dom Casmurro, and Aires.

The strongly defined social reality of the countryside, the communal life that does not allow the degree of duplicity possible in the city, marriage, a child, all these are bonds that attach the individual to reality. They preclude the withdrawal and the questioning of social meanings that may turn the individual into a spectator and theoretician (instead of a pragmatic person). They divert (see Pascal) the narrator from the skeptical crisis threatening to arise in an early period of his life.

***

Antero (from "O anjo Rafael" ["The angel Rafael"]) is a character of this period who at first sight seems to anticipate Brás Cubas: "Cansado da vida, descrente dos homens, desconfiado das mulheres e aborrecido dos credores . . . determinou um dia despedir-se deste mundo" (MJ I 29) ("Bored with life, disbelieving of men, distrustful of women and upset by his creditors . . . he one day decided to bid farewell to this world"). The skeptical life-view is, however, still far from appearing in Machado's fiction. The omniscient narrator disqualifies the protagonist on the spot: there are no substantial motives for such an act, he says, and Antero's talk of suicide is nothing but the result of his too limited experience of men and the world: "Por ter tratado até então com alguns bonecos sem consciência" (MJ I 29) ("For having so far dealt only with a few puppets short of consciousness"). So, because the character has hitherto lived in the social milieu of impersonality and strategy, he attributes meaninglessness to the world on the basis of his limited life experience.

Antero's main limitation is his failure to perceive that there is an alternative to social men—"puppets short of consciousness"—who are not that different from himself. And then he meets Celestina, the alternative to the "half-dozen love traders" who made him "distrustful of women," and, by extension, of life itself. (Celestina was raised completely apart from the external social world.) Her edifying presence changes the *tolo* into "um bom homem, quando não passava de um homem inútil e mau" (MJ I 64) ("a good man, [whereas] before [he] was but a useless and evil [person]").

Antero becomes a *homem de espírito,* a singular individual, able to live apart from the "puppets short of consciousness," that is, the *tolos.* Celestina (in Portuguese her name means "heavenly" or "from heaven") converts him from the realm of false appearances to the realm of true essences, from the world of instrumentality to the world of morality. As a philosopher who is a secondary character in the short story says, social life is the locus of "opinion," not of "truth," and "[a] opinião pública é um muro em branco: aceita tudo quanto lhe escrevem . . . quer venha da mão de um garoto, quer da de um homem de bem" (MJ I 69) ("public opinion is like a blank wall: it accepts everything that one writes on its surface, no matter whether it comes from a child's hand or from the hand of a virtuous man").

The philosopher's distinction between opinion and truth is a good occasion for a brief indication of Machado's later path toward skepticism. This same truth is rendered problematic during Machado's second phase in the short story "O segredo do bonzo" ("The Bonze's Secret"). In this story truth is conceived merely as "convenient," because public opinion (belief) is what really matters in the world. Skepticism takes over completely a bit later in *Dom Casmurro,* when truth is completely darkened and characters and readers are left only with very precarious (groundless) opinions.

Comparison of "The angel Rafael" with *Epitaph* clarifies the nature of the aforementioned skeptical crisis. According to the dogmatic Machado of this first phase, social life is opposed to the intimate life of marriage as "opinion" (which is short of epistemological ground) is opposed to "truth." Insofar as marriage becomes social and is ruled by the logic of opinion in *Epitaph,* truth is rendered problematic. In the character's understanding of this twist, we observe the skeptical crisis of the Machadian character and the birth of the skeptical life-view. Still pursuing this comparison, we recall that both Antero and Brás Cubas "die." Antero—who is considered deceased by public opinion because his absence from the social stage is preceded by his written announcement of his intention to commit suicide—is "dead" for social life but is born again for the authentic and essential life of marriage. Brás Cubas is dead *tout court.* For him there is no life other than that ruled by "opinion." The only mode of "life" available to him is pure authorship (he is careful to explain that he is a "deceased author" not in the sense that he is an author who has died, but because he has become an author only after his death). This difference is also expressed in the differing literary forms of the two pieces. Insofar as there is a distinction between truth and opinion in "The angel Rafael," there is also a distinction between the omniscient narrator who utters true statements and the character who opines. With the advent of the skeptical life-view, the point of view of the omniscient narrator is replaced by the restricted one of the protagonist. The following is an example of the author's omniscient intervention in the story: "O Dr. Antero pensou que sim, e eu, na qualidade de romancista, direi que pensava bem" (MJ I 54) ("Dr. Antero thought yes, and I, in the capacity of the author, say that he was right"). This capacity is absent from the three novels in which a skeptical life-view can be identified. This change in literary form presupposes the definition and development of the skeptical character. And if we compare Brás Cubas, for example, with Antero, we find that Brás Cubas has a theoretical density that Antero lacks completely, and that Brás Cubas's superior qualities of observation and authorship are also absent in Antero. We therefore conclude that besides the access to truth by the omniscient narrator, the undeveloped nature of the character is a factor inhibiting his taking over the narration.

***

Female characters are paradigmatic in Machado's fiction. In the essay and early short stories from 1861 to 1871, women are divided between those who prefer *tolos,* that is, those oriented to the outward life, and those oriented to domestic peace and who prefer *homens de espírito.* Among the former, one could highlight the female characters of the short story "O que são as moças" ("What girls really are"), to whom emotional interest has priority over moral behavior. This is also the case of Diana (from a story titled after her), who conceals her face to appear prettier than she really is in order to obtain a good marriage, and of Onda ("Onda" ["Wave"]), whose volatility and vivacity suggest to the narrator the sea metaphor that Machado explores later with Capitu.

Diana, Onda, and others are, however, exceptions in Machado's early fiction. This is indeed the only period during his productive life in which female characters oriented to intimate life outnumber those oriented to social life. In most short stories of the period, "domestic life" is presented as transparent, without any trace of the duplicity and strategy that characterize social life. Yet, duplicity and strategy are precisely those aspects of life that seem to interest Machado most. Even in this period of predominance of domestic peace, strategies are frequently employed either for its establishment (e.g., in "Linha reta e linha curva" ["Straight line and curved line"] or for its rebuilding (e.g., in "A mulher de preto" ["Woman in black"]).

The theme of the paradox of woman is basic in "Straight line and curved line." Tito, the main male character, presents himself to Emília as unable to love and as opposed to marriage. In trying to disprove the image of an affected and vain man of society that Emília had drawn of him on an earlier occasion, he presents himself as someone totally sincere and natural: he does not care for politeness, flattery, and speeches. Actually, this is but a strategy to conquer Emília (the "curved line"). Years before, he had frankly and directly let her know of his love; his failure at that time was complete. The narrator proposes thereby the paradox of woman: "[A linha curva] [à]s vezes é o caminho mais curto" (OC 2: 151) ("The curved line is sometimes the shortest way"). It is also worth noting the power of appearances in human interaction and the sophistication of the duplicity in question. That which appears to be a genuine nonsocial singularity is nothing but a self-image deliberately constructed for the strategic aim of sentimental conquests.

To sum up the 1861–71 period: if, on the one hand, the moral positivity of domestic peace is often portrayed, on the other hand, the negativity of social life (duplicity and strategy, i.e., lack of morality) is no less noticeable. That this was Machado's obsession in this early period of his career is clear from the selection he made of short stories of this period for his first published volume. Strategy—usually immoral—is the common feature of all the short stories selected. The protagonist's performance in *"Miss Dollar"* is disastrous. His strategies are all equivocal, and only by chance, and after much effort, does he conquer Margarida. In "Woman in black," it is Madalena who reconquers her husband, thanks to her skillful manipulation of his best friend, the naive Estévão. A complex conspiracy against the protagonist's emotional aspirations is the core of "Frei Simão" ("Friar Simão"). Luiz Soares (protagonist of a short story named after him), Gomes (from the short story enitled "O segredo de Augusta" ["Augusta's secret"]), Emílio (from "Confessions of a young widow"), and Tito ("Straight line and curved line") all adopt the strategic life-view. They all make use of complex and immoral strategies in order to achieve their aims. Luiz Soares and Gomes behave cynically. They try to marry wealthy women only to get the economic means to continue their libertine lives. Emílio, as we saw, is a "vulgar seducer only a bit more skillful than others." Tito tries the strategy of being natural and indifferent in order to conquer the woman who despised him when he acted nonstrategically.

Yet, it must be recalled that although remote and often established strategically, there is still a place for transparency, truth, and morality in the private realm of marriage. Machado's position here is like that portrayed by Sextus as the dogmatist's ideal: possession of the truth is directly associated with the attainment of happiness (in Machado, marriage). As a result of this possession, tranquility or peace of mind (in Machado, domestic peace) follows as the state of mind and spirit enjoyed by the happy and virtuous person. According to Sextus, this tranquility is so longed for—given the disturbing and conflicting appearances of the changeable world (in Machado, the appearances of social life)—that it constitutes the ultimate end pursued by all philosophers, that is, it actually is happiness, not a mere consequence of it. Machado seems to share this view, for the short stories examined above strongly suggest that marriage is the means for securing this tranquility. Of course, as Sextus would quickly point out, such tranquility is grounded on a poor foundation, for the dogmatist is too hasty in finding an essence. His tranquility holds only because he is not reflective and open minded enough to see the gaps in his naive lifeview. Indeed, one cannot find any thinking character in Machado's early fiction. We have seen in this chapter the practical background of this absence. If we take into account the importance of marriage in the construction of reality in the modern world and agree with Peter Berger and Hansfried Kellner that "to be 'at home' in society entails, *per definitionem,* the construction of a maritally based subworld" (Berger and Kellner 19), we can conclude that in this period (1) the preconditions for withdrawal necessary for the constitution of the observer are absent and—given the strength of reality provided by marriage—(2) no skeptical life-view can be developed. A skeptical life-view arises in Machado's fiction when the Celestinas are replaced by the Virgílias of his second phase, when marriage becomes part of the outward life. When that which was considered the true reality is seen as just another deceitful appearance. When the equation of happiness or goodness with marriage can no longer be maintained.

Chapter Two

The Short Stories and
First Novels
from 1872 to 1878

The view of social life present in Machado's fiction from 1872 to 1878 is not essentially different from that of the 1861–71 period. However, a decisive change occurs in his view of marriage. Domestic peace becomes fragile, far more vulnerable to the duplicitous and changeable outward life. Likewise, female characters who are oriented to social life are more elaborated and central than in the previous decade. And although the possibility of truth and morality is not excluded, it certainly becomes more remote. Despite these changes, it is important to note that there is no essential difference between these two periods as there is between Machado's fiction before and after *Epitaph*. In the period examined in this chapter—from 1872 to 1878—one finds many short stories with situations equivalent to those analyzed in the previous chapter. The stories that exhibit a solid domestic peace in this period are, however, very few. Furthermore, only after 1871 does one find short stories in which marriage is clearly problematic.

The short story "Ernesto de Tal" ("Ernesto Doe") illustrates well the opposition between the naive and strategic life-views and the appeal of the social man to woman. Rosina manipulates the feelings and emotions of the naive Ernesto, managing to keep him committed and in love while she tries to seduce a *tolo*. With respect to the latter,

> [não] havia ninguém, pelo menos, naquelas imediações, que tivesse mais elegância na maneira de arquear os braços, de concertar os cabelos, ou simplesmente de oferecer uma xícara de chá. (OC 2: 207; see Appendix 14)

Rosina's strategy is facilitated by Ernesto's naïveté.

> Rosina sufocou um grito; . . . dos olhos rebentaram-lhe duas grossas lágrimas. Ernesto não podia vê-la chorar; por mais cheio de razões que estivesse, . . . curvava-se logo e pedia-lhe perdão. . . .
>
> A moça ouviu ainda muitas coisas que lhe disse Ernesto, e a todas respondeu com um ar tão contrito e palavras tão repassadas de amargura, que o nosso namorado sentiu quase rebentarem-lhe as lágrimas dos olhos. Os de Rosina estavam já mais tranqüilos. (OC 2: 218–19; see Appendix 15)

The precarious condition of the naive character, vulnerable to sudden change, trapped in the conflicting web of appearances spun by women, causes the disturbances that point to the necessity of attaining *ataraxia*. Ernesto's oscillations are later intensified and developed in the direction of skepticism in Brás Cubas, and even more in Dom Casmurro. In both cases, the woman, respectively Virgília and Capitu, is in control of the interaction. As for the men, each attains authorship by the end of his life and adopts a skeptical point of view that constitutes the solution to the disquietude suffered by the naive character. This solution is consolidated in Aires, a skeptic and an author from the outset.

"Aires e Vergueiro" ("Aires and Vergueiro"), "Antes que cases" ("Before you get married"), "Um homem superior" ("A superior man"), and "O machete" ("The little guitar") are short stories of this period in which the corruptive action of the outward life on the core of domestic peace is mercilessly portrayed by Machado. In the first story, Aires steals his best friend's money and his wife, with whom the friend used to enjoy a perfect domestic peace. In commenting on the episode, the narrator remarks that "[a] fortuna varia como a mulher" (OC-1937 11: 47) ("life varies like women"). The problem of fortune shifting over time is addressed by Machado especially through female characters. "Nada é eterno neste mundo" (OC-1937 11: 50) ("Nothing is eternal in this world"). This saying marks the disappearance in Machado's writing of the last alternative to the realm of treacherous changes because from this point on dissimulation and treason are found even in marriage. As noted above, in *Dom Casmurro* the problem of woman's instability raises the question of temporality. With Bento, fictional author of *Dom Casmurro,* the perplexity, disturbance, and reflection of the character who faces woman's instability and changing temperament over time become the very axis of the novel. We can thus measure the difference of elaboration between Bento and Vergueiro. Whereas Bento uses his relationship with Capitu to philosophize about time, Vergueiro does not reflect on his experience or derive any value from it.

Alfredo in "Before you get married" is a naive man who dreams of a marriage lived apart from social life. He meets a widow whose beauty and reserve persuade him that she is the right person with whom to build domestic peace. The engagement proceeds according to the strictest pattern of privacy and respect. But once married, the former widow, Angela, proves to be, contrary to all previous appearances, completely oriented toward outward life:

> Angela era um turbilhão.
> A vida para ela estava fora de casa. . . . Não havia baile a que faltasse, nem espetáculo, nem passeio, nem festa célebre, e tudo isto cercado de muitas rendas, jóias e sedas, que ela comprava todos os dias, como se o dinheiro nunca devesse acabar. (MJ I 115–16; see Appendix 16)

The picture of marriage here is contrary to that found in the short stories of Machado's first period from 1861 to 1871. For Angela, marriage means full participation in the social life. This new picture dominates Machado's fiction from this point to the end. Marriage becomes the means of access to intense social life for most of Machado's female characters after Angela: Guiomar (*A mão e a luva* [*The Hand and the Glove*]), Iaiá Garcia (*Iaiá Garcia* [*Iaiá Garcia*]), Virgília (*Epitaph*), Sofia (*Philosopher or Dog?*), Capitu (*Dom Casmurro*), and Fidélia (*Counselor Ayres' Memorial*).

A previous remark made in the context of comparing *Dom Casmurro* with "Aires and Vergueiro" also holds here. The crucial difference between Alfredo and Bento is that Alfredo (of the first phase) does not evolve, as Bento (of the second) does, into Dom Casmurro. Instead of becoming an author and developing observational and reflective skills, Alfredo lets himself be dominated by Angela (as Bento is by Capitu before breaking with her), for, as is the case with Capitu, "all power was in [Angela]" (MJ I 116). Putting it in terms of the categories suggested in this study, we can say that naive and strategic perspectives are irremediably opposed. No skeptical alternative is available to resolve their conflict. All the *homem de espírito,* Alfredo, can do in this context is to despair of his ethical-romantic dreams, pay Angela's bills, and put up with her parties.

Female characters of Machado's first phase lack the complexity and definition of those of his second. Angela's variable behavior does not constitute a problem of intelligibility, nor does it appear as elements of beauty and attractiveness, as it does with Capitu. Angela's orientation to social life is open and outrageous, while Capitu's is subtle and dubious. Carlota's ("Aires and Vergueiro") unfaithfulness is certain; Capitu's is totally uncertain. What in the first phase is false appearance covering the truth becomes in Machado's second phase an opaque appearance that problematizes the truth. The advent of the skeptical life-view brings with it a finer elaboration of the strategic one.

***

Marriage is not the only thing that changes its significance in this period. Whereas Machado could hardly disguise his condemnation of the *tolo*'s strategic life-view in "Women's preference for *tolos,*" he now takes a more sympathetic view of the strategic life-view. This new attitude is noticeable, for example, in the short story entitled "Um homem superior" ("A superior man"). The plot is very similar to the plots of the short stories previously examined. A seducer destroys domestic peace by employing the gifts of a social man. His interest is merely economic: he is after the means to continue his libertine life. His success comes at the expense of the happiness of the seduced, who does not find in her marriage with him the domestic peace she had hoped for. Despite the protagonist's instrumental action, his manipulations and dissimulations, Machado calls him "a superior man":

> Como! E a moralidade? A minha história é isto. . . . Não me proponho a castigar ninguém. . . . Clemente Soares nenhuma punição teve, e eu não hei de inventar no papel aquilo que se não dá na vida. Clemente Soares viveu festejado e estimado por todos, até que morreu de apoplexia, no meio de muitas

> lágrimas, que não eram mais sinceras do que ele foi durante
> sua vida. (OC-1937 11: 109; see Appendix 17)

Machado's concluding irony discloses his realistic understanding of the place in the world of characters who exemplify the strategic life-view. This realism leads him away from the condemnatory attitude toward the strategic life-view that he exhibits in his earliest short stories.

The theme of "The little guitar" is that of the outsider. In this case, the outsider is a particular *homem de espírito*: the artist, whose medium is the cello. His divorce from the world is dramatized by the decision of his wife (Carlota) to leave him for a guitar player. As in most of Machado's stories of this period, domestic peace is secured only during the time Carlota and the cellist live far from the outward life. "Moravam ambos em lugar afastado, . . . alheios à sociedade que os cercava e que os não entendia" (OC 2: 857) ("They lived in a remote place, . . . indifferent to the society that surrounded and did not understand them"). Contact with society mediated by the guitar player causes Carlota to change her allegiance from the remoteness and tranquility of domestic peace to the amusement and diversion of the outward life. The short story has the same triangular structure as "Women's preference." The musicians are contrasted after the manner of their instruments' opposition. The cellist—*homem de espírito*—is an intellectual, melancholic, and solitary person. The guitar player—a *tolo*—is popular, social, and sensual. The woman prefers the guitar. Her relationship with her husband is significant:

> Inácio gostava de *ouví-la* e *vê-la;* amava-a muito, e, *além disso,* como que precisava às vezes daquela expressão de *vida exterior* para entregar-se . . . às especulações do seu espírito. (OC 2: 858; emphasis added; see Appendix 18)

Even though withdrawn in domestic peace, the *homem de espírito* needs the stimulation provided by outward life and embodied in woman in order to give birth to his philosophical or artistic creation. We shall see in the last chapter that Counselor Aires gives up his project of a reclusive life style because of the necessity of seeing and hearing the world. Above all, woman (Flora in *Esau and Jacob* and Fidélia in *Counselor*

Ayres' Memorial) is the *homem de espírito*'s aesthetic object. Counselor Aires's aesthetic experience of the world and woman is the *raison d'être* of his literary activity.

We shall see that Brás Cubas (Chapter Five) and Bento (Chapter Six) move toward this stance, which becomes their solution to their problematic situation as outsiders. Brás Cubas, Dom Casmurro, and Counselor Aires find in authorship an alternative position to their divorce from the female characters (that is, from the world). This is the main difference between Machado's two phases. Whereas the cellist goes crazy when Carlota abandons him, Brás Cubas, who experiences repeated break-ups with women throughout his life, takes the theoretical alternative of philosophizing about the human condition and writing his autobiography. After Capitu's departure for Europe, Bento becomes Dom Casmurro, a memorialist author. The definitive and most effective solution is to be found, however, in Aires. Aires becomes reconciled with old age during the events narrated in *Counselor Ayres' Memorial,* thereby defining himself as a spectator. Aesthetic and cognitive distance, which is just a supplementary aspect in the cellist's relationship with woman, becomes the crucial characterization of Aires and the definitive solution to the *homem de espírito*.

Although in a nontheoretical way, "The little guitar" anticipates the doctrine of "Pomadism" that will be elaborated in "The Bonze's Secret." The decisive criterion of value in social life is appearance, not intrinsic merit. The narrator describes the guitar player's performance as follows:

> Todo ele acompanhava a gradação e variações das notas; inclinava-se sobre o instrumento, retesava o corpo, pendia a cabeça ora a um lado, ora a outro, alçava a perna, sorria, derretia os olhos ou fechava-os nos lugares que lhe pareciam patéticos. Ouvi-lo tocar era o menos: vê-lo era o mais. Quem somente o ouvisse não poderia compreendê-lo. (OC 2: 861; see Appendix 19)

In "The Bonze's Secret," the truth of the bonze's doctrine is verified by the narrator, who, although a mediocre musician, manages to achieve tremendous success during a concert

> com o só recurso dos ademanes, da graça em arquear os braços para tomar a charamela, que me foi trazida em uma

bandeja de prata, da rigidez do busto, da unção com que alcei os olhos ao ar, e do desdém e ufania com que os baixei à mesma assembléia, a qual neste ponto rompeu em um tal concerto de vozes e exclamações de entusiasmo, que quase me persuadiu do meu merecimento. (OC 2: 327; see Appendix 20)

This performance is one of the experiments that corroborate Pomada's doctrine that what something or somebody is believed to be, not what it, he, or she really is, is the real gear driving the (social) world.

"The Bonze's Secret," published right after *Epitaph of a Small Winner,* was written at the same time as other "theoretical" short stories by Machado, such as "O espelho, esboço de uma nova teoria da alma humana" ("The looking glass") and "Education of a stuffed shirt." Its similarity with "The little guitar," written about fourteen years before, and with other short stories written even earlier, shows that the young Machado already held the view of social life about which he "theorizes" later in his second phase. What is lacking in "The little guitar" (as in all short stories of Machado's first phase), is a theoretical stance capable of giving philosophical expression to his view. The advent of the skeptical life-view, of the spectator, and of the literary form of the memoir provided the conditions for the expression of this view. Within the fictional framework of Machado's works, this required the elaboration of an "outsider" character. To the extent that this character develops through Machado's short stories and novels, he becomes a spectator and finally takes up the "authorship" of novels and short stories. The expression of the reflective dimension comes, therefore, from within the fictional universe of short stories and novels. It is thus reasonable to speculate that were this stance available to the cellist, authorship would have been available to him as an alternative to madness.

***

Machado's first novels, written between 1872 and 1878, overlap the years when the stories covered in this chapter were written. Following the method of comparing works from Machado's two phases that has been used with the short stories, the earlier novel *Ressurreição (Resurrection)* will be contrasted to the later *Dom Casmurro;* then *The Hand and the*

Glove will be contrasted to *Epitaph;* and finally a brief note will be made on *Iaiá Garcia.*

Two characters in *Resurrection* indicate two different developments of the *tolo* character. Moreirinha emphasizes the "vulgarity" of the type.

> Era ele galanteador por índole e por sistema; . . . Ninguém melhor do que ele sabia lisonjear o amor-próprio feminino; ninguém prestava com mais alma esses leves serviços de sociedade, que constituem muita vez toda a reputação de um homem. Dirigia os piqueniques, comprava o romance ou a música da moda, . . . levava os pianistas aos saraus, tudo isso com um modo tão serviçal que era de se ficar morrendo por ele. (OC 1: 125–26; see Appendix 21)

This kind of "social agent" is, however, displaced from the forefront of Machado's fiction, becoming, from this novel on, a secondary and grotesque character. The gestation of a reflective dimension in Machado's work is exhibited in the greater importance and complexity of a second-stage development of the *tolo.* This emphasizes the strategic understanding of social life (which can be granted to the *tolo* in "Women's preference" only on a very intuitive level), and the strategic actions aimed at the accomplishment of social, economic, and sentimental projects. Luís Batista is this character in *Resurrection.* He is one of the vertices of the sentimental triangle which frames the novel.

The basic relation here, as in most Machadian fiction, is that which holds between the disillusioned *homem de espírito*—Félix—and the major female character—Lívia. Machado says in the preface to the first edition of the novel that he did not "quis fazer romance de costumes; . . . [mas] o esboço de uma situação e o contraste de dois caracteres" (OC 1: 114) ("want to write a novel of morals; . . . [but] to outline a situation and the contrast between two characters"). As in almost all of his novels—with the possible exception of *Helena* and *Philosopher or Dog?*—the contrast among the characters determines the plot. Machado's reference to "contrast" well indicates which relationship interests him most: not the affinity between woman and the *tolo* in the strategic life-view, but the tension between woman and the *homem de espírito,* who will adopt the skeptical point of view in Machado's second-phase fiction.

Lívia, however, belongs to a period in which there are still women who reject the outward life. Her preference is not for Luís Batista but for the disillusioned Félix. Félix tells Lívia that he used to be "crédulo como tu" ("credulous like you are"); his mind "criara um mundo seu, uma sociedade platônica, em que . . . o amor [era] a lei comum" ("created its own world, a Platonic society, in which . . . love [was] the common law"). But after some deceptions (presumably emotional ones such as those referred to in Machado's earlier stories), he reveals that his

> espírito ficou árido e seco. Invadiu-me então uma cruel misantropia, a princípio irritada e violenta, depois melancólica e resignada. Calejou-se-me a alma a pouco e pouco, e o meu coração literalmente morreu. (OC 1: 153–54; see Appendix 22)

Félix hopes that by getting involved with Lívia, he will experience "resurrection" (renewed belief in the value of life) like that noted in the narrator of "Happiness through marriage" and in Antero of "The angel Rafael." Lívia represents the possibility of truth and morality in conjugal life as an alternative to outward life. Yet, during the period under examination, such "resurrection" has already become problematic. Social life and its agents such as Luís Batista have become more subtle and corruptive. Taking advantage of Félix's jealousy and of his "distrust in people's sincerity," Luís Batista,

> [o]bservador e perspicaz, e ao mesmo tempo sem paixões nem escrúpulos, percebeu . . . que quanto mais o amor de Félix se tornasse suspeitoso e tirânico, tanto mais perderia terreno no coração da viúva, e assim roto o encanto, chegaria a hora das reparações generosas com que ele se propunha a consolar a moça dos seus tardios arrependimentos. (OC 1: 144; see Appendix 23)

Luís Batista has an intuitive understanding of the finite nature of human feelings and commitments. He also has a practical strategical knowledge of the channels of social interaction. His plan is to act in such a way as to cause Félix to think that he enjoys a secret relationship with Lívia. The narrator compares this situation with that in Othello and notices the sophistication of his character's procedure as compared with Iago's.

> A dificuldade era certamente maior e mais delicada [pois Iago calunia Desdêmona diretamente a Otelo], mas o pretendente tinha em larga escala as qualidades precisas para ela. Era-lhe necessário afetar com a moça uma intimidade misteriosa, mas discreta, sem aparato, antes cercada de infinitas cautelas, tão hábil que ela não percebesse, mas tão claramente dissimulada que fosse direto ao coração de Félix. (OC 1: 145; see Appendix 24)

Luís Batista's plan is feasible because Lívia is a woman alien to the opacity and ambiguity of social life. The point here is that dissembling in social life constitutes its "clear," that is, essential, procedure. This procedure is necessary not only to prevent Lívia's perception of Luís Batista's machinations but also, and especially, in order to trigger Félix's suspicions. Machado illustrates here the paradox that a large number of meaningful relationships in social life unfold in precisely this manner. Note that social life has here become more sophisticated than in previous short stories. It is no longer a matter of grotesque affectation as denounced in "Women's preference." Luís Batista's behavior makes it more difficult to determine what lies beyond visible appearances, although such determination is still possible: Lívia is *indubitably* faithful to Félix. Later in *Dom Casmurro,* the network of interactions becomes so obscure and filled with dissembling that any reasonable determination of what lies beyond visible appearances is impossible. At that point, no truth about the intimate dispositions of the female character is discernible.

Félix's doubts, unlike Dom Casmurro's, do not arise from a skeptical situation but from his own inability to discern the truth.[1] Félix is a weak character who lets himself be entangled in the net of the false appearances of social life. In this novel, written previous to the development of the skeptical life-view, the narrator exercises his omniscient authority, distinguishing truths from false appearances: "Entendamo-nos, leitor: eu, que te estou contando esta história, posso afimar-te que a carta [que comprometia Lívia] era efetivamente de Luís Batista" (OC 1: 189) ("Let's make it clear, reader: I, who am telling you this story, enjoy circumstances such that I can assure you that the letter [which implicated Lívia] was actually written by Luís Batista"). No such assurance is available in *Dom Casmurro.*

And this is the key element that makes *Dom Casmurro* a masterpiece. *Resurrection* would be closer to *Dom Casmurro* if Félix were the narrator, writing his memories or autobiography. The underdeveloped nature of the character distanced from social life (Félix, the *homem de espírito*), and the still-present possibility of truth beyond the false appearances (the ethical woman Lívia)—in short, the absence of the skeptical life-view—explain the absence for Félix of the alternative of being outsider, observer, and thinker. Although it is difficult to access due to the misguiding and deceitful logic of social life, the truth is still available in *Resurrection*. One can detect Machado's evolution toward skepticism by comparing, on the level of subject matter, Lívia's transparency with Capitu's opacity; and, on the observer's level, Félix's fragility with Dom Casmurro's density.

> Félix é que não iria parar ao claustro. . . . [Se o desenlace] profundamente o abateu, rapidamente se lhe apagou. O amor extinguiu-se como lâmpada a que faltou óleo. (OC 1: 192; see Appendix 25)

Félix's forgetfulness shows his fragility. He is incapable of adopting the reflective position of a Brás Cubas, Dom Casmurro, or Aires. Unlike the narrator-characters, Félix does not move from the naive to the skeptical point of view. Not being a *tolo* holding the strategic life-view, he is finally displaced from Machado's fictional universe.

***

The triangular structure is finally fixed in *The Hand and the Glove*. The woman is definitively construed as a character oriented to social life. The strategic life-view she adopts is far more complex than that outlined in "Women's preference." The *homem de espírito*—Estévão—becomes even weaker than Félix and finally disappears from the center of the narrative. The *tolo*—Luís Alves—is no longer a "puppet short of consciousness," but a smart, ambitious, determined, and strategic type. Finally, the woman—Guiomar—fits, like a glove to the hand, this improved version of the *tolo* character (from now on better called strategic). One notices, however, that, although far more complex, the fundamental relation is still the same as that presented in "Women's preference."

Besides the stronger elaboration of the strategic life-view, a further modification is that Machado now looks at this life-view with more sympathy than before (as noted above in the short stories of this period). Social life is no longer portrayed as negatively as it is in the 1861–71 narratives. Moreover, as also noted about the short stories of the period, the meaning of marriage is turned upside down. It is now the entrance to the agitated life of society. The naive proposal that marriage constitutes domestic peace apart from social life, which is positive in Machado's earliest short stories, no longer attracts the female characters from 1872 onward. It is rather the boldness and determination of a Luís Alves or Lobo Neves (*Epitaph*)—guarantees that social status, power, and "diversion" will be secured—that now explain the woman's preference for the strategic man. Guiomar "coldly" chooses Luís Alves.

> Demais, o primeiro passo do homem público estava dado; ele ia entrar em cheio na estrada que leva os fortes à glória. Em torno dele ia fazer-se aquela luz, que era a ambição da moça, a atmosfera, que ela almejava respirar. . . . em Luís Alves via ela combinadas as afeições domésticas com o ruído exterior. (OC 1: 252; see Appendix 26)

This combination becomes, from this point to the later Machado's novels and short stories, the ideal of most of his female characters, although, if forced to choose, the "bustle of noise outside" is always preferred over "domestic warmth."

Although in *The Hand and the Glove* and in short stories of this period ("Before you get married," "A superior man," "The little guitar") marriage already belongs to the realm of social life, it is not yet an object of the narrator's reflection, as it is in the novels belonging to the second phase. In Machado's later period (1879–1908), all the negativity already identified in social life is discovered also in marriage.

The development of a skeptical life-view in the second phase constitutes a denunciation of the limited and dogmatic wisdom and conviction that are typical of the strategic life-view. Instrumental reason does not criticize the validity of the ends pursued through social actions. Its job is to look for the best available means. One of the basic features of Luís Alves is his obstinacy, which propels him to accomplish sentimental conquests and to succeed in projects of social ascension. When Guiomar alludes to this characteristic of his, Luís Alves replies: "Justamente, é uma idéia fixa. Sem idéia fixa não se faz nada bom neste mundo" (OC 1: 248) ("Precisely; it is an *idée fixe*. Without a definite idea nothing good can be done in this world" [HG 85]).

Differentiating himself from Lobo Neves, who certainly would agree with Luís Alves's view, Brás Cubas advises his readers: "Deus te livre, leitor, de uma idéia fixa" (OC 1: 514) ("God deliver you, dear reader, from a fixed idea" [E 23]). According to the Pyrrhonians, belief in the value of ends is a major source of disturbance and anxiety. As we shall see, this is what Brás Cubas has in mind in giving this piece of advice. So, whereas social ends are criticized from a moralizing point of view in the short stories of the 1861–71 period, in Machado's second phase the criticism of ends reappears but from a skeptical point of view: the point then is not that those ends are morally wrong, but that ends-in-view, conceptions of the good, no matter what, are disruptive of one's tranquility.

Guiomar's strategy is as efficient as Rosina's ("Ernesto Doe") and Clemente's ("A superior man"). When her wealthy godmother asks her which man she prefers, Guiomar says the godmother's nephew, Jorge. But she says it in such a tone of voice and context that the godmother quickly concludes that her nephew is not Guiomar's real choice. The godmother reads Guiomar's answer as a self-abnegating one: the goddaughter would be willing to sacrifice her life for the godmother's sake. She rejoices over the girl's willingness to sacrifice, but makes her marry Luís Alves instead.

> Mas por que o nome de Jorge lhe roçou os lábios? A moça não queria iludir a baronesa, mas traduzir-lhe infielmente a voz de seu coração, para que a madrinha conferisse, por si mesma, a tradução com o original. Havia nisto um pouco de meio indireto, de tática, de afetação, estou quase a dizer de hipocrisia, se não tomassem à má parte o vocábulo. Havia, mas isto mesmo lhes dirá que esta Guiomar, sem perder as excelências de seu coração; era do barro comum de que Deus fez a nossa pouco sincera humanidade; e lhes dirá também que, apesar de seus verdes anos, ela compreendia já que as aparências de um sacrifício valem mais, muita vez, do que o próprio sacrifício. (OC 1: 263; see Appendix 27)

Guiomar intuitively knows that social interactions take place through a game of appearances in which success presupposes duplicity, manipulation, and dissimulation. This is Machado's main theme in the period under consideration. The point is no longer the denunciation of the *tolo* by the *homem de espírito,* but the objective focus on the strategic nature of social life. Machado says in the foreword to the 1874 edition of the novel that

> o desenho de tais caracteres,—o de Guiomar, sobretudo,—
> foi o meu objeto principal, se não exclusivo, servindo-me a
> ação apenas de tela em que lancei os contornos dos perfis.
> Incompletos embora, terão eles saído naturais e verdadeiros?
> (OC 1: 196; see Appendix 28)

To conclude this commentary on *The Hand and the Glove,* note that the *homem de espírito* agonizes in this period in order to be replaced in 1879 by the skeptical observer. Because this is the vertex of the triangle critical of social life, there is no wonder that a critical life-view in Machado's fiction obtains from 1861 to 1871 and from 1879 to his death (1908). During the transitional period discussed in this chapter (1872–78), one notices the greater relevance of Guiomar (and to a lesser degree, of Luís Alves). The strategic life-view is the one most defined at this point. The reference to Guiomar's strategic intuitive knowledge—"the appearance of the sacrifice is oft-times worth more than the sacrifice itself"—indicates that given the absence of the skeptical reflective perspective, in conveying his message the narrator adopts the available perspective that is most developed. In the second phase, with the constitution of the skeptical life-view, Machado theorizes about the intuitive understanding exhibited by Guiomar, in works such as the short story "The Bonze's Secret."

***

In order to conclude this chapter, I will make a brief note on *Iaiá Garcia.* In this novel, the last of Machado's first phase, the change in the meaning of marriage and the definitive consolidation of woman as a character belonging to the realm of the outward life are most clearly indicated. The novel focuses on the replacement of Estela—one of the last female characters still belonging to the family of those "spiritual women" found in the short stories from 1861 to 1871—by Iaiá Garcia as the central character. Iaiá Garcia, like Guiomar, is oriented to the outward life. Female characters like Estela, who "não dispunha da arte de combinar a paixão espúria com a tranquilidade doméstica" (OC 1: 473) ("was not endowed with the art of combining illicit passion with domestic tranquility" [IG 118]), no longer have a central place in Machado's fiction.[2] This art turns out to be the basic feature of Machado's female characters in the novels written after *Iaiá Garcia*. Iaiá, unlike Estela,

> achou no casamento a felicidade sem contraste. . . . Se antes de casar . . . possuía o abecedário da elegância, depressa aprendeu a prosódia e a sintaxe; afez-se a todos os requintes da urbanidade, com a presteza de um espírito sagaz e penetrante. (OC 1: 506; see Appendix 29)

There is a correspondence between the opposing female characters and the two contrary meanings of marriage. Estela's marriage (domestic peace) is problematic and precarious—she does not love her husband, who dies by the midpoint of the novel. Iaiá's marriage (outward life) is, on the contrary, promising. When she marries, Iaiá sets out to enjoy the "turbilhão das coisas" (OC 1: 489) ("the carousel of life" [IG 141]). We shall see in the second part of this study how troublesome this "carousel" turns out to be and how fragile is the happiness of marriage when it is part of social life. The transformation of marriage into the very core of social life provides the occasion for the rise of skepticism and furnishes Machado's skeptical characters a privileged field where human misery is probed.

Chapter Three

Problematic Characters

The Skeptic's Ancestors

The *homens de espírito* are the earliest ancestors of the skeptics in Machado's fiction. Four major features distinguish them from the *tolos:* (1) they are removed from women, i.e., social life; (2) their precarious condition is a result of the first feature; (3) their uniqueness is in contrast with the homogeneity of the *tolos,* i.e., they are individuals instead of social persona; and (4) they will not or cannot act strategically. The skeptical lifeview is the solution to the problematic situation of the *homem de espírito.* Once he adopts this attitude, the character's uniqueness and divorce from social life are intensified. At the same time, his condition as outsider ceases to be problematic to the extent that spectating and reflection are consolidated. The character moves from a situation in which he is alienated from social life to another in which he becomes an inquirer about and observer of its nature. In these ancestors from the early part of Machado's first phase we find only a problematic uniqueness and, in a few cases, a slight interest in reflection, though not reflection itself.

The problematic characters can be divided into two groups. We begin with those who, having gone through the bitter experience of separation (which usually occurs as sentimental failures and deceptions), find a way out of their precarious condition by finally finding a domestic peace that is an alternative to and remote from social life. These *homens de espírito* find women who belong to the realm of truth and morality.

Three short stories with characters falling into this group of *homens de espírito* who experience a happy resolution have already been mentioned. Machado calls F. S., the narrator of "Happiness through marriage," and Menezes, of "Woman in black," "skeptics" and "misanthropes." F. S. is so called because he was despised by a girl for his introverted and reflective personality. Menezes thought he was a victim of human hypocrisy, expressed in the alleged unfaithfulness of his former wife. F. S.'s disappointment leads him to Pascal and Ecclesiastes. Menezes is described by an acquaintance as a "misantropo, e um cético [que] não crê em nada, nem estima ninguém. Na política como na sociedade faz um papel puramente negativo" (OC 2: 61) ("misanthrope, a skeptic who does not believe in anything, nor care for anybody. In politics as in society, he plays only a negative role"). The allusion to his "negative role" reveals his condition well: condemning social life and inwardly exiled from it. Fernando, of "Fernando and Fernanda," also suffers a disillusionment when he sees that his beloved is well adjusted to the social life he despises. The problematic situation of the three characters is resolved, however, by their finding women who do not prefer the *tolos*. Before this happy outcome, while still in their problematic state, F. S. and Menezes show signs of having a reflective inclination that, however, does not translate into elaborated thought. All we know concerning this reflection is that they read and devote their lives to study and reflection. In F. S.'s case we find a speech in which his own pain and resentment overshadow the bit of philosophy one might find in it; as for Menezes, his qualification as a "skeptic" reveals that Machado holds at this point a still crude and embryonic notion of skepticism.

Other problematic characters of this group can be discerned in other short stories. For instance, the protagonist of "Último dia de um poeta" ("A poet's last day") suffers from his beloved's preference for a *tolo* to such a degree that he comes very close to dying. He escapes death when he finds out that she was forced to prefer the *tolo*. While sick, close to death, he delivers a pessimistic speech whose theme is later developed by Machado in *Epitaph*. The address on nature in the following excerpt, once deprived of its lachrymose pitch, resembles Brás Cubas's delirium:

> Ó mãe cruel, que não honras a morte dos teus filhos com uma lágrima de dor e um suspiro de mágoa. . . . Parece que te apraz criá-los para matá-los, produzi-los com uma ilusão, absorvê-los com um desengano, verdadeira condenação dos

que aguardavam esse desengano e acreditaram nessa ilusão.
(MJ III 208; see Appendix 30)

The poet's pessimism vanishes, however, when he discovers the objective and circumstantial causes of his suffering.

A second group of problematic characters is composed of those who also have experienced the bitterness of life but, unlike those of the first group, do not find domestic peace. Beginning again with those already mentioned, one could cite the "angel Rafael," who goes crazy when he convinces himself of his wife's unfaithfulness and shuts himself and his daughter away from any contact with the external world. His case is like that of "Woman in black." A false appearance (a love letter kept by his wife but which was not addressed to her) leads him to believe in her unfaithfulness and, therefore, in the hypocrisy and evil of mankind.

When Inácio's wife ("The little guitar") leaves him for the guitar player, preferring the movement and cheerfulness of the outward life to the tranquility of domestic peace, Inácio realizes that life, *tout court,* is indistinguishable from this social life. Unable to bear this discovery he, like the "angel Rafael," goes mad.

Friar Simão ("Friar Simão") is another character who withdraws from the world. He becomes a monk and closes himself in a cloister, mortified by the strategies that precluded him from marrying the woman he loved. His final words before a premature death are: "—Morro odiando a humanidade!" (OC 2: 152) (" 'I die hating humankind!' ").

Valério ("Valério"—1864) is a character tortured by his incompatibility with "society." The woman he falls in love with prefers a *tolo*. He develops a friendship with a politician who uses Valério's literary skills but denies him help when he badly needs it. When he helps the politician's daughter, she despises and humiliates him in return. His incompatibility with social life makes him doubt the meaning of life.

> Quando Valério meditava sobre as condições da sua existência, a sua mocidade sem risos, o seu futuro sem esperanças, lançava um olhar melancólico para o suicídio, como a solução razoável do problema da vida, e perguntava entre si se a moral que desarma o braço do homem não era

> simplesmente uma moral de convenção. (OC-1937 19: 10;
> see Appendix 31)

Valério's singularity presupposes personal suffering and leads him toward a beginning of reflection. This reflection is clearly an embryonic form of skepticism. The point that morality is not universal and rational but relative to particular cultures and conventional is a traditional skeptical position that was heavily emphasized by Montaigne and Pascal (Machado's most likely sources.)[1] As with the other problematic characters, Valério's suffering is not mitigated by reflection. He ends up killing himself.

The number of cases of suicide and madness in Machado's early fiction points from the beginning to the difficulty of finding tranquility in marriage. Madness and suicide are the only "alternatives" for the problematic character who does not find domestic peace. When Machado begins to disbelieve in the possibility of domestic peace, practical alternatives are unfeasible. The alternative must be, therefore, theoretical. From Brás Cubas to Aires we shall see this development of reflection—here only referred to—finally separated from direct personal suffering. In Brás Cubas, for example, the emphasis is not on an embryonic reflective attitude, a mere by-product of failures, but rather on human misery, philosophically uncovered. This new state is due to the spectator's stance—unavailable to the problematic characters—which provides an alternative reflective standpoint in the fictional universe.

Machado's stress on physical features in some of these characters shows their still undeveloped state. In what follows, some of those who exhibit incipient traits of reflective, skeptical thought are briefly mentioned.

In the short story titled "Sem olhos" ("Deprived of eyes"), the narrator refers to a doctor whose aspect was so "extraordinary" and whose manners so "unique" "que a gente tinha prazer em o conversar e atrair, quando menos por sair um pouco da vulgaridade dos outros homens" (OC-1937 19: 107) ("that it was a pleasure to bring him closer and to talk with him, at least in order to escape for a little while from the vulgarity of the other men").

Mr. Belém ("Um esqueleto" ["A skeleton"]) is "um homem extremamente singular" (OC 2: 814) ("a truly unique man").

Although he does not exhibit any reflection in the short story, we are told that he has written a theological treatise and made astronomical discoveries. "[Q]uando ele meditava, ficava com olhos como de defunto. . . . O estudo o abatera muito, e os desgostos também" (OC 2: 815) ("While meditating, his eyes looked like those of a deceased man. . . . His studies—and his griefs— took a lot out of him"). Madness takes over completely when Mr. Belém decides to live with his deceased wife's skeleton. He resists the dissolution, in this case from natural causes, of his domestic peace. Like the others, he commits suicide. He prefers death to life without truth and an ethical relationship.

Captain Mendonça, in the short story by the same name, attracts the narrator at once, for "encontrar um original no meio de tantas cópias de que anda farta a humanidade, não é uma fortuna?" (MJ III 166) ("to find an original amid so many copies within humanity! Isn't this a treasure?"). The original is once more a crazy philosopher and scientist. Although far more a madman than a philosopher, Captain Mendonça holds the doctrine that "a vaidade . . . não é mais que a irradiação da consciência; à contração da consciência chamo eu modéstia" (MJ III 177) ("pride . . . is nothing more than the expansion of consciousness; its contraction I call modesty"). Here this thought is merely announced. Later, in Machado's short story "Elogio da vaidade" ("Praise of pride"), the idea is developed philosophically after the fashion of Erasmus's *Praise of Folly*.

Another madman of this group is a character who thinks he is Marcus Brutus ("Decadência de dois grandes homens" ["The downfall of two remarkable men"]). He also makes some skeptical remarks: "Toda a filosofia pode ser verdadeira; a ignorância dos homens é que faz de uma ou de outra crença da moda" (MJ II 30) ("Any philosophy can be true; it is man's ignorance that makes one or another the fashionable persuasion").[2] Other remarks recall Ecclesiastes: "[A] vida é uma eterna repetição. Todos inventam o inventado" (MJ II 33) ("Life is an eternal repetition. Everybody creates what has already been created"). The reflective dimension he presents is, however, limited to these few remarks. The major part of his uniqueness is sheer madness.

In summary, the characteristic feature of these ancestors of Machado's skeptics is a hint of skepticism, which, however, is the by-product of personal grief and even physical deformation.

Besides, their personalities are utterly problematic. They are madmen and/or suicidal.

The conclusion is that at the end of the first phase of Machado's fiction, the strategic life-view—mostly elaborated in the 1872–78 period—is fairly advanced, while the naive life-view—characteristic of the short stories from 1861 to 1871—has been transformed. This naive life-view will disappear to make room for the skeptical life-view in the second phase. In the stories of 1861–78, the naive life-view is held by problematic characters. These, however, will be superseded in the fictional universe of the short stories. This probably explains why Machado does not include any of these short stories whose protagonists are problematic characters—with the single exception of "Friar Simão"—in the two volumes of short stories he published during the first phase. As remarked above, most of the stories he included in the volumes deal with strategies. The likely reason for this exclusion is the very problematic condition of these characters. Later, when a solution is found for the problematic characters, they come to the forefront of Machado's fiction. The uniqueness of the skeptical character is only hinted at in the first phase; it is not elaborated.

***

Machado's evolution toward skepticism is clarified when the problematic characters of the first phase are compared to the outsiders of the second. When we turn to the latter, we find sophisticated characters, elaborated observers with an ironical and skeptical outlook. Not many of these characters of the second phase will be discussed because detailed analysis of the three major ones appears in Chapters Five, Six, and Seven of this study. The present inquiry will be limited to three second-phase short stories: "Último capítulo" ("Final Chapter") of 1883; "Papéis velhos" ("Old journals"), published in 1899; and "Questões de maridos" ("A question of husbands"), published posthumously. They are—the first two in particular—Machadian masterpieces in which well-developed skeptical characters appear.

"Final Chapter" is a short autobiography in which Matias Deodato—who is about to commit suicide—explains his apparently nonsensical will: Matias wants all his estate to be converted into new shoes and boots to be distributed among unhappy people. He summarizes his own misfortune in the autobiography: the premature death of his parents, professional dissatisfaction, an unhappy marriage, romantic betrayals, and other disenchantments that led him to doubt the possibility of happiness in this world and finally to the decision to finish himself off. About the time he makes this decision, Matias casually notices "um homem bem trajado, fitando a miúdo os pés" (OC 2: 386) ("a well-dressed man who frequently stared down at his feet as he walked" [DV 64]). The man was an acquaintance of his. Like himself, he had been quite unlucky and unhappy in life. Yet, Matias observes that this man

> ia risonho, e contemplava os pés, digo mal, os sapatos. Estes eram novos, de verniz, muito bem talhados. . . . Ele levantava os olhos para as janelas, para as pessoas, mas tornava-os aos sapatos. . . . Ia alegre; via-se-lhe no rosto a expressão da bem-aventurança. Evidentemente era feliz; e, talvez, não tivesse almoçado; talvez mesmo não levasse um vintém no bolso. (OC 2: 386; see Appendix 32)

Our philosopher narrator then wonders if happiness is a new pair of boots. Noticing that nothing in the world—social and political problems and all human miseries—"vale, para ele, um par de botas" ("is worth a pair of boots"), he concludes that the walking man "breathes" and "shines along with" the boots,

> ele calca com elas o chão de um globo que lhe pertence. Daí o orgulho das atitudes, a rigidez dos passos, e um certo ar de tranquilidade olímpica . . . Sim, a felicidade é um par de botas. (OC 2: 386; see Appendix 33)

With these considerations Matias reveals the rationale of his will. He gives it a philosophical ground.

> Não é outra a explicação do meu testamento. Os superficiais dirão que estou doido, que o delírio do suicida define a cláusula do testador; mas eu falo para os sapientes e para os malfadados. . . . Eia, caiporas! que a minha última vontade seja cumprida. Boa noite, e calçai-vos! (OC 2: 386; see Appendix 34)

Like many problematic characters in Machado's first phase, the outsider Matias kills himself. But the differences here are remarkable.

First, note that Matias, the narrator, differentiates himself from the eccentric and mad fellows of the first phase. He displays sharp lucidity in understanding the outward *modus operandi* of social life: the power of a new pair of boots lies in their being a source of social recognition, by their worth in the public sphere of the street where boots are proudly exhibited. Putting it in terms of Jacobina's categories in "The looking glass" (also of Machado's second phase), the new and elegant boots, like the uniform in Jacobina's story, is an "outward soul" capable of stamping a positive social identity on its wearer. Notice that Matias underlines the fact that the walking man stares at his boots, not at his feet. We see in this detail his skepticism concerning the existence of any human essence beyond social appearances. In "The looking glass," Jacobina, absolutely alone on a remote farm, searches for his image in a looking glass and sees only a shadow. Completely in panic, Jacobina finally puts on his military uniform to recover his image.

When we contrast Matias of "Final Chapter" with characters from "Captain Mendonça," "A skeleton," "The downfall of two remarkable men," and similar stories of the first phase, we realize that reflection has replaced madness. The philosophical view of the narrator denounces the irrationality, misery, and precariousness of life. Reflection and self-consciousness bring a dimension of greatness to human misery, but the latter continues to be overwhelming.[3] The human condition boils down to external social artifacts. Appearances rule over essence. Outward images predominate over inward entities such as spirit, morality, and truth. The final irony conveys this message: human happiness is, contrary to the doctrine of the Stoics, not a virtuous life but a new pair of boots. This now not only is understood by the outsider, but also is made explicit by him. Despite hints of a reflective attitude in the problematic characters of the first phase, reflection itself is not present. All one finds is a litany of failures and misfortunes. In "Final Chapter," besides this unhappy litany, there are remarkable reflections concerning the human condition.

Like the three protagonists analyzed in the second part of this study, Matias Deodato is the narrator of the story. He relates the circumstances that led him to death's door. In contrast, only two of the many problematic characters of the first phase are narrators. This corroborates the hypothesis that a reflective dimension requires first-person narration and that the very act of taking the stance of a narrator is part of the solution for a character who rejects social life and is seeking another position. The ultimate position is that of the skeptical author, but this solution is still not complete in "Final Chapter." Matias Deodato does commit suicide. Moreover, his position is still that of a dogmatist; he has a positive view about the value of human life. The solution becomes more effective in *Epitaph*—Brás Cubas has an identity, however peculiar: he is a "deceased author." But its final establishment occurs with Aires, who is an observer, skeptic, and living author.

To return to Matias, he is like the man he observes in the street in terms of unhappiness. Yet, Matias responds to his need in a different manner. Whereas the boot man reconciles himself to the human condition by identifying himself, probably in an unconscious manner, with this condition, the narrator understands—and rejects—its value. His comprehension could have led him to manipulate the social mechanisms that bring success and recognition: he could have bought an elegant pair of boots for himself. In refusing the strategic life-view, like the view taught in "Education of a stuffed shirt," Matias rejects social life. (Recall that the alternative of marriage, that is, of an essence, is no longer available in the second phase.) Despite his understanding, he sticks to his fatal decision. Perhaps it would be more accurate to talk of impossibility instead of refusal. The awareness of the precariousness of life precludes its strategic manipulation. This is possibly one of the reasons why the reflective dimension does not blend with the strategic life-view. As early as "Women's preference for *tolos*," Machado hints at this impossibility. It also explains Brás Cubas's failures to adopt the strategic life-view. By the same token, we understand the advice given in "Education of a stuffed shirt" to the effect that non-instrumental reflection compromises the strategy of the "stuffed shirt," so it must be avoided at all costs. Like Brás Cubas, Matias Deodato limits himself to the writing of his autobiography, in which he points to the absurdity of life. We can, therefore, conclude that besides the disappearance of the alternative of a marriage based on truth, virtue, and tranquility, refusal to adopt (or the impossibility of adopting) the strategic life-view is another precondition for the development of the skeptical perspective.

***

Whereas Matias Deodato emphasizes the pessimistic aspect, Brotero (in "Old journals") stresses the proper Pyrrhonian effect of adopting the skeptical life-view. Brotero is a congressman who has just been passed over in the composition of the new Cabinet even though his name had been mentioned among the Cabinet ministers as a very likely presence in the new Administration. Disappointed and upset, he writes to the prime minister, announcing his break with the Government. During the long night preceding the remittance of the letter, he examines some "old journals" of his. One of these contains a letter written in his youth in which he stated his willingness to kill himself because of an unhappy love.

> Nada faltava a essas cartas; lá estava o infinito, o abismo, o eterno. Um dos *eternos,* escrito na dobra do papel, não se chegava a ler, mas supunha-se. A frase era esta: "Um só minuto do teu amor, e estou pronto a padecer um suplício et . . ." Uma traça bifara o resto da palavra; comeu o *eterno* e deixou o *minuto.* Não se pode saber a que atribuir essa preferência, se à voracidade, se à filosofia das traças. (OC 2: 623; see Appendix 35)

Brotero then measures the distance between his present and past feelings concerning the matter of this juvenile letter. The moth and his memory make him realize the precariousness of human feelings and emotions, given their temporality. He notices that those promises and dispositions of the past are now completely irrelevant and meaningless to him. He then concludes that his radical break with the Administration, which will certainly bring costly sequels such as public ridicule and the hardship of being in the Opposition, is too hasty and naive a move. After all, his letter of rupture will later become just another "old journal" like the one he has just examined. As soon as he has this insight, he calms his spirit and tears up the letter.

Brotero's awareness of time allows him to avoid the negative consequences resulting from thoughtless and hasty actions caused by passions. Besides, his awareness also helps him to mitigate these very passions. His attitude is typically Pyrrhonian. Brotero compares the value of the old with that of the new letter and realizes that they are equipollent. One is no more valuable than the other (Sextus, PH 1.190). Both are equally meaningless from the standpoint of ultimate human finitude. Equipollence makes Brotero suspend judgment (*epoche*) with respect to the external (intrinsic) value of the matters addressed in the letters. During the whole night, Brotero is undecided and in mental confusion. With the discovery of the equipollence of the letters, he reaches the stage where "[the skeptics] found that quietude, as if by chance, followed upon their suspense, even as a shadow follows its substance" (PH 1.29).

Machado here sheds light on the axiological foundation of the Pyrrhonian life and on the subtle passage experienced by the Pyrrhonian from suspension of judgment (*epoche*) to tranquility (*ataraxia*). This ethical aspect of Greek skepticism has recently been the object of much interest and scholarship. Myles Burnyeat, Julia Annas, and Martha Nussbaum have emphasized that detachment from values is crucial in Pyrrhonian *ataraxia* (Brotero finds tranquility because he mitigates— detaches himself from—the value of being a minister of state). Avner Cohen and Oswaldo P. Pereira distinguish doubt from *epoche,* stressing the therapeutic aim of Pyrrhonism, viz., to cure the anxiety caused by doubts (Brotero's distressing night: to break or not with the Government?). David Sedley and Gisella Striker have argued that *ataraxia* must come unexpectedly (Brotero does not examine his old journals in order to attain tranquility; tranquility comes unexpectedly).

***

One thus finds in Machado's second phase the skeptical character with a correspondingly skeptical life-view. We can then pause for a moment to assess Machado's development toward a progressively more elaborated skepticism. The "skeptic" Daniel ("Qual dos dois?" ["Which of the two?"]) from the first phase, whose basic feature is apathy and even mental laziness, becomes the Pyrrhonian Brotero. Moreover, the skeptical characters of the second phase are no longer those exotic characters completely alienated from social life, but observers and thinkers. Finally, whereas Daniel is the only character of the first phase with skeptical traits, in the short stories of the second, besides Brotero, there are Matias Deodato ("Final Chapter"), Jacobina ("The looking glass"), Frei Lourenço ("Lágrimas de Xerxes" ["Xerxes's tears"]), Camilo ("A cartomante" ["The fortuneteller"]), Coimbra ("O escrivão Coimbra" ["The notary Coimbra"]), Fidélis ("Galeria póstuma" ["Posthumous gallery"]), and especially Moraes Pancada ("A question of husbands").

Moraes Pancada receives letters from his two recently married nieces. The letters from the niece who married a man known as a model of virtue are full of complaints, criticism, and regret. In those from the other, who married a man with a quite dubious moral reputation, Moraes Pancada finds only expressions of happiness, praise, and satisfaction. After the Pyrrhonian manner, the uncle opposes one set with the other and concludes: "—O subjetivo . . . o subjetivo . . . Tudo através do subjetivo . . ." (OC 2: 942). "[U]m e outro, ao passarem pelo espírito das mulheres, mudavam de todo" (OC 2: 945) (" 'Subjectivity . . . subjectivity . . . Everything through subjectivity. . . . Each [husband], in passing through [his wife's] spirit, was transformed completely' ").

Since this passage through the spirit (mind) is a precondition for every cognitive act, there being no alternative access to external reality, and since the object is completely changed during its cognition, how can statements about external reality be made? This example confirms what the reader has by now certainly realized, namely, that Machado's epistemological concerns are, above all, about ethics, and that his skepticism develops from his struggle with ethical questions. The question indirectly raised by Moraes Pancada is: how does one distinguish good from evil?

To conclude this chapter, a note must be added about the failure by critics to notice the skeptical life-view in Machado's short stories written after *Epitaph*. Alfredo Bosi, for example, presents a comprehensive overview of the short stories that Machado published in collections. In discussing "The looking glass," Bosi says that "[o] que separa . . . o narrador da história narrada, é, simples e brutalmente, a passagem de classe, o aprendizado das aparências" ("what lies between . . . the narrator and the story narrated is a change in class situation, the learning of social appearances"). This passage, according to

Bosi, "empenha o futuro inteiro do eu narrador" ("engages the whole future of the narrator's self") and is fundamentally a passage "da inexperiência ou da ingênua franqueza à máscara adulta" ("from inexperience or frank naïveté to the mature mask") (Bosi 447–48). But the Jacobina who uses the mask (who is attached to his uniform) is not the Jacobina who tells his story. The former is a character who holds the strategic life-view; the latter is a philosopher who reflects upon and theorizes on his past experience and on that of others. Besides the transition noted by Bosi from the naive to the strategic life-view, there is another one: from the strategic to the skeptical life-view.

Chapter Four

The Revised Short Stories

Adjusting the Narrative
to the Skeptical Point of View

Machado de Assis is a master of the short story. He wrote a very large number of them, mostly under his own name, but many—especially the less elaborated early ones—under pseudonyms. The short stories served as a kind of laboratory in which he sketched and experimented with forms, themes, and characters. This procedure is most clearly seen in some short stories that he rewrote for republication. The most noticeable thing in this procedure is Machado's search for a narrative focus that best gives expression to the reflective dimension he develops throughout his fiction.

Our first example brings together two very early pieces. "O país das quimeras" ("The country of chimeras") is probably one of the earliest short stories written by Machado. In 1866, this story appears again as "Uma excursão milagrosa" ("A miraculous journey"). The plot is the same in both versions. Having just gone through a disillusioning love affair, a roving poet, Tito, "travels" to the very strange "country of chimeras." This "trip" takes place under an ambiguous state of consciousness: a transient state between sleep and waking. Not unlike Brás Cubas shortly before his death, Tito goes through a kind of delirium. There is indeed a parallel in their experiences. Brás Cubas returns to ordinary consciousness to find himself facing his cat (OC 1: 522). Tito, on returning from his "journey," is facing his dog (OC 2: 770). Tito's trip is a concrete and real exemplification of the "trips" (fancies) undergone by poets and people who are distracted from reality by chimeras (empty reflections and imaginations). One notes, however, Machado's philosophico-ontological point in that the "country of chimeras" is the place where the "real" chimeras of the social world are engineered. In the "country of chimeras," man's occupations are unmasked as arbitrary, precarious, and formal. Those chimeras have a function: to make sure that individuals do not face their original nothingness. The following are some of Tito's observations about this strange but revealing country.

1. "[É o país] para onde viaja três quartas partes do gênero humano" (OC 2: 765) ("It is a country visited by three-fourths of the human species"). Note that during this early period of Machado's fiction a minority of people still do not travel to the "country of chimeras." Tito returns wiser from his trip. He now can distinguish the chimerical, that is, the *tolo,* from those "que têm miolos na cabeça" ("who have brains in their heads"), that is, the *homens de espírito.* However, he returns also "unhappier and poorer," for this is "a sorte de todos quantos entendem dever dizer o que sabem; nem se compra por outro preço a liberdade de desmascarar a humanidade" (OC 2: 770) ("the fate of all those who think they should tell what they know; and this is the price one has to pay for unmasking humanity").

Machado still conceives at this point of an essence beyond the false appearances of social life. Although chimerical, this appearance is strong enough to punish and to reduce to a minority those "who have brains in their heads."

2. The ontological fragility of social reality requires that the interactions be highly formalized and ritualized.

> O *Gênio das bagatelas* . . . estava sentado em um trono de casquinha, tendo de ornamento dois pavões, um de cada lado. . . . Todos aqueles pavões, de minuto a minuto armavam-se, *apavoneavam-se,* e davam os guinchos de costume. . . . não se dá naquele país o ato mais insignificante sem que esta formalidade seja preenchida. (OC 2: 765; see Appendix 36)

3. Tito finally finds the room where the most important activity of the country takes place.

> [M]uitos quiméricos à roda de mesas discutiam os diferentes modos de inspirar aos diplomatas e diretores deste nosso mundo os pretextos para encher o tempo e apavorar os espíritos com futilidades e espantalhos. Esses homens tinham ares de finos e espertos. Havia ordem do soberano para não entrar naquela sala em horas de trabalho; uma guarda estava à porta. A menor distração daquele congresso seria considerada uma calamidade pública. (OC 2: 768; see Appendix 37)

Making up amusements to occupy people's lives, no matter what, is a matter of existential security. The aim is to fill the void of existence. Pascal's influence here as elsewhere is clear:

> the sole cause of man's unhappiness is that he does not know how to stay quietly in his room. . . .
> The only good thing for men therefore is to be diverted from thinking of what they are, either by some occupation which takes their mind off it, or by some novel and agreeable passion which keeps them busy, like gambling, hunting, some absorbing show, in short by what is called diversion. (La 136)

4. Precariousness is another major characteristic of the "country of chimeras":

> mas quando ia falar reparei que as duas [interlocutoras] se haviam tornado mais delgadas e vaporosas . . . desfaziam[-se] como se fossem feitas de névoa. . . . Dentro de pouco eu senti que me faltava o apoio aos pés e vi que estava solto no espaço. (OC 2: 769–70; see Appendix 38)

Once more Pascal (La 199): the experience of the abyss follows the understanding that the occupations of life are but fragile chimeras filling empty space.

"A miraculous journey" has only two substantial differences from "The country of chimeras," yet these differences are significant enough to justify the change of title and to render the second version a much better short story. The first is the addition of a couple of introductory pages in which Machado explains the meaning of the peculiar "trip" his character takes. He contrasts it with some other literary journeys. This procedure anticipates the narrator's awareness of the epistemological possibilities of such a trip. (In Chapter Five we shall see how this awareness is developed in *Epitaph*.) After alluding to ordinary trips that involve spatial displacement, the author cites "sedentary trips" like Tito's: "*Viagem à Roda do Meu Quarto,* e a *Viagem à Roda do Meu Jardim,* de Maistre e Alphonse Karr" (OC 2: 759) ("*The trip around my room,* and *The trip around my garden,* by Maistre and Alphonse Karr").

Anticipating Brás Cubas, who, as Machado says in the prologue to the third edition of *Epitaph*, "viajou à roda da vida" (OC 1: 510) ("traveled around life"), and Plácido, who "viajou à roda de si mesmo" ("traveled around himself") ("Viagem à roda de mim mesmo" ["Journey around myself"]), Machado indicates the peculiarity of his hero's journey. Geographic displacement—the "country of chimeras" is on another planet—is an epistemological device employed in order to generate the withdrawal and estrangement usually experienced by travelers and necessary to the formation of the spectator and the reflective attitude.

> Todavia, apesar das estradas que o nosso viajante percorreu, dos condutores que teve e do espetáculo que viu, não se pode deixar de reconhecer que o fundo é o mais natural e possível deste mundo. (OC 2: 759; see Appendix 39)

The second modification is a formal adjustment made so the short story can better convey the epistemological possibilities inherent in Tito's journey. Whereas the narrator of "The country of chimeras" is omniscient throughout, in "A miraculous journey" the author gives the narrative focus to the traveler.

> Aqui deixa de falar o autor para falar o protagonista. Não quero tirar o encanto natural que há de ter a narrativa do poeta reproduzindo as suas próprias impressões. (OC 2: 763; see Appendix 40)

The modifications in the narrative focus and in the title are both meaningful. "The country of chimeras" emphasizes the objective place where the character goes. The emphasis of "A miraculous journey" lies in the subjective impressions of the character caused by his journey and the country. This change anticipates the literary evolution undertaken by Machado toward the skeptical perspective. Whereas the narrative focus of all novels belonging to the first phase is omniscient, the action of the plot being their strongest element, most novels of Machado's second phase are narrated in the first person. This facilitates the expression of the protagonist's impressions. A skeptical perspective requires a restricted point of view that is possible only in first-person novels. The basic characteristic of the omniscient narrator is his unlimited knowledge of characters' intentions, motivations, and destinies. In transforming "The country of chimeras" into "A miraculous journey," Machado shows that he is searching—in a quite early period of his literary activity—for a literary form that can best give expression to a skeptical standpoint.

***

Another revised short story is titled "Rui de Leão" in its first version of 1872 and "O imortal" ("The immortal one") in the second version of 1882. Rui de Leão attains immortality when he takes an elixir of life given to him by an Indian. After living for almost three centuries, he gets bored and tries—without success—to bring his life to an end. He finally manages to escape immortality when he finds an antidote to the elixir he had taken.

The modifications in the second version show the development of the spectator and of the reflective dimension that characterizes Machado's second phase. The narrative focus, omniscient in the first version, is restricted in the second. The narrator of the second version is Rui's son, witness of part of his life. This modification facilitates the presentation of the immortal one's own point of view, which is a fundamental element of the short story insofar as Rui's immortality gives him a vantage point for perceiving the utter meaninglessness and precariousness of the many human diversions (Pascal, La 132–39). The changes Machado makes in the plot reveal his interest in this anthropological investigation. The change of titles also indicates this interest. Whereas in "Rui de Leão" the emphasis is on the many amusing episodes in the life of the character, the main emphasis in "The immortal one" is on the point of view made possible by immortality and on the immortal one's thoughts about the temporal nature of life. Whereas the character in the first version achieves multiple successes in the numerous occupations in which he engages during his long life, in the second version the character's odyssey becomes unstable, with lows and highs: he has moments of glory, but his many painful moments of fall and failure are always emphasized. A contemporary of Brás Cubas, the immortal one is shaken like a baby's rattle throughout his life (as, in *Epitaph*, Pandora shakes humankind). Misery, fragility, and immorality are the features of life highlighted in the second version.

> Tinha visto morrer todas as suas afeições. . . . Outras afeições e não poucas o tinham enganado; e umas e outras, boas

> e más, sinceras e pérfidas, era-lhe forçoso repeti-las, sem
> trégua, sem um respiro ao menos, porquanto, *a experiência*
> *não lhe podia valer contra a necessidade de agarrar-se a*
> *alguma coisa, naquela passagem rápida dos homens e das*
> *gerações.* Era uma necessidade de vida eterna; sem ela,
> cairia na demência. Tinha provado tudo, esgotado tudo; agora
> era a repetição, a monotonia, sem esperanças, sem nada (o
> grifo é nosso). (OC 2: 900; emphasis added; see Appendix 41)

Immortality affords a description of the finite nature of time and
generates a tragic consciousness: a longing for eternal life on
the one hand and consciousness of the fragility of life on the
other. Once more we notice the theme of Ecclesiastes—"nothing new under the sun." Machado's originality in construing a
point of view that allows this glimpse of the vanity of humankind must, however, be emphasized. A similar construction is
observed in the chapter "The Delirium" of *Epitaph*. The itali-
cized portion of the citation above indicates the resemblance
of Rui's mood to that of Brás Cubas in the delirium. The similarity does not obscure, however, the crucial difference. Rui's
stance is a problematic one arising from the combination of his
sharing the ordinary man's aspirations with his awareness of
the vanity of these aspirations. His understanding makes him
different from ordinary mortal men who identify noncritically
with their desires and ambitions, with people and projects, and
who lack an enlarged perspective on the fragility of all these
things in the flow of time. In Brás Cubas, one finds a first tentative solution to this contradiction. Dead, he no longer longs
for eternity. His attitude toward life is merely reflective. It is
therefore quite revealing that Rui is not the narrator, even in the
second version.

***

The final revised short story to be addressed has the same title
in both versions. It was titled "Uma visita de Alcibíades"
("Alcibíades's visit") when it first appeared in 1876 and also
when it reappeared in 1882. As in the previous cases, the
reelaboration is aimed at better expressing the observer's point
of view, that of a modern man receiving a visit from an ancient
Greek.

In the 1876 version, the narration starts in the third person,
with Alvares about to report the strange visit he received to a

circle of friends at a party. At this point the focus moves to the character, who tells of his meeting with Alcibíades. In this version, the meeting took place when Alvares was dressing to go to a ball.

In the 1882 version, there is a formal modification and a change in the plot. The short story becomes a letter to the Chief of Police. Because of this modification, Alcibíades's visit is no longer the anecdote it is in the first version, where the extraordinary event, and not its epistemologico-skeptical possibilities (cultural relativism), is emphasized. The second version is a serious report written in the first person. The epistolary form highlights the character of the narrator and makes room for his philosophical commentaries, which are absent from the first version, for such commentaries are not appropriate in social conversations. The philosophy is again one that emphasizes the temporal dimension of the human condition. In the short story under consideration, this dimension is expressed, above all, in the changeable and fragile nature of customs and beliefs. Thus the skeptical narrator-character at one point tries to soothe a disturbed Alcibíades, confused by modern customs (for when the narrator puts on his tie, Alcibíades thinks he is going to hang himself).

> Cada século, meu caro Alcibíades, muda de danças como muda de idéias. (OC 2: 354; see Appendix 42)

Part 2
Machado's Second Phase
(1879 to 1908)

Chapter Five

Epitaph of a Small Winner

The Deceased Writer

The analysis presented in Chapter Four showed that the key element in the short stories that Machado de Assis revised for second publication is a search for a point of view appropriate for exhibiting a reflective dimension. Similarly, in *Epitaph* Machado has Brás Cubas take a point of view that is the solution for the problematic situation of the *homem de espírito*. At this point, where Machado's pessimism is at its highest, the *homem de espírito* has no place in real life. He thus becomes the basic formal element of the novel. This solution represents a revolutionary turn in Machadian—and Brazilian—fiction. Scholars unanimously point out that what makes *Epitaph* a masterpiece is its narrative point of view. My analysis begins with Brás Cubas's initial remark—reiterated by Machado in the prologue to the third edition—about the status of his work.

> Trata-se, na verdade, de uma obra difusa, na qual eu, Brás Cubas, se adotei a forma livre de um Sterne, ou de um Xavier de Maistre, não sei se lhe meti algumas rabugens de pessimismo. Pode ser. Obra de finado. Escrevi-a com a pena da galhofa e a tinta da melancolia. . . . Acresce que a gente grave achará no livro umas aparências de puro romance, ao passo que a gente frívola não achará nele o seu romance usual. (OC 1: 511; see Appendix 43)

For Brás Cubas, the singularity of his work, which he qualifies as philosophical, lies in its reflective content. Within the fictional context of his life, his autobiography is a serious attempt at capturing the central events and features of that life. These features account for the "peevish pessimism" (E 17) that he indicates as distinguishing his work, on the one hand, from those novels that were models for his own, and on the other hand, from the romantic novels then fashionable in Brazil. The criterion for selection of the events to be included in the autobiography is not merely factual, but philosophical: he selects those events that portray human misery. Once reconsidered in the writing of the autobiography, these events appear as illustrations of the reflective dimension—philosophical view—that is being generated in Machado's fiction and, as has been demonstrated, is closely related to Pascal's thought.

Epitaph highlights the first stage of the Pyrrhonian's journey: *zetesis*. This is the most philosophical stage, for it is the occasion on which philosophical doctrines are subjected to critical examination. In Brás Cubas's case, the philosophical doctrine subjected to *zetesis* is Quincas Borba's "Humanitism." As pointed out by Barreto Filho, Humanitism is a caricature of philosophical systems and doctrines in general, and in particular, of the philosophies of history fashionable in Brazil during the late nineteenth century—Darwinism, Comte's positivism, and Spencer's social evolutionism. What has not been noticed thus far by scholars is that the element of these philosophies that Brás Cubas assails is the Stoicism that Machado identifies behind the secularized and scientific outward appearance of the "nova tendência intelectual" (OC 3: 810) ("new intellectual tendency"). These Stoic elements are the following: determinism, rationalism, a providential view of nature, and an optimistic view of human nature—the divinization of the human species. Brás Cubas's skepticism, therefore, attacks fundamental features of the Hellenistic doctrine that was historically the main target of the Greek skeptics.

The skeptic's *zetesis* must be distinguished from the usual philosophical argumentation that aims at the establishment and proof of doctrines. Brás Cubas refers to this philosophical—but not dogmatic—aspect of *zetesis* when he specifies the status of his book:

> obra supinamente filosófica, de uma filosofia desigual, agora austera, logo brincalhona, coisa que não edifica nem destrói, não inflama nem regela, e é todavia mais do que passatempo e menos de que apostolado. (OC 1: 514; see Appendix 44)

He emphasizes the *philosophical* nature of his work at the same time that he distinguishes it from the optimistic philosophical works of his time. "Apostolado" ("preachment") probably refers to Comte's positivism, one faction of which became a church in Brazil the year before the publication of *Epitaph* (Paim 440).

Although Brás Cubas's work is antidogmatic, it is not completely skeptical. The other two stages in the Pyrrhonian's journey—*epoche* and *ataraxia*—although not altogether absent in *Epitaph,* are fully defined only in later novels. Brás Cubas's rejection of Humanitism does not lead him to suspend judgment but to assume a contrary philosophical position. He distinguishes true from false appearances and holds a pessimistic view of human nature in contrast to the optimism of the "new intellectual tendency."

The "peevish pessimism" does not, however, overshadow the "free form of a Sterne or of a Xavier de Maistre" (E 17) that Brás Cubas adopted. This free form, which reveals a fundamental meaning of his narrative, is the "solution"—skeptical—to a Pascalian-inspired anthropology without the religious dimension that in Pascal recovers meaning for the human condition. The "Melancholy" that Brás Cubas experienced in life is transformed into "ink" for the deceased writer's "pen of Mirth." The free narration—the irony and the humor—that accompanies the analysis of human misery (for melancholy, included in the autobiography during the selection process, results from awareness of the emptiness that human agitation tries to fill) is the last meaningful activity available for the disenchanted *homem de espírito* who refuses both social life and Pascal's faith.

Another feature—"work of a man already dead"—needs further commentary because it refers to the author's stance.[1] Brás Cubas inverts the chronology of his life by beginning with the events that preceded his death. This inversion has epistemological significance. In the first chapter—"The Death of the Author"—he describes his funeral and establishes his condition as a deceased writer, the point of view from which the reflective dimension unfolds. His death marks his passage from the strategic life-view, which he pursues until his life comes to an end, to the skeptical life-view from which the book is written. Brás Cubas then goes on to relate his last meeting—after many years of separation—with Virgília. This provides him an occasion for emphasizing the implacable destructive power of time (a central theme of the novel). After the meeting, he is seized by a "delirium" that summarizes and universalizes the philosophy exhibited in the autobiography.

In the first chapter, a crucial passage indicates Brás Cubas's first motivation for beginning his autobiography with the end of his life: "eu não sou propriamente um autor defunto, mas um defunto autor, para quem a campa foi outro berço" (OC 1: 511) ("properly speaking, I am a deceased writer not in the sense of one who has written and is now deceased, but in the sense of one who has died and is now writing, a writer for whom the grave was really a new cradle" [E 19]). The difference is fundamental. Although Brás Cubas wrote a few articles, poems, and maxims during a certain period of his life, they have no relevance in the novel. With the exception of a few maxims, these writings are only mentioned in passing. In the passage above, Brás Cubas stresses the fact that his death defines his stance as an author. The meaningful authorship is that of the autobiography itself, an authorship that is only born with his death. The condition of being deceased is the point of view that frames the analysis of his life, of the other characters, and of life in general. This point of view cannot be adopted by a living character at this period in Machado's fiction. This impossibility is consistent with Pascal's view of humankind and with the view exhibited in Machado's first phase: *divertissement* precludes the understanding of human nature. Before the creation of Brás Cubas, Machado's characters were entangled in these distractions and so could not attain a reflective perspective. Because at this period at the end of Machado's first phase the power of social life is absolute (see Chapter Two), the withdrawal necessary to allow an observational and reflective attitude must be radical but distinct from the suicidal and insane condition of the problematic characters analyzed in Chapter Three. Only a deceased writer meets these conditions. Only a deceased writer does not amuse and agitate himself. He is radically divorced from the unstable social life at the same time that, unlike the problematic character, he maintains a lucid mental condition. He is thus in a position to observe the finiteness that underlies life, to which his own condition of deceased writer attests.

Brás Cubas's trajectory is a progressive but difficult and painful withdrawal from social life, which corresponds to his progressive approach to authorship. His journey from one life-view to another is analyzed below. The precariousness of the human condition is revealed to him whenever his projects are destroyed and his agitation arrested. As his trajectory develops, this second factor increasingly predominates over his insertion in social life until he is totally immobilized in death. At this point, the naive and strategic life-views of the living Brás Cubas—belief in the realization and intrinsic value of projects—step aside, and the skeptical perspective of the deceased writer takes their place. The transition from the naive to the skeptical life-view is propelled by the failures of the living character; insofar as they paralyze Brás Cubas's activity (agitation), they push him to the reflective attitude. Reference was made above to the advice given by the "stuffed shirt" that reflection is a major obstacle to the success of the strategic life-view. Because it reveals the human misery that the "stuffed shirt" manipulates for his own advantage, this reflection can make him melancholic and, therefore, unmotivated to employ his strategies. This is exactly what happens to Brás Cubas. Melancholy stops him from attaining the strategic life-view he is pursuing, nurturing instead the skeptical one.

Although Brás Cubas does not go along with Pascal's attempt to convert libertines, he does present a normative critique of the strategic life-view. In ceaselessly braking the narrative, he attempts to halt the reader's agitation and bring him or her to a reflective attitude in a movement parallel to Brás Cubas's own life experience.[2]

As for Brás Cubas-author's practical situation, it differs from that of Brás Cubas-character in that as a deceased writer, he is free from the perturbations that affected the living character. There is no disturbance because there is no life. This first version of the skeptical life-view is therefore only a literary and philosophical point of view. The solution to the problem of the *homem de espírito* is therefore still partial at this point. It is only theoretical, for *ataraxia* is reached only in death. This corresponds to a traditional criticism of Pyrrhonism, recently raised by Myles Burnyeat, Julia Annas, and Jonathan Barnes, that Pyrrhonism is a paradoxical way of life because it aims at detachment from all the values and beliefs that alone give meaning to and promote survival in life. In a literal sense, Brás Cubas is a skeptic who cannot live his skepticism. This situation changes in *Dom Casmurro*. Besides representing the point of view of the novel, Bento Santiago is also a living character, although a "casmurro," i.e., antisocial, pessimistic, and misanthropic. Only in the third and last stage, with Counselor Aires, is this practical alternative consolidated.

The deceased writer's theoretical distance facilitates his philosophical view. His final assessment of his relationship with Virgília well exemplifies the distance that lies between the naive life-view he had at the time he met her and the philosophical one exhibited by the deceased writer. In the "ardent and brief" first kiss, he signals the

> prólogo de uma vida de delícias, de terrores, de remorsos, de prazeres que rematavam em dor, de aflições que desabrochavam em alegria,—uma hipocrisia paciente e sistemática, único freio de uma paixão sem freio,—vida de agitações, de cóleras, de desesperos e de ciúmes, que uma hora pagava à farta e de sobra; mas outra hora vinha e engulia aquela, como tudo mais, para deixar à tona as agitações e o resto, e o resto do resto, que é o fastio e a saciedade: tal foi o livro daquele prólogo. (OC 1: 567; see Appendix 45)

The autobiographical literary form is crucial for this understanding. It allows the chronological distance that alone opens the perspective of the ultimate (metaphysical) meaning of the relationship. Since, as Brás Cubas says, in "umas memórias, como estas[,] . . . só entra a substância da vida" (OC 1: 542) ("memoirs, such as these, . . . only the substance of my life is set forth" [E 68]), that which is included is precisely the meaningless agitations and concupiscence that "[agitam] o homem como um chocalho" (OC 1: 521) ("[shake] man like a baby's rattle" [E 34]), revealing the precariousness of humankind. The narrator's method is to synthesize in himself the summary of the passions that annihilate humankind.

The autobiographical form allows the display of characters and events during his lifetime—meetings and new meetings with the same characters later—pointing to the essential temporal predicament of life. The autobiography also allows Brás

Cubas to express his philosophy in the many commentaries he inserts in the narrative. These interruptions make it harder for the reader to amuse him- or herself with the story, for the reader, according to Brás Cubas, is far more interested in the action—agitation—than in the pessimistic commentary on the events. Brás thus addresses his reader:

> Tu tens pressa de envelhecer, e o livro anda devagar; tu amas a narração direta e nutrida, o estilo regular e fluente, e este livro e o meu estilo são como os ébrios, guinam à direita e à esquerda, andam e param, resmungam, urram, gargalham, ameaçam o céu, escorregam e caem . . . (OC 1: 581; see Appendix 46)

Authorship functions in *Epitaph,* as in *Dom Casmurro* and in *Counselor Ayres' Memorial,* as a distraction from the boredom of eternity. The authors of the three memoirs are outside the dimension of time. In a certain sense they are outside practical life, *locus* of the strategic and naive life-views.

> Começo a arrepender-me deste livro. Não que ele me canse; eu não tenho que fazer; e, realmente, expedir alguns magros capítulos para esse mundo sempre é tarefa que distrai um pouco da eternidade. Mas o livro é enfadonho, cheira a sepulcro, traz certa contração cadavérica. (OC 1: 581; see Appendix 47)

Authorship constitutes the *modus vivendi* of these characters. This is literally Brás Cubas's situation—he is a deceased writer. In Dom Casmurro and, later, in Aires one sees a progressive, although distanced, return to the sphere of practical life.

Note the perspective determined by his condition as deceased writer in Brás Cubas's evaluation of his book. Life appears "tedious" when seen without the chimerical illusions that distract and keep people busy. The philosophy of precariousness and death that he presents "smells of the tomb." *Rigor mortis* well expresses the narrator's immobility that results from his failure, while alive, to realize his projects and aspirations.

Note also that the literary form of the work is related to Brás Cubas's "existence" strictly as an author. His "existence" is realized in his narrative. His style—insertion of many parenthetical comments in the narrative, thereby constantly interrupting the plot—corresponds to what constituted the general pattern of his life: a history characterized by constant deviations and falls from the common bourgeois social trajectory (preparation in college for a profession that brings social status, a wife, children, and professional and social success). The linking of life to style reveals the deceased writer's attempt to revive the dead sensations by narrating them. For example, his style in telling the story of the later period of his life expresses the monotony and boredom that characterized it.

> Já se vai sentindo que o meu estilo não é tão lesto como nos primeiros dias. . . . O que eu quero dizer não é que esteja agora mais velho do que quando comecei o livro. A morte não envelhece. Quero dizer, sim, que em cada fase da narração da minha vida experimento a sensação correspondente. (OC 1: 623, 625; see Appendix 48)

Death means to Brás Cubas recollection and reflection on his past life. The position of this Machadian skeptical philosopher is contrary to that of the philosopher as described by Plato. Brás Cubas is not located in the changeable world of time, recollecting eternal ideas, but in the realm of the eternal, trying to recollect the changeable phenomena of the world of time. But note that Brás Cubas's realm of the eternal has nothing to do with the Platonic world of perfectly intelligible forms of good, truth, and beauty. In Brás Cubas's world, these are mere illusions that fooled the *homem de espírito*. His point, however, is that he is better off as a deceased writer than he was (or everybody is) as a living person because now he enjoys *ataraxia*. Because he is deceased, he no longer suffers the disturbances and griefs that are unavoidable in life. Note that according to Burnyeat and Annas, only by being completely "dead" to everyday life—were this ever possible—would the Pyrrhonian reach *ataraxia*. Brás Cubas finds this possibility in writing. In working on his book, he converts the disturbance and melancholy he suffered while alive into ink for his "pen of Mirth." While he was alive, melancholy was inevitable; as a deceased writer, he has the alternative of transforming melancholy into jest. This escape from pain is the function of deceased authorship in a period of Machado's fiction when tranquility is no longer available in the morality and truth of marriage.

Creiam-me, o menos mau é recordar; ninguém se fie da felicidade presente; há nela uma gota da baba de Caim. Corrido o tempo e cessado o espasmo, então sim, então talvez se pode gozar deveras, porque entre uma e outra dessas duas ilusões, melhor é a que se gosta sem doer. (OC 1: 516; see Appendix 49)

In this comment, Brás Cubas exhibits a Pascalian type of skepticism. From a metaphysical standpoint, reality cannot be distinguished from illusion. Human reality is but a brief spasm of being in the immensity of the infinite universe. "For, after all, what is man in nature? A nothing compared to the infinite, a whole compared to the nothing, a middle point between all and nothing, infinitely remote from an understanding of the extremes" (Pascal, La 199). Once the illusory ontology of human reality is demystified—and Pascal's alternative of faith excluded—it becomes clear that the best position is that of the deceased writer who is fully aware of the human predicament.

The condition of deceased writer makes sincerity and objectivity possible in the report and analysis of his own motivations. Sincerity is a presupposition of the *autobiographical* genre. Objectivity is a presupposition of the *philosophical* autobiography. Both make possible the analysis of the hidden, vicious motives that master human behavior. Moreover, sincerity represents the ethical possibility of transparency that is the alternative to the deceitful and hypocritical social life that at this point is hegemonic, for marriage no longer means domestic peace.

Talvez espante ao leitor a franqueza com que lhe exponho e realço a minha mediocridade; advirta que a franqueza é a primeira virtude de um defunto. Na vida, o olhar da opinião, o contraste dos interesses, a luta das cobiças obrigam a gente a calar os trapos velhos, a disfarçar os rasgões e os remendos, a não estender ao mundo as revelações que faz à consciência. . . . Mas, na morte, que diferença! que desabafo! que liberdade! Como a gente pode sacudir fora a capa, deitar ao fosso as lentejoulas, despregar-se, despintar-se, desafeitar-se, confessar lisamente o que foi e o que deixou de ser! Porque, em suma, já não há vizinhos, nem amigos, nem inimigos, nem conhecidos, nem estranhos; não há platéia. O olhar da opinião, esse olhar agudo e judicial, perde a virtude, logo que pisamos o território da morte; não digo que ele se não estenda para cá, e nos não examine e julgue; mas a nós é que

não se nos dá do exame nem do julgamento. Senhores vivos,
não há nada tão incomensurável como o desdém dos finados.
(OC 1: 543–44; see Appendix 50)

Indifference (*adiaphoria*) is a major end pursued by Pyrrho and
his followers. Brás Cubas seems to agree with Burnyeat that
only death can fully bring this blessed pleasure. Since for the
Hellenistic philosophers in general, the goal of indifference and
tranquility is an ethical one, Brás Cubas's book has a moral
input. Brás Cubas, the author, is a descendant of the *homens de
espírito*. Narration occupies the place of ethical behavior characteristic of the *homens de espírito,* behavior that at this point
is no longer possible. Because the alternative to social life is
now narration, this narration expresses a philosophical dimension committed to the truth. Brás Cubas's position is unlike
Plato's, but it is also unlike the Sophist's. The latter reacts to
skepticism by turning to pragmatic politics and rhetoric (the
life-view corresponding to sophistry is the strategic one).
Because nonpragmatic reflection presupposes sincerity, it is
unavailable to the individual entangled in the trap of social life.
Attention to the development of Machado's fiction and to the
content of the reflective dimension generated in this development suggests that Kinnear, Nunes (*Craft*), and Schwarz are
wrong to question Brás Cubas's reliability.

It is important to emphasize that since Brás Cubas's skeptical perspective is committed to the values of truth and morality,
it must be distinguished from Pyrrhonism, although, like
Pascal, Brás Cubas uses Pyrrhonism in presenting his view.
Note also the pessimism underlying even this possibility of
morality: the only ethical behavior possible is the sincere
report of the insincerity and manipulation that structure the behavior of those alive. Brás Cubas is a moral skeptic. He doubts
the possibility of a moral *life* but not of a moral *perspective*.[3]

The Delirium

The last experience reported by Brás Cubas before his death is
his famous delirium, presumably his last experience as a living
person. It is reported, however, like his funeral and the last
meeting with Virgília, in the beginning of his autobiography.
There is an epistemological reason for such inversion. Because

it is his last experience, and because it occurred under an extraordinary state of consciousness, it signals the passage from the live Brás Cubas to the deceased writer. During the delirium, Brás Cubas loses both his last illusions (breaking with the naive life-view) and his hopes of success in life (breaking with the strategic life-view) to adopt finally the skeptical life-view. Besides marking this passage, the delirium summarizes, intensifies, and universalizes the philosophical view that his life corroborates. The following are the major skeptical and Pascalian aspects of this philosophy.

1. Reason is powerless with respect to metaphysical questions. Reason is utterly unable to clarify the meaning of the human condition. In the delirium, Reason steps aside and Folly takes its place. Brás Cubas tells "Nature or Pandora" (E 32) that he cannot understand her: "tu és absurda, tu és uma fábula. Estou sonhando, decerto, ou, se é verdade que enlouqueci, tu não passas de uma concepção de alienado, isto é, uma coisa vã, que a razão ausente não pode reger nem palpar" (OC 1: 520) ("You are an absurdity, a fable. I am surely dreaming, or, if in truth I have gone mad, you are nothing but a psychopath's figment, a vain and empty thing, which reason, being absent, cannot govern" [E 33]).

Pascal emphasizes the weakness of reason with respect to metaphysical questions. God is above—for some other skeptical fideists even against—reason. Nature, including reason, is corrupted by Original Sin—a mystery that reason cannot grasp (La 131 and 695). Unlike Brás Cubas, the skeptical fideists introduce faith as the alternative to reason. In *Epitaph,* the function of faith is exercised by Folly, which thereby gains epistemological significance. Instead of sheer madness, Folly represents the moment of Brás Cubas's highest lucidity, with which he becomes the skeptical deceased writer.

2. The skeptical object of problematic cognition is, above all, represented by woman—as pointed out in the first part of this study. Pandora is a woman whose opacity is an intensification and projection of the whole nature of this basic feature of Machado's female characters.

> Caiu do ar? destacou-se da terra? não sei; sei que um vulto imenso, uma figura de mulher me apareceu então. . . . Tudo

nessa figura . . . escapava à compreensão do olhar humano, porque os contornos perdiam-se no ambiente, e o que parecia espesso era muita vez diáfano. Estupefato, não disse nada. (OC 1: 519; see Appendix 51)

The relationship between Brás Cubas and Nature is a skeptical cognitive one. As far as the object of this cognitive relation is concerned, one notes Aenesidemus's trope based "on the quantities and formations of the underlying objects" (HP 1: 37). As far as the subject is concerned, one notes the *apraxia* (immobility) frequently reported as striking the Pyrrhonian. Brás Cubas's reference to his initial silence recalls the Pyrrhonian *aphasia*, the impossibility of making statements about the object under examination.

3. Stupefaction and *aphasia* bring to Brás Cubas the awareness of his own fragility as well as the consciousness of human fragility in general. "[M]e sentia eu o mais débil e decrépito dos seres" (OC 1: 520) ("I felt like the weakest and most decrepit of beings" [E 33]). Pyrrhonism—a view that shows the opacity of the world and its creator (a view that Pascal "Christianizes" in his doctrine of the hidden God)—is used as a propaedeutic to the moral aim of humiliating man's pride. For Pascal and other skeptical fideists, a major manifestation of pride is the philosophical attempt at certain knowledge of God and nature. A major way of crushing man's pride is, therefore, to show the vanity of philosophy. Brás Cubas is taken to the top of a mountain; from there he observes the parade of the centuries. From this distanced point of view he can transcend particular historical formations and attain the universal view of Ecclesiastes that nothing is new under the sun. Brás Cubas is compelled by Pandora to

ver os séculos que continuavam a passar, velozes e turbulentos, . . . Cada século trazia a sua porção de . . . verdade e de erro, e o seu cortejo de sistemas, de idéias novas, de novas ilusões; em cada um deles rebentavam as verduras de uma primavera, e amareleciam depois, para remoçar mais tarde. Ao passo que a vida tinha assim uma regularidade de calendário, fazia-se a história e a civilização, e o homem, nu e desarmado, armava-se e vestia-se, . . . criava a ciência, que perscruta, e a arte que enleva, fazia-se orador, mecânico, filósofo, corria a face do globo, descia ao ventre da terra, subia à esfera das nuvens, colaborando assim na obra misteriosa,

com que entretinha a necessidade da vida e a melancolia do
desamparo. (OC 1: 521–22; see Appendix 52)

Note the epistemological status of the delirium. This enlarged vision that precedes the writing of the autobiography
enables Brás Cubas to identify the misery and vanity lying
behind the diversions of the characters (including himself) in
his posthumous review of life. Brás Cubas notes that despite
the fact that "[o]s séculos [desfilassem] num turbilhão" ("the
ages moved along in a whirlwind" [E 34]),

> porque os olhos do delírio são outros, eu via tudo o que
> passava diante de mim,—flagelos e delícias,—desde essa
> coisa que se chama glória até essa outra que se chama
> miséria, e via o amor multiplicando a miséria, e via a miséria
> agravando a debilidade. Aí vinham a cobiça que devora, a
> cólera que inflama, a inveja que baba, e a enxada e a pena,
> úmidas de suor, e a ambição, a fome, a vaidade, a melancolia,
> a riqueza, o amor, e todos agitavam o homem, como um
> chocalho, até destruí-lo, como um farrapo. (OC 1: 521; see
> Appendix 53)

The eyes of delirium are those with which Brás Cubas reinterprets his life, selecting the substance that he includes in the
autobiography. Brás Cubas's trajectory—which comes to an
end in the delirium—can be understood as the process of the
constitution of these eyes (see the following section). Brás
Cubas identifies all these afflictions that shake man (including
himself while he was still alive) like a baby's rattle. One of
the best examples of this procedure is the aforementioned
"prologue" in which Brás Cubas summarizes the substance of
his relationship with Virgília: "a life of nervousness, of anger,
of despair, of jealousy" (E 108). These and other afflictions
shook Brás Cubas "like a baby's rattle until they transformed
him into something not unlike an old rag" (E 34), his present
moment of moribund raving. The hypothesis here proposed is
that the movement of the "baby's rattle" is an oscillation
between two poles: on the one hand, the tension between hope
("the worst of all evils") and belief in the value of the pursued
good (fame), and on the other, the failures caused by the
afflictions. The "baby's rattle" is Brás Cubas's spirit or mind,
while the "shaking" indicates a disturbance that calls for
ataraxia.

4. After pointing to the misery and finiteness of the human predicament, Brás Cubas in his delirium moves to criticism of contemporary philosophies. Their optimism and dogmatism sharply contrast with his vision of human misery.

> Meu olhar, enfarado e distraído, viu enfim chegar o século presente. . . . [V]inha ágil, destro, vibrante, cheio de si, um pouco difuso, audaz, sabedor, mas ao cabo tão miserável como os primeiros. (OC 1: 522; see Appendix 54)

The qualifications refer to the philosophies of history already mentioned. Note the irony: the present age is, according to these philosophies—and Comte's positivism, in particular—the dawn of the highest moment of humankind. By contrast, Brás Cubas verifies that the current age is as miserable as earlier ages. He refutes with his own life—and with that of the other observed characters—the view, held by Pascal to be presupposed in all philosophical systems, that human beings can overcome their fallen and sinful condition by means of their own intellectual endeavors (Pascal, La 140–43, 131, and 149). This point is clear in Brás Cubas's empirical—through his own life—refutation of Quincas Borba's Humanitism. Quincas Borba's doctrine caricatures precisely the excessive pretension, enthusiastic optimism, and strong dogmatism that most of Machado's contemporaries draw from the evolutionary philosophies of the nineteenth century. We shall see that Brás Cubas's central criticism of Humanitism is that as a "new idea" or philosophy, it is but a "new illusion."

The profile of the nineteenth century portrayed in Brás Cubas's delirium attacks the "new ideas." The incongruity between the presumption claimed and the actual precariousness—which is intensified in the treatment of Humanitism—resembles the characterization of many *tolos,* "stuffed shirts," and pupils of the bonze. For example, the characterization of the nineteenth century is strikingly similar to that of the "guitar player" ("The little guitar"), a character belonging to the sphere of outward social life: "[E]ra nada menos que um exemplar daquela falange acadêmica fervorosa e moça animada de todas as paixões, sonhos, delírios e efusões da geração moderna" (OC 2: 860) ("He was just another example of that academic, young, and enthusiastic phalanx, motivated by all passions, dreams, deliriums, and effusions of the modern generation"). Brás Cubas himself is, in his youth, also an example of this modern generation—"estroína, superficial, tumultuário e petulante" (OC 1: 540) ("I was a harebrained scholar, superficial, tumultuous, and capricious" [E 65]). Both are recent college graduates; they feign a knowledge that they lack, are adamant in defending political ideals of freedom and equality in which they do not believe, and pretend to have noble feelings when they are, in fact, rascals. Outward social life, the *locus* of these characters, is a web of dissembling and mystification that conceals their utterly empty lives. This duality is precisely what Brás Cubas observes in contemporary philosophies or in the enthusiasm they arouse in his contemporaries. In a procedure similar to Pascal's, Brás Cubas unmasks this duality. In particular, he points to the absurdity of Quincas Borba's attempt to divinize humanity in his Humanitism.

Evidence that Pascalian pessimism underlies *Epitaph* can be found in a piece of literary criticism written by Machado at the time of the novel's publication. Machado observes the birth of "uma nova geração poética, geração viçosa e galharda, cheia de fervor e convicção" ("a new poetic generation, an exuberant and elegant generation, full of fervor and conviction"). He then stresses the dogmatic aspect of this generation by relating it to the "desenvolvimento das ciências modernas" ("the progress of the modern sciences").

> Os naturalistas, refazendo a história das coisas, vinham chamar para o mundo externo todas as atenções de uma juventude, que já não podia entender as imprecações do varão de Hus; ao contrário, parece que um dos caracteres da nova direção intelectual terá de ser um otimismo . . . triunfante. . . . a ordem geral do universo parece-lhe a perfeição mesma. A humanidade que ela canta em seus versos . . . é um deus. . . . A justiça . . . nos é anunciad[a] em versos subidos de entusiasmo. . . . É o inverso da tradição bíblica; é o paraíso no fim. . . . [M]as em suma, venham eles [os poetas da nova geração] e cantem alguma coisa nova,—essa justiça, por exemplo, que oxalá desminta algum dia o conceito de Pascal. (OC 3: 809–12; see Appendix 55)

Machado describes the enthusiasm felt by Brazilian poets for what has been called the "Brazilian Enlightenment." The influence of social evolutionism (Spencer), Darwinism, and positivism (Comte) in Brazil by Machado's time generated the belief that "a modernização do Brasil dependia da adesão sem reservas ao pensamento científico e do abandono das disputas teológicas e metafísicas" (Barros) ("Brazil's modernization required absolute commitment to scientific thought and neglect of the theological and metaphysical controversies"). It must be said that the "Brazilian Enlightenment" was not characterized by an actual development of science but by faith in its capacity to solve all philosophical, metaphysical, and social problems. Machado denounces his contemporaries' faith in a "science" conceived as a kind of secular redemption.

5. Recovering from the delirium, Brás Cubas notes that "foi assim que me encaminhei para o *undiscovered country* de Hamlet, sem as ânsias nem as dúvidas do moço príncipe, mas pausado e trôpego como quem se retira tarde do espetáculo. Tarde e aborrecido" (OC 1: 512) ("thus I started on the road to Hamlet's 'undiscovered country,' with neither the anxiety nor the doubts of the young prince, but slow and halting, like a person who has lingered in the theatre long after the end of the performance. Tardy and jaded" [E 20]). The manner in which Brás Cubas leaves the theater of life indicates the style of *Epitaph*. The deceased condition immediately transmutes into the condition of author.

From the Naive to the Skeptical Life-view

Brás Cubas's childhood does not receive much of the auto-biographer's attention. A more detailed account is provided of his youth, when Brás Cubas first steps in the pathway of libertines (*tolos*) such as those analyzed in previous chapters of this study. A woman distracts him from this strategic direction, pushing him to the naive one. Completely in love with Marcela, Brás Cubas believes in the woman's pledges of love and fidelity, gives her expensive gifts, and engages in a relationship in which he is manipulated. He recalls one occasion in which he had "ímpetos de a estrangular, de a humilhar ao menos, subjugando-a a meus pés. Ia talvez fazê-lo; mas a ação trocou-se noutra; fui eu que me atirei aos pés dela, contrito e súplice" (OC 1: 535) ("an impulse to strangle her or at least to humiliate her by making her grovel at my feet. I started to do the latter; but somehow the act reversed itself in the doing, and I threw myself at her feet, contrite and supplicant" [E 56]).

In Brás Cubas's first meaningful interaction with a woman (Marcela), his naïveté and subjection come to the surface, resembling Ernesto's griefs and oscillations in front of Rosina in "Ernesto Doe" (see Chapter Two). The relationship is similar to the one described in "Women's preference for *tolos*" in the following passage: "Ei-lo [o *homem de espírito*] obrigado a ajoelhar-se aos pés de uma mulher para quem é nada o mérito de caminhar pouco e pouco atrás de sua sombra" (OC 3: 970) ("Here is [the *homem de espírito*] obliged to fall on his knees before a woman for whom there is no merit in one's following her shadow"). The explanation for this relationship is also found in "Women's preference": the person who does not love, that is, the person who relates outwardly with his or her behavior, is the one who dominates. Duality is the key to understanding the strategic character's success.

Brás Cubas begins his long series of failures when, in an attempt to end his relationship with Marcela, his father forces him to go to Europe. This negative experience is compounded by the girl's refusal to go with him. Her attitude seems to Brás Cubas to be totally inconsistent with her previous behavior and appearances. He then realizes for the first time the deceitful nature of social appearances and of the hidden interests that rule social interactions. "Marcela amou-me durante quinze meses e onze contos de réis; nada menos" (OC 1: 534) ("Marcela loved me for fifteen months and eleven contos; nothing less" [E 55]). This is the exact value of the relationship, its substance, once the passions and afflictions—love, jealousy, etc.—that shook Brás Cubas like a baby's rattle are abstracted. This statement reveals the deceased writer's consciousness of human precariousness.

At this early moment in his life, it can already be observed that the fixed ideas (projects and beliefs) that are the secret of the strategic Luís Alves's success in *The Hand and the Glove* are problematic in this work. Brás Cubas's first fixed idea is to persuade Marcela to go with him. He tries to accomplish this by offering her expensive jewels. Marcela accepts the jewels, but does not show up at the harbor. A second fixed idea follows the first.

> Três dias depois segui barra fora, abatido e mudo. Não
> chorava sequer; tinha uma idéia fixa ... Malditas idéias
> fixas! A dessa ocasião era dar um mergulho no oceano,
> repetindo o nome de Marcela. (OC 1: 537; see Appendix 56)

Brás Cubas curses the fixed ideas because they are completely
incompatible with the world where they must be realized. As
he says shortly before death, there is nothing as fixed in the
world as the fixed ideas. Brás Cubas's skeptical crisis then
begins to show its first signs. What begins to leap into the ocean
is not Brás Cubas, but his beliefs.

A succession of disastrous episodes then follows. On a ship
to Portugal, Brás Cubas first meets a madman who has lost his
daughter, then witnesses the death of the captain's wife. However, he soon removes these manifestations of melancholy from
his consciousness. Brás Cubas still entertains many projects,
ambitions, and hopes—that is, fixed ideas. The skeptical life-
view is still far away.

> [A] ambição desmontava Marcela. Grande futuro? Talvez
> naturalista, literato, arqueólogo, banqueiro, político, ou até
> bispo,—bispo que fosse,—uma vez que fosse um cargo, uma
> preeminência, uma grande reputação, uma posição supe-
> rior. ... [E]studei [as matérias acadêmicas] muito medio-
> cremente, e nem por isso perdi o grau de bacharel; deram-mo
> com a solenidade do estilo. ... era um acadêmico estróina,
> superficial, tumultuário e petulante, dado às aventuras,
> fazendo romantismo prático e liberalismo teórico, vivendo
> na pura fé dos olhos pretos e das constituições escritas ...
> sentindo já uns ímpetos, uma curiosidade, um desejo de
> acotovelar os outros, de influir, de gozar, de viver,—de
> prolongar a Universidade pela vida adiante ... (OC 1: 540;
> see Appendix 57)

Brás Cubas's attachment to and belief in fame as the *summum
bonum* displaces the melancholy that threatened to engulf him
at Marcela's defection and in the episodes that occurred during
his trip to Europe. As for many other of Machado's libertine
characters, so for the newly graduated Brás Cubas, to be a lawyer is nothing more than to be entitled to a prestigious social
role. Social roles are nothing but devices to "fill up" the emptiness of life. The deceased writer denounces the duality and
unmasks himself to reveal the falseness of social appearances.

His procedure is Pascalian: "Make no mistake about it. What else does it mean to be Superintendent, Chancellor, Chief Justice, but to enjoy a position in which a great number of people come every morning from all parts and do not leave them a single hour of the day to think about themselves?" (La 136)

After being immersed in the "lights" of the century at Coimbra University, Brás Cubas returns like the century, "agile," "vibrant," "proud," and "learned" (E 36). The fragility of the graduate's impetus and, therefore, the groundlessness of the optimism of the "nova direção intelectual" (OC 3: 810) ("new intellectual direction") come to the surface right after the death of his mother. Brás Cubas verifies two basic features of the world: irrationality ("o cancro é indiferente às virtudes do sujeito" ["cancer is wholly indifferent to the virtues of the patient"]) and pain ("Longa foi a agonia, longa e cruel, de uma crueldade minuciosa, fria, repisada, que me encheu de dor e estupefação") (OC 1: 542–43) ("Long was her agony, long and cruel, with a minute, cold, repetitious cruelty that filled me with pain and stupefaction" [E 69–70]). This traumatic experience and the perplexity it causes him upsets his hitherto superficial trajectory. The main effect of the experience on him is cognitive. "Confesso que tudo aquilo me pareceu obscuro, incongruente, insano . . ." (OC 1: 543) ("It all seemed obscure, incongruent, insane . . ." [E 70]). Brás Cubas's cognitive state facing his mother's death is similar to his cognitive state facing Marcela's refusal to go with him to Europe, which is identical with his cognitive state facing Nature or Pandora in the delirium. The particular experience with his mother is an empirical verification of the philosophical view exhibited in the delirium: unintelligibility, stupefaction, impossibility of making assertions or judgments, that is, the view contrary to "the new intellectual direction." Brás Cubas then begins to deal with the "problem of life and death [that] had never troubled [his] mind" (E 70). The outcome of his reflection on the problem is that he begins to withdraw from outward social life. He retires to Tijuca, a place that was at the time isolated from the city of Rio de Janeiro.

> Renunciei tudo; tinha o espírito atônito. Creio que por então
> é que começou a desabotoar em mim a hipocondria. . . .
> Ninguém me visitava; recomendei expressamente que me
> deixassem só. (OC 1: 544–45; see Appendix 58)

Brás Cubas is, from this point on, repeatedly and with increasing intensity, shaken like a baby's rattle. He is jerked from the melancholy that arises out of his awareness of human fragility, to the desire to engage in life, and from that to another experience of human fragility that brings him back to melancholy. His father's project, to make him a congressman and happily married man, is one more force that shakes Brás Cubas. This duality is indicated in chapter 26, "The Author Is Undecided":

> Uma parte de mim mesmo dizia que sim, que uma esposa formosa e uma posição política eram bens dignos de apreço; outra dizia que não; e a morte da minha mãe me aparecia como um exemplo da fragilidade das coisas, das afeições, da família. (OC 1: 546; see Appendix 59)

But soon the "yellow flower" of melancholic reflection "withdrew into its bud and left the field to another flower, less yellowish and not at all morbid—the love of fame" (E 78). Brás Cubas decides to implement his father's project. Marriage and politics are the two main axes of social life of Machado's second phase. Brás Cubas's father's advice to his son presupposes the bonze's doctrine and reproduces the advice given by the "stuffed shirt" to his son. Brás Cubas's father offers his son the strategic life-view:

> —Teme a obscuridade, Brás; foge do que é ínfimo. Olha que os homens valem por diferentes modos, e que o mais seguro de todos é valer pela opinião dos outros homens. (OC 1: 548; see Appendix 60)

The project does not succeed because Brás Cubas lacks the conviction and willpower—that is, ideas fixed enough—that are necessary to propel the strategic character in social life. Shortly after his decision to accomplish the project, Brás Cubas again comes across human misery, which renders him unwilling to act. He meets Eugênia.

> Uns olhos tão lúcidos, uma boca tão fresca, uma compostura tão senhoril; e coxa! Esse contraste faria suspeitar que a natureza é às vezes um imenso escárnio. Por que bonita, se coxa? por que coxa, se bonita? Tal era a pergunta que eu vinha fazendo a mim mesmo . . . sem atinar com a solução do enigma. (OC 1: 552; see Appendix 61)

It is on this occasion that Brás Cubas meets again the formerly "beautiful Marcela," now deformed by the pox. While these enigmas and paradoxes cause him perturbations and hallucinations—he has a vision of the young and beautiful Virgília (his fiancée-to-be) deformed by aging and pox—the determined and ambitious Lobo Neves appears and steals Virgília and the political career from him. As noted by the "stuffed shirt," reflection on the human predicament deters pragmatic action and accomplishment. Like Luís Alves in *The Hand and the Glove,* Lobo Neves brings with him the perspective of social status and fame that seduces women: "A Marchioness, for I Shall Be a Marquis" (ch. 43). The new failure increases Brás Cubas's estrangement from reality that is structured by these basic axes and ushers in the character's skeptical crisis. At this point, the first major deviation in Brás Cubas's trajectory occurs. Instead of immersing himself in outward social life, Brás Cubas begins to become its observer. This situation prevails until he is forty years old. The chapter that summarizes this period has a clarifying title: "The Recluse."

> Vivi meio recluso, indo de longe em longe a algum baile, ou teatro, ou palestra, mas a mor parte do tempo passei-a comigo mesmo. Vivia; deixava-me ir ao curso e recurso dos sucessos e dos dias, ora buliçoso, ora apático, entre a ambição e o desânimo. Escrevia política e fazia literatura. . . . Quando me lembrava do Lobo Neves, que era já deputado, e de Virgília, futura marquesa, perguntava a mim mesmo por que não seria melhor deputado e melhor marquês do que o Lobo Neves. (OC 1: 562; see Appendix 62)

This quotation illustrates three stages in the construction of the observer in Machado's fiction: (1) the reclusive life he leads suggests the *casmurro* life of Bento, the author; (2) his setting himself adrift in the ebb and flow of the days points to Counselor Aires's attitude in life; and (3) the activity of writing indicates that this is now the alternative to the external social life, which at this point includes marriage. Stages 1 and 3 are not well defined yet, and stage 2 refers not to Aires's tranquil state, but to Brás Cubas's mental oscillations between agitation and apathy. His mental disturbance is neutralized only when his interest in the *summum bonum* of fame is annulled by his verification of the ultimate and irreparable fragility of life.

Brás Cubas's displacement from social life, together with the fact that this displacement is not compensated for by the enjoyment of domestic peace, helps to construct the observer's stance that denounces the fragility and duality of life. Brás Cubas reconquers Virgília, now a married woman. Because she is not willing to give up the hope of becoming a marchioness, they establish an adulterous relationship that intensifies the immorality, duplicity, and distress that characterize social life. When Brás Cubas relates the story of this period of his life, it is precisely this ethical aspect that he emphasizes. As shown above, in Brás Cubas's evaluation of his love affair with Virgília, these qualifications constitute the "substance" of his main relationship with a woman, that is, with the world.

Interaction with Virgília facilitates the constitution of the skeptical life-view. Woman is the main object of reflection in Machado's fiction. As soon as the relationship begins, Brás Cubas raises the question of why "[a]gora, que todas as leis sociais no-lo impediam, agora é que nos amávamos deveras" (OC 1: 569) ("now that all the laws of society forbade it, now at last we were really in love" [E 111]). Brás Cubas suggests that feelings of love are gratuitous and that immoral interests rule the instituted social relationships. On another occasion, Virgília reacts to a secondary character's courtship: "—Que importuno! dizia ela fazendo uma careta de raiva" (OC 1: 569) (" 'He's so importunate!' she said, and she made an angry face" [E 111]). After witnessing her moral indignation, Brás Cubas describes his astonishment:

> Estremeci, fitei-a, vi que a indignação era sincera; então ocorreu-me que talvez eu tivesse provocado alguma vez aquela mesma careta, e compreendi logo toda a grandeza da minha evolução. Tinha vindo de importuno a oportuno. (OC 1: 569; see Appendix 63)

One notes, behind the humor, Brás Cubas's intellectual perplexity with the paradox of time and woman. Meaningful things, things that have value, are born and die in the flow of time. They are precarious, for there is no reason for their coming to be at particular times. The world is a world of becoming, not of being. The opportunity or importunity of things does not depend on the external reality of things and persons, but instead on their random and gratuitous emergence in time.[4]

Brás Cubas gets closer to skepticism as experience upsets his naive life-view. From the point of view of the naive character, the woman's (Virgília's) behavior appears utterly paradoxical. Brás Cubas proposes an end to the dissembling to which they are subjected in social life and a break from all the chains that social life poses to their love. His idea is to flee society to some remote countryside. He invites Virgília to leave her husband and join him in "a little house" withdrawn from all social life. In other words, Brás Cubas proposes "marriage" with the meaning it had during the first period of Machado's first phase: the *locus* of "domestic peace," apart from the hypocrisy and stress of the "outward life" of society. Virgília's answer is a perfect example of the strategic life-view. (Remember that Virgília belongs to a phase in Machadian fiction in which women are strongly oriented to social life): "—Pensei nisso, acudiu Virgília; uma casinha só nossa, solitária, metida num jardim, em alguma rua escondida, não é? Acho a idéia boa; mas para que fugir?" (OC 1: 576) (" 'I've been thinking about it,' said Virgilia. 'A little secluded house with a garden, all to ourselves, hidden away on some out-of-the-way street, isn't that it? I like the idea; but why should we run away?' " [E 123]).

From the standpoint of the naive life-view that Brás Cubas holds at the time, Virgília's statement is contradictory. The "little secluded house" means, within this framework, precisely the rejection of, the alternative to, the duality and immorality of society. Virgília, however, does not share this life-view. She reconciles the secluded house, domestic peace, with the immoral sphere of social life. Brás Cubas's naive beliefs, which begin to sink in the ocean when he is separated from Marcela, receive other and stronger blows from his relationship with Virgília. It is during the period of his life signaled by the "little house" that Brás Cubas most often performs immoral actions. It is then that Dona Plácida crosses Brás Cubas's path. He subjugates the character's moral values by persuading her to be the "official" resident of the "little house." He makes her a mediator of adulterous love. It is also during this period that he corroborates the highly immoral "law of the equivalence of windows" (ch. 105). Because it causes guilt, an immoral action is like a window closed in one's conscience. But the conscience is aired when another window is opened, that is, when a moral action is performed. This "law," like most moral insights exhibited by Brás Cubas, is drawn from Pascal and La Rochefoucauld, whose ethical views are consistent with Augustinian emphasis on the corruption of Man caused by the Fall: even the apparently most virtuous actions are immoral, truly virtuous action being possible only through grace.

But not everything in Brás Cubas's life at this time is negative. He makes Virgília pregnant. He is exultant: "Um filho! Um ser tirado do meu ser! Esta era a minha preocupação exclusiva daquele tempo. . . . Sentia-me homem" (OC 1: 596) ("A child! A being derived from my own being! This was the exclusive subject of my thoughts. . . . I felt that I had just become a man" [E 156]). But again, this is not reality but another "fixed idea" like the previous ones: a fixity in complete tension with the fragility of being.

> Uma tarde, após algumas semanas de gestação, esboroou-se todo o edifício das minhas quimeras paternais. . . . Eu encostei-me à janela, o olhar para a chácara, onde verdejavam as laranjeiras sem flores. Onde iam elas as flores de antanho? (OC 1: 600; see Appendix 64)

Recovered, Virgília and he resume the love affair. New episodes continue to shake Brás Cubas's naive life-view, always checked by Virgília's strategic life-view. Then Lobo Neves receives an anonymous letter denouncing his wife (the letter does not name the lover). Brás Cubas, who is present at Virgília's denial of the affair to her husband, is perplexed by her coldness and indignation. Brás Cubas's reaction already reveals the cynicism that follows from his loss of naïveté.

> Não lhe disse nada; era ocioso ponderar-lhe que um pouco de desespero e terror daria à nossa situação o sabor cáustico dos primeiros dias; mas se lho dissesse, não é impossível que ela chegasse lenta e artificialmente até esse pouco de desespero e terror. (OC 1: 601; see Appendix 65)

Here we see that the erosion of the naive life-view brings forth a dramatic view of society. Human interactions appear as a spectacle (see the commentary on the "delirium" in the previous section). But despite these setbacks, Brás Cubas still aspires to a more important role in the spectacle.

> [E]u galgara os quarenta anos, e não era nada, nem simples eleitor de paróquia. Urgia fazer alguma coisa, ainda por amor de Virgília, que havia de ufanar-se quando visse luzir o meu nome . . . (OC 1: 602; see Appendix 66)

The relationship with Virgília is, however, nearing its end. An episode related in chapter 61 attests to this decay and makes Brás Cubas once more aware of the fragility of passions and the mental disturbance that they produce. He finds a note from Virgília in the "little house." She asks him to come to her secretly at her house during the night. To that end she indicates a lower section of the wall surrounding her house that can be jumped. He thinks the situation is ridiculous but is ready to go, when Dona Plácida tells him that the note is an old one. Brás Cubas then recalls that, indeed, in the beginning of the love affair he had made the visit. "Guardei o papel e . . . Tive uma sensação esquisita" (OC 1: 609) ("I had put the note away and . . . I felt a queer sensation" [E 179]). Human fragility is implied by the tremendous power an old piece of paper exerts on the spirit. The reader will remember that in "Old journals" (see Chapter Three), through such old notes Brotero understands the precariousness of things and attains *ataraxia*.

Brás Cubas's separation from Virgília constitutes another major step taken by the character in the direction of the top of the mountain referred to in the delirium. Separation from woman means separation from the world. At this point the character changes his position in the novel. This separation of the narrator from the female character also occurs in the two novels that are discussed in the next two chapters of this study. In each particular context, the separation indicates the place of the spectator and the degree of his definition. Brás Cubas separates from Virgília, and although his life is then restricted to remembrance, writing, and reflections, these elements are not significant in the narrative. Another indication that the spectator is still not consolidated is Brás Cubas's attempt to adopt the strategic life-view. The spectator is more developed in *Dom Casmurro;*

when Bentinho separates from Capitu, he becomes Dom Casmurro, the author of the narrative.

When Bentinho becomes Dom Casmurro, and, to a lesser degree, when Brás Cubas separates from Virgília, they withdraw from the temporal dimension of life. An existential gap thus arises between the authors and women (the world). When Aires separates from Fidélia at the end of *Counselor Ayres' Memorial,* the advanced stage in the constitution of the spectator and the skeptical life-view means that Aires's distance from the world is more psychological than spatial. As a result, unlike Brás Cubas and Dom Casmurro, what Aires loses when he separates from woman is not the existential bridge with the world, but an object of study and aesthetic contemplation. In Brás Cubas's case, the separation means the return of melancholy and the sharpening of his consciousness of temporality.

> A partida de Virgília deu-me uma amostra da viuvez. Nos primeiros dias meti-me em casa. . . . Era tudo: saudades, ambições, um pouco de tédio, e muito devaneio solto. Meu tio cônego morreu nesse intervalo; item, dois primos. . . . Morriam uns, nasciam outros: eu continuava às moscas. (OC 1: 612; see Appendix 67)

The oscillations of his spirit are by no means halted during this period. Brás Cubas is again pulled from his melancholy and motivated to life by "three forces" (E 183). The first is a project undertaken by his sister, who, in the role of his deceased father, plans to bring him back to ordinary reality through marriage with her friend Nhan-loló. Another is his desire for "agitar-me em alguma coisa, com alguma coisa e por alguma coisa" (OC 1: 615) ("the hurly-burly of an active life" [E 187]). The third is the philosopher Quincas Borba and his edifying Humanitism. Brás Cubas is then initiated into Quincas Borba's Stoicism with a Comtean-Spencerian face. The doctrine contains views radically contrary to what has been the substance of Brás Cubas's life. However, exactly because the doctrine is optimistic, Brás Cubas adheres to it and in the philosopher and his philosophy, he finds the motivation to try to accomplish something positive in life.

> Entre o queijo e o café, demonstrou-me Quincas Borba que o seu sistema era a destruição da dor. A dor, segundo o

Humanitismo, é uma pura ilusão. . . . . Não basta certamente a adoção do sistema para acabar logo com a dor, mas é indispensável; o resto é a natural evolução das coisas. Uma vez que o homem se compenetre bem de que ele é o próprio Humanitas, não tem mais do que remontar o pensamento à substância original para obstar qualquer sensação dolorosa. (OC 1: 614; see Appendix 68)

Furthermore, pain is an illusion because given that "Humanitas"[5]—both principle and *telos* of humankind—"[é] a substância criadora e absoluta, cada indivíduo deveria achar a maior delícia do mundo em sacrificar-se ao princípio de que descende" ("is the creative substance, every individual ought to be delighted to sacrifice himself to the principle from which he descends"). The existence of evil is not a problem in the system, according to Quincas Borba, because it does not diminish "o poder espiritual do homem sobre a Terra, inventada unicamente para seu recreio dele, como as estrelas, as brisas, as tâmaras e o ruibardo" (OC 1: 614–15) ("our dominion over the earth, which, with everything in and about it—the stars, the breezes, the exotic date-palm, and the common garden rhubarb—was created solely for our pleasure" [E 187]).

Humanitism is a caricature of one aspect of Comte's positivism and Spencer's social evolutionism that Pascal identifies in all philosophical systems, namely, Stoicism. By Stoicism here is meant not the particular Greek school *per se,* but a pantheistic life-view that conceives of man—in particular, man's intellect—as possessing the same ontological status traditionally attributed to God, and of nature as designed for man. From the Renaissance, this view was associated with Stoicism (Bouwsma). That providentialism is the central thesis of Humanitism is clear from the above quotation and from the chicken wing example in the following passage:

Quincas Borba . . . [t]inha uma asa de frango no prato, e trincava-a com filosófica serenidade. . . . —[A] fome (e ele chupava filosoficamente a asa do frango), a fome é uma prova a que Humanitas submete a própria víscera. Mas eu não quero outro documento da sublimidade do meu sistema, senão este mesmo frango. Nutriu-se de milho, que foi plantado por um africano, suponhamos, importado de Angola. Nasceu esse africano, cresceu, foi vendido; um navio o trouxe, um navio construído de madeira cortada no mato por

> dez ou doze homens, levado por velas, que oito ou dez
> homens teceram, sem contar a cordoalha e outras partes do
> aparelho náutico. Assim, este frango, que eu almocei agora
> mesmo, é o resultado de uma multidão de esforços e lutas,
> executados com o único fim de dar mate ao meu apetite. (OC
> 1: 614; see Appendix 69)

This account recalls the Stoicism of Hellenistic philosophy. Porphyry reports Chrysippus's view that "the pig has been born for the natural end of being slaughtered and eaten. When this happens to it, it achieves its natural end, and is benefited" (Long and Sedley 329). The providentialism of Humanitism goes further than the Stoic's insofar as Quincas Borba cynically includes the instrumental use of other men.

Nothing can be more erroneous than to suppose that Brás Cubas, *the deceased writer,* holds Quincas Borba's doctrine. Brás Cubas, the living character, indeed becomes a disciple of the philosopher from this point up to his death, but the transition from the strategic life-view of the living Brás Cubas to the skeptical view of the deceased writer must be acknowledged. Humanitism is one of the main targets of the skeptical deceased writer. And note that this is quite consistent with the traditional opposition between Stoics and skeptics. The Stoics were the Hellenistic philosophers most attacked by the Greek skeptics. During the revival of these Hellenistic philosophies in the modern era, Neo-Stoicism was one of the main targets of Pascal's skepticism. In *Epitaph,* the living character Brás Cubas is the main piece of empirical evidence that Brás Cubas-author cites to mock and refute Quincas Borba's system. Up to the point where he becomes Quincas Borba's friend, Brás Cubas's life has been quite inconsistent with Humanitism. After he encounters Quincas Borba, it becomes even more so.

The Stoicism in Quincas Borba's Humanitism also appears in the function that he has in Brás Cubas's life. The philosopher combats Brás Cubas's melancholy and motivates him, in a first movement, to marry and have children, and in a second, to return to politics. Cicero reports that according to the Stoic Cato, these are precisely the things the philosopher should do. "[S]ince we see that man is created with a view to protecting and preserving his fellows, it is in agreement with this nature that the wise man should want to play a part in governing the state and, in order to live the natural way, take a wife and want children by her" (Long and Sedley 349). Motivated by Quincas Borba, Brás Cubas decides to marry Nhan-loló.

> Sim, cumpria ser pai. A vida celibata podia ter certas vantagens próprias, mas seriam tênues, e compradas a troco da solidão. Sem filhos! Não; impossível. . . . O filósofo [Quincas Borba] ouviu-me com alvoroço; declarou-me que Humanitas se agitava em meu seio, animou-me ao casamento, ponderou que eram mais alguns convivas que batiam à porta, etc. (OC 1: 615–16; see Appendix 70)

A while later, Quincas Borba encourages Brás Cubas to begin an opposition political newspaper with an editorial line inspired by the principles of Humanitism. "[P]rometia curar a sociedade, destruir os abusos, defender os sãos princípios de liberdade e conservação" (OC 1: 629) ("[I]t promised to cure the ills of society, to destroy misrule, to promote liberty and security" [E 211]).

Human misery is, however, implacable, and "the new intellectual direction" fails to overcome Pascal's view (see the previous section). Brás Cubas fails in both efforts. First to die is the newspaper.

> O primeiro número do meu jornal encheu-me a alma de uma vasta aurora, coroou-me de verduras, restituiu-me a lepidez da mocidade. Seis meses depois batia a hora da velhice, e daí a duas semanas a da morte, que foi clandestina, como a de Dona Plácida. No dia em que o jornal amanheceu morto, respirei como um homem que vem de longo caminho. (OC 1: 632; see Appendix 71)

The hour of Nhan-loló's death—and with it, the brief hope of procreation—comes even quicker. She is struck down by an epidemic shortly before the wedding date. Both episodes *show* that the "natural way" is not that pointed out by the Stoic Cato but that presented to Brás Cubas in the delirium. They also attest to the radical discontinuity between "fixed ideas" and reality. Projects, aspirations, and hopes are completely inconsistent with the perishable and fragile things of the world. The events are clear refutations of Humanitism. As a result, Brás Cubas returns to melancholic reflection on the "problem of life and death."

> [N]ão cheguei a entender a necessidade da epidemia, menos
> ainda daquela morte. Creio até que esta me pareceu ainda
> mais absurda que todas as outras mortes. Quincas Borba,
> porém, explicou-me que epidemias eram úteis à espécie,
> embora desastrosas para uma certa porção de indivíduos. . . .
> Chegou a perguntar-me se, no meio do luto geral, não sentia
> eu algum secreto encanto em ter escapado às garras da peste;
> mas esta pergunta era tão insensata, que ficou sem resposta.
> (OC 1: 619; see Appendix 72)

The problem of evil was one of the main challenges posed by the Greek skeptics to the Stoics' providentialism. Quincas Borba attempts to solve it by appealing to the social evolutionism then in vogue. Even more remarkable in the passage is the incongruity between the philosopher's explanation of everything—even of the most absurd events—and Brás Cubas's inability to understand. Not only is Nhan-loló's death absurd, but so are Quincas Borba's explanation and question. Brás Cubas's response—as when faced with Marcela's refusal to go with him to Europe, his mother's death, the loss of Virgília's unborn child, etc.—is silence: the impossibility of making a judgment (*aphasia*).

We must now return to a moment of Brás Cubas's life before the opposition newspaper and Nhan-loló's death. This moment shows a strategic Brás Cubas, motivated to enter the bustle of social life and pursuing fame. He is a congressman, colleague of Lobo Neves, and aspires to an appointment in the Cabinet as a minister:

> A onda da vida trouxe-nos à mesma praia, como duas bote-
> lhas de náufragos, ele contendo o seu ressentimento, eu
> devendo conter o meu remorso; e emprego esta forma sus-
> pensiva, dubitativa ou condicional, para o fim de dizer que
> efetivamente não continha nada, a não ser a ambição de ser
> ministro. (OC 1: 620–21; see Appendix 73)

Indeed, Brás Cubas abandons his illusions concerning ethical attitudes and actions. He no longer dissembles about his past love affair with Virgília (ch. 131, "Concerning a Calumny"), nor is he sorry for his vicious life (ch. 129, "No Remorse"), and he exhibits an intuitive comprehension of the bonze's doctrine, namely, that appearing virtuous is more relevant and effective than actually being virtuous. His former naive life-view steps aside, and the strategic one steps in. The strategic life-view, however, soon also fails. After a melancholic crisis resulting from his casual meeting with Virgília (the meeting makes him meditate on the finiteness of relationships and of everything else), Quincas Borba once more reanimates him, making the Stoic point that happiness is obtained when the sage submits to the laws of nature.

> —Que diacho! é preciso ser homem! ser forte! lutar! vencer! brilhar! influir! dominar! . . . Trata de saborear a vida; e fica sabendo que a pior filosofia é a do choramigas que se deita à margem do rio para o fim de lastimar o curso incessante das águas. O ofício delas é não parar nunca; acomoda-te com a lei, e trata de aproveitá-la. (OC 1: 624; see Appendix 74)

Once more shaken by life like a baby's rattle, Brás Cubas resolves to play his last card to gain public attention and be nominated to the Cabinet. To this end he delivers in the pulpit of the House of Representatives the famous speech of the biretta (ch. 137, "A barretina" ["The Shako"]). The speech, delivered with fervor, is the quintessence of rhetoric, but it is also very well argued, with premises leading to the right conclusions and with neat images illustrating the point of view being defended. In summary, a masterpiece from the aesthetic point of view. The supreme humor is that the elaborate speech is intended to show the ministers and congressmen Brás Cubas's outrage over the unimportant issue of the size of the biretta used by the soldiers of the National Guard. The political result is, of course, disastrous. The speech reveals the strategic life-view Brás Cubas adopts for the occasion. He understands that appearance and rhetoric are the means of interaction in the outward life, where fame is pursued. However, the speech also reveals his distance from the strategic life-view. He completely lacks the talent of the "stuffed shirt." Were he really a strategic character and not a naive one, a descendant of the *homens de espírito* of Machado's first phase, he would have employed his literary and rhetorical talents in a speech dealing with some issue considered relevant by the social and political *milieu*. The subject matter of the speech demonstrates Brás Cubas's skeptical vocation. The deceased writer's message is that once the "substance of life" is distilled, once human activities are seen as "diversions," there is no point in distinguishing relevant from irrelevant matters in the world. The social value of things is annihilated: "demonstrei que [o assunto da barretina] não era indigno das cogitações de um homem de Estado" (OC 1: 624) ("I pointed out that [the problem of the biretta] was not unworthy of a statesman's consideration" [E 203]). The speech leaves Brás Cubas even further from the Cabinet, for he soon loses his seat in the House. With this additional failure to succeed in social life, he again becomes melancholic and removes himself to Tijuca.

Nearing the end of his life, Brás Cubas is still searching for fame. He finally obtains a dim and temporary success, but in a melancholic way: he engages in philanthropy, where he shines against the background of misery (ch. 157, "The Most Brilliant Phase"). In pointing out that his holding of executive offices in a philanthropic organization makes this "the most brilliant phase of [his] life" (E 221), the deceased author reveals how distant he is from the naive life-view. He implies that offices are worthy not for their intrinsic merit but because they fill the emptiness in human life. As in the episode of the biretta, once the substance of life is distilled, the idea of social value becomes meaningless, and there is no distinguishable difference between the offices of minister of state and director of a philanthropic organization.

While engaged in this social work, Brás Cubas sees the formerly "gorgeous Marcela" in a poor hospital, dying, "ugly, thin, decrepit . . ." (E 222), and meets again Eugênia, now living in a very poor neighborhood, "as lame as when I had left her and much sadder" (E 222). He also reencounters the philosopher Quincas Borba, again a beggar and now also mad, who dies in Brás Cubas's house a few days later, "jurando e repetindo sempre que a dor era uma ilusão" (OC 1: 637) ("swearing repeatedly that pain and grief were illusions" [E 223]).

These meetings of Brás Cubas with pain, death, and misery, and, in particular, the ironical death of the creator of Humanitism, constitute definitive refutations of the system. The numerous instances of pain and grief verified by Brás Cubas contradict the philosopher's optimistic denial of their existence.

The contrast between Quincas Borba and Brás Cubas is symbolized in the question of fatherhood. We have seen Quincas Borba's insistence on motivating his then disciple Brás Cubas to have children. According to Humanitism, "there is only one genuine misfortune: not to be born" (E 185). This is in direct contrast with Brás Cubas's final evaluation of his life: "ao chegar a este outro lado do mistério, achei-me com um pequeno saldo . . . Não tive filhos, não transmiti a nenhuma criatura o legado da nossa miséria" (OC 1: 637) ("upon arriving on this other side of the mystery, I found that I had a small surplus, . . . I had no progeny, I transmitted to no one the legacy of our misery" [E 223]).

At the end of the chapter entitled "Oblivion," the deceased author addresses a hypothetical lady who was preeminent during previous administrations and then meets "Oblivion," "personagem tão desprezado e tão digno, conviva da última hora, mas certo" (OC 1: 623) ("so despised and yet so worthy a personage—a guest who may arrive late but who never fails to come" [E 201]).

> [S]e é digna de si mesma . . . não busca no olhar de hoje a mesma saudação do olhar de ontem, quando eram outros os que encetavam a marcha da vida, de alma alegre e pé veloz. *Tempora mutantur.* Compreende que este turbilhão é assim mesmo, leva as folhas do mato e os farrapos do caminho, sem exceção nem piedade; e se tiver um pouco de filosofia, não inveja, mas lastima as que lhe tomaram o carro, porque também elas hão de ser apeadas pelo estribeiro OBLIVION. Espetáculo, cujo fim é divertir o planeta Saturno, que anda muito aborrecido. (OC 1: 623; see Appendix 75)

The philosophy of Brás Cubas (the deceased writer) is one that understands *tempora mutantur.* It is the antithesis of Humanitism and most metaphysical systems that look at the world, as Spinoza says, *sub specie aeternitatis.* (The basic principle of Humanitism is *Humanitas,* principle and *telos* of humankind, which means that, as Quincas Borba says, from a metaphysical standpoint, death is not real; it is the return of Humanitas to Humanitas.) The contradiction between the deceased author's and Quincas Borba's philosophies becomes crystal clear when we compare the quotation above with Quincas Borba's claim that "the earth . . . was created solely for our pleasure" (E 187). Brás Cubas's philosophy is similar to the skeptical fideism that denounces man's philosophical pretension that his fallen condition can be overcome by means of reason alone. The essential difference between Quincas Borba's and Brás Cubas's views is that Brás Cubas rejects what Quincas Borba intensifies, namely, the ultimate philosophical end, according to Pascal and other Christian thinkers, of divinizing or redeeming humankind. Machado does seem to see this as a basic feature of the "new intellectual direction." This direction, he says, "is the inverse of the biblical tradition: paradise is at the end" (see previous section). The peculiarity and interest of the view exhibited in Machadian fiction is that unlike Pascal and the skeptical fideists, Machado does not find a solution in the transcendence inherent in religion. Since his skeptical characters are not fideists, faith is not brought into the picture. His solution is to be found, as *Epitaph* and the following novels show, in a combination of Pyrrhonian and aesthetic life-views.

To come back to Brás Cubas's meetings during his "brilliant phase," I note that, comparing it with earlier periods of his life, while misery remains and increases (Eugênia), or returns (Quincas Borba), beauty and excitement die (Marcela). The autobiographic literary form is well designed to capture this substance of life: finiteness, degeneration, diversion, and agitation (like a baby's rattle). The temporal axis of the autobiography is fitted to the essential temporal dimension of life (*tempora mutantur*). The autobiography allows the exposition of the character's mental and spiritual oscillations and the paradoxes that develop in time: beauty, hope, and life at one moment; degeneration, despair, and death at another.

If the deceased writer is above all, as it is argued in this study, a philosopher, why did he decide to write an autobiography instead of a philosophical treatise? The answer lies in the kind of philosophy he holds. Memory is the form best suited to his philosophy. Conversely, traditional metaphysical treatises are suitable for the kind of philosophy held by Quincas Borba, who, indeed, wrote "quatro volumes manuscritos, de cem páginas cada um, com letra miúda e citações latinas" (OC 1: 614) ("four manuscript volumes of one hundred pages each, in a fine hand and with numerous quotations from the Latin" [E 186]).

Before concluding this analysis of Brás Cubas's trajectory, his discovery of "the plaster" to cure melancholy must be examined. The plaster was his last "fixed idea" and the indirect cause of his death. It was also his last attempt to become famous. We suggest that this fixed idea is Brás Cubas's discovery and application of the bonze's doctrine. The "existência necessária" ("necessary existence") is that of belief (opinion), not reality (OC 2: 325). The application of the bonze's doctrine would make possible the cure of melancholy. No actual reality is necessary to produce such healing because belief alone could do the job. This interpretation is consistent with *Dom Casmurro,* where belief is viewed as the basic factor in human life (see Chapter Six). As the bonze says, reality is secondary, not at all essential to produce the desired pragmatic effects. The plaster could destroy melancholy in the same way that the noseless people who received "metaphysical noses" continued to use handkerchiefs. The plaster, i.e., the bonze's doctrine, would cure melancholic people by converting them into fellows of the bonze or "stuffed shirts." To use the categories proposed in this study, the problem of the *homens de espírito* would be resolved by their transition from the naive to the strategic life-view. This solution presupposes, therefore, the suspension of ethics.

> Um tio meu, cônego . . . costumava dizer que o amor da glória temporal era a perdição das almas, que só devem cobiçar a glória eterna. Ao que retorquia outro tio, oficial de um dos antigos terços de infantaria, que o amor da glória era a coisa mais verdadeiramente humana que há no homem, e, conseguintemente, a sua mais genuína feição.
>
> Decida o leitor entre o militar e o cônego; eu volto ao emplasto. (OC 1: 513; see Appendix 76)

In this passage, Brás Cubas verifies the equipollence of contrary judgments. Equipollence is symbolized in the fact that the two opinions are held by opinionated people of the same rank: two uncles.[6] The anthropological background is Christian (Augustinian) as conceived by the Jansenists and Pascal. The basic feature of human beings is love (*charitas*)—in Pascal, "heart"—that can be directed either to oneself (self-love) and other created things or to God. Brás Cubas, who comes to skepticism at the end of his life, suspends judgment, thereby rejecting both views. As the Pyrrhonian says, one is no more persuasive or true than the other. Instead of worrying about which of these conceptions of the *summum bonum* is true, he turns to his plaster. The Pyrrhonians claim that the result of this procedure is *ataraxia*. *Ataraxia* is a pagan end, alien to the Christian context represented by the conceptions of goodness held by the two uncles. *Ataraxia* is exactly what Brás Cubas is after. The plaster is, after all, the medicine designed to cure the melancholy and disturbance caused by the failure to attain the desired fame.

However, this *ataraxia* is not the Pyrrhonian one nor has Brás Cubas suspended judgment yet about goodness, as the reference to his uncles would suggest. This suspension occurs only after his death. When he conceives his plaster, he still believes—and is pursuing—what he takes to be the supreme good: fame. Brás Cubas adopts at this point the strategic life-view: he attempts to attain fame by fraudulent means. Because fame is not a result of having some intrinsic merit but the result of public recognition, Brás Cubas endeavors, like the bonze's disciples and the "stuffed shirts," to manipulate public opinion. Human fragility, however, once more prevails. Like Humanitism before, the bonze's doctrine is also refuted. Therefore, not only the naive but also the strategic life-view is overthrown in Brás Cubas's death bed. Brás Cubas then adopts the skeptical life-view.

> Senão quando, estando eu ocupado em preparar e apurar a minha invenção, recebi em cheio um golpe de ar; adoeci logo, e não me tratei. Tinha o emplasto no cérebro; trazia comigo a idéia fixa dos doidos e dos fortes. Via-me, ao longe, ascender do chão das turbas, e remontar ao céu, como uma águia imortal, e não é diante de tão excelso espetáculo que um homem pode sentir a dor que o punge. . . . creio haver provado que foi a minha invenção que me matou. . . . Tinha saúde e robustez. Suponha-se que, em vez de estar lançando os alicerces de uma invenção farmacêutica, tratava de coligir os elementos de uma instituição política, ou de uma reforma religiosa. Vinha a corrente de ar, que vence em eficácia o cálculo humano, e lá se ia tudo. Assim corre a sorte dos homens. (OC 1: 516; see Appendix 77)

The reference to the fragility of human plans (the fragility of strategic reason and of philosophical reason—Quincas Borba goes crazy in the end) signals the transition to the skeptical perspective. The deceased writer's message is clearly that of Sextus Empiricus (M 11: 110–67). Attachment to values and conceptions of goodness ultimately bring unhappiness because the dogmatist gets disturbed and worried during his efforts to attain or maintain what he believes is good and in avoiding or in trying to be released from what he believes is evil.

The fundamental, generic "fixed idea" responsible for all the disastrous particular fixed ideas Brás Cubas had in his lifetime is the belief in fame as the *summum bonum*. Sextus claims that

> it is by pursuing earnestly and with extreme persistence what he himself believes to be the good and desirable that each man unwittingly falls into the evil lying next door. Thus for instance . . . the man who supposes fame to be desirable earnestly strives for fame, and the earnest striving for fame is love of fame; therefore the supposition that fame is desirable and good by nature serves to generate a great evil, love of fame. (M 11: 121–23)

The cause of Brás Cubas's disturbance and unhappiness—and the indirect cause of his death—was his belief in the supreme value of fame. Note the presence of the point emphasized by skeptical fideist authors, who stress human fragility and crush human pride: "The current of air would have come along just the same and, with its efficacy greater than that of human plans, would have carried everything off with it" (E 59). This causal relation between "fixed ideas" and death is quite consistent with the Pyrrhonian position. The fixed idea, a strong conviction (the idea of the plaster), took over his mind, making him inattentive to vital affections (a current of air). For this reason Brás Cubas curses the "fixed ideas" (E 59). In recollecting his life, he notes the relativity of fixed ideas (beliefs) to particular circumstances and times, and as a deceased writer, stops believing in their validity, thereby achieving Pyrrhonian *ataraxia*. The deceased writer is no longer subjected to the depressions and excitement that disturbed the living character. Brás Cubas undoes Pascal's reconstruction of Pyrrhonism. Pascal, realizing the unchristian character of the Pyrrhonian's search for tranquility and indifference, insists that humans must be *supremely* interested in their own salvation. Given the unavailability of this religious option, Brás Cubas returns to the Greek skeptic's practical ends. This return is most interesting because Machado probably was not directly acquainted with Sextus, but had Pascal as his main source of information about Pyrrhonism. Brás Cubas's position, although contrary to Pascal's, is as radical: *absolute* indifference and detachment that is symbolized by his deceased condition. It will be up to Brás Cubas's skeptical successors—Dom Casmurro and Counselor Aires—to find tranquility and detachment without having to pay the price of life. Brás Cubas is a skeptic who cannot live his skepticism.

Brás Cubas's *Zetesis*

Brás Cubas's *zetesis* is an inquiry into social life. Although more skeptical than the analysis of social life one finds in Machado's first phase, Brás Cubas's *zetesis* is not typically Pyrrhonian as are Dom Casmurro's and Counselor Aires's inquiries. It has been argued above that in Machado's first phase, the domestic peace of marriage is opposed to the stir and bustle of social life in the same way that truth is opposed to opinion, transparency to dissembling, and morality to immorality. Although the outward life already includes marriage in the second period of Machado's first phase, it was noted that domestic peace is still possible, although increasingly less probable. It has just been pointed out that in *Epitaph,* social life becomes hegemonic, and therefore filled with dissembling, opinion, and immorality.

As also indicated, the view of social life as dual, as a place where the intentions and dispositions of the individuals are always hidden and often contrary to the external behavior they exhibit, can be seen beginning with the very earliest short stories written by Machado. This view does not change essentially at the point when social life becomes hegemonic. The duality social appearance / subjective reality is therefore still basic in *Epitaph.* Although this subjective reality is no longer expressed in a transparent way by living characters, it is still presupposed in the deceased writer's critique of social life. This perspective must therefore be distinguished from the Pyrrhonian because a subjective reality, although subjugated, is still assumed.[7] Brás Cubas's *zetesis* is therefore less Pyrrhonian and more Augustinian-

Jansenist and Pascalian. His analysis is backed by a Christian anthropology that emphasizes the corruption of humankind, the corruption of social life being the result of this basic human predicament.

Brás Cubas justifies, in the chapter entitled "O estrume" ("The Fertilizer"), his instrumental action with respect to Dona Plácida. He made her the mediator of his adulterous love by giving her an endowment (Dona Plácida is an ethical character but also very poor).

> Dona Plácida estava agora ao abrigo da mendicidade [graças a] os meus amores . . . donde se poderia deduzir que o vício é muitas vezes o estrume da virtude. O que não impede que a virtude seja uma flor cheirosa e sã. (OC 1: 585; see Appendix 78)

The last two sentences constitute an ironical and neat figurative expression of the Jansenists' stress on the corruption caused by the Fall. Even actions that on the surface seem very virtuous have roots in the corrupted heart of Man. The Jansenists' point is that fallen human beings cannot act virtuously without the intervention of divine grace. Machado draws this view from Pascal and La Rochefoucauld.[8] In *Epitaph,* this theme appears—without any reference to this possibility of genuine virtue through grace—in a few other occasions, such as when Cotrim publishes the benefits produced by his philanthropic actions in order, he says, to motivate others to do the same.

It is important to keep in mind that the deceased writer's inquiry is a moral one. His interest is neither to provide a sociological theory of the structures of human interaction nor to apologize for the lack of morality by appealing to the necessity of communal life. This second point is particularly important because it is a mistake easily committed by those who do not distinguish the life-view of the living Brás Cubas from that of the deceased writer. The living Brás Cubas uses his moral theories to avoid guilt. The deceased writer uses himself when alive and other characters to expose this Pascalian-Jansenist anthropology. Society offers alibis that ease the consciences of concupiscent individuals. (Philanthropy is an excellent example because it is a typical benevolent action that is shown to have a selfish ground.) The living Brás Cubas utilizes these alibis; the deceased writer denounces them. In the tradition of the *homens de espírito* of the first phase, Brás Cubas denounces the lack of morality in social life.

A second qualification of social life, presented in the chapter entitled "A ponta do nariz" ("The Tip of the Nose"), exemplifies Brás Cubas's method. The chapter is a commentary on the resentment he felt toward a poet who was a better poet than he was. He sublimates his resentment by looking at the tip of his nose.

> Cada homem tem necessidade e poder de contemplar o seu próprio nariz, para o fim de ver a luz celeste, e tal contemplação, cujo efeito é a subordinação do universo a um nariz somente, constitui o equilíbrio das sociedades. (OC 1: 563; see Appendix 79)

Brás Cubas illustrates the theory with the example of a hypothetical hatter who loses his customers to a neighboring hatter.

> Mortifica-se naturalmente; mas vai andando, concentrado, com os olhos para baixo ou para a frente, a indagar as causas da prosperidade do outro e do seu próprio atraso, quando ele chapeleiro é muito melhor chapeleiro do que o outro chapeleiro . . . Nesse instante é que os olhos se fixam na ponta do nariz. (OC 1: 563; see Appendix 80)

The equilibrium of society is not grounded on altruistic impulses but on the mystifying power of self-love that is capable of reinterpreting reality, depriving it of aspects that are uncomfortable to the individual and could lead him or her to conflict and to the eventual fragmentation of the social body. Note the Pascalian view of the Fall in the background: the ultimate source of this self-love is man's willingness to be like God ("with the sole purpose of seeing the divine light," "the subordination of the universe to one nose," etc.).

Brás Cubas's thought resembles Erasmus's *Praise of Folly*. Erasmus is another figure in the revival of skepticism in association with faith in the early modern period. Erasmus's *Praise of Folly* is consistent with the skeptical fideist tradition that develops Paul's view that Christian faith is foolishness compared to Greek wisdom. As in Pascal, Stoicism is particularly attacked by Erasmus in *Praise of Folly*.

The point noted by Brás Cubas in the passage above is that it is Folly, instead of Wisdom, that holds society together because Folly provides that the individuals do not become aware of their own mediocrity.

> [T]hose who, while differing in no respect from the meanest tinker . . . yet by virtue of my lovely companion Philautia [self-love], they lead a pleasant life. There will always be other fools, too, to admire specimens of this breed as if they were gods. (Erasmus 59)

A secondary character makes the same point. Jacob is the most honest man Brás Cubas meets in his life, yet while Brás Cubas is visiting him, Jacob lies repeatedly. He first asks his servant to tell another visitor that he is not at home. Then, because the visitor seems willing to wait for him, he instructs the servant to tell another lie. Questioned by Brás Cubas about his behavior, Jacob argues that "a veracidade absoluta [é] incompatível com um estado social adiantado, e que a paz das cidades só se podia obter à custa de embaçadelas recíprocas . . ." (OC 1: 594) ("absolute truth is incompatible with an advanced state of society and that peace and order can only be achieved at the cost of reciprocal deceit . . ." [E 152]).

Social life is conceived as the place of deceit and false appearances. Unlike the view held in Machado's first phase, however, in *Epitaph* deceit and false appearance are seen as necessary to the very existence of society. Pascal's influence is again remarkable.

> Man is therefore nothing but disguise, falsehood and hypocrisy, both in himself and with regard to others. He does not want to be told the truth. He avoids telling it to others, and all these tendencies, so remote from justice and reason, are naturally rooted in his heart. (La 978)

Brás Cubas derives the foundations of social life from Pascal's Christian anthropology. According to Brás Cubas, social life is the negative, immoral "outward life." The sincerity and transparency that were possible in the sphere of "domestic peace" are now seen as absent from all human interaction. They are, however, presupposed. These ethical predicaments are theoretically rescued by the deceased writer, who reveals the vicious roots that structure social life. The author Brás Cubas realizes the morality that is still achievable and is committed to the truth that is still available at this point. This theoretical rescue of truth and morality is no longer available to Dom Casmurro, who is completely disconnected from the subjectivity of the other characters of the novel. His narrative is therefore less philosophical—inasmuch as he does not make statements about the nature of social and human life—and more skeptical.

The explanation for the impossibility of transparency in social life—as well as the logic of this life—is clearly stated in the chapters "A opinião" ("Public Opinion") and "A solda" ("The Solder"). Brás Cubas tells of a casual meeting he had with Lobo Neves in Ouvidor Street (the heart of Rio in the period of the novel). When they met, Lobo Neves was aware of Brás Cubas's past love affair with Virgília.

> Lembra-me que estava retraído, mas de um retraimento que forcejava por dissimular. Pareceu-me então . . . que ele tinha medo—não medo de mim, nem de si, nem do código, nem da consciência; tinha medo da opinião. Supus que esse tribunal anônimo e invisível, em que cada membro acusa e julga, era o limite posto à vontade do Lobo Neves. Talvez já não amasse a mulher; . . . Cuido . . . que ele estaria pronto a separar-se . . . mas a opinião, essa opinião que lhe arrastaria a vida por todas as ruas, que abriria minucioso inquérito acerca do caso, que coligiria uma a uma todas as circunstâncias, antecedências, induções, provas, que as relataria na palestra das chácaras desocupadas, essa terrível opinião, tão curiosa das alcovas, obstou à dispersão da família. Ao mesmo tempo tornou impossível o desforço, que seria a divulgação. Ele não podia mostrar-se ressentido comigo, sem igualmente buscar a separação conjugal; teve então de simular a mesma ignorância de outrora, e, por dedução, iguais sentimentos. (OC 1: 610; see Appendix 81)

Public opinion requires the dissembling of the truth, which is the evil-aggressive-concupiscent feelings that cannot appear as such in the sphere of social life. Note that Antero's philosophy (see the commentary on "The angel Rafael" in Chapter One) that one should ignore public opinion is viewed as completely naive in *Epitaph*. Disregard for community values is now a position available only to *deceased* writers. Antero believes that social life can be ignored because he finds domestic peace in marriage, the alternative to social life during Machado's early first phase. To Antero, marriage means release from the rule of public opinion. In Lobo Neves's case, it is precisely his marriage that subjects him to this tyranny.

Note that although repressed by social life, there is a subjective reality assumed by Brás Cubas: human depravity. The situation is dual, paradoxical, and ironical. As Brás Cubas says, "terrifying public opinion" produced the benefit of precluding the destruction of "domestic peace." Brás Cubas theorizes about this point—that evil causes generate beneficial consequences—in the following chapter, "The Solder."

> A conclusão, se há alguma no capítulo anterior, é que a opinião é uma boa solda das instituições . . . tanto na ordem doméstica, como na política. Alguns metafísicos biliosos têm chegado ao extremo de a darem como simples produto da gente chocha ou medíocre; mas é evidente que, ainda quando um conceito tão extremado não trouxesse em si mesmo a resposta, bastava considerar os efeitos salutares da opinião, para concluir que ela é a obra superfina da flor dos homens, a saber, do maior número. (OC 1: 610–11; see Appendix 82)

Brás Cubas's irony resembles Erasmus's in *Praise of Folly*. Belief or opinion is supposedly an inferior cognitive state (Plato). It is nonetheless supreme in the fallen human condition. And note that there is no alternative of wisdom or knowledge apart from the denunciation of human intellectual and moral weakness such as Pascal's and Brás Cubas's. The point is the rejection both of ordinary opinion (which is intrinsically nonsense) and of the philosophical criticism of the latter (for nonsense gives the right measure of the present human condition). Although Brás Cubas rejects the philosophical criticism of ordinary opinion, he is by no means apologizing for the latter. His position is similar to the following one held by Pascal:

> *Cause and effect.* Constant swing from pro to con. Thus we have shown that man is vain to pay so much attention to things which do not really matter, and all these opinions have been refuted. Then we showed that all these opinions are perfectly sound, so that, all these examples of vanity being

perfectly justified, ordinary people are not as vain as they are said to be. Thus we refuted the opinion which refuted that of the people. But we must now refute this last proposition and show that it is still true that the people are vain, although their opinions are sound, because they do not see the truth when it is there, and assume things to be true when they are not, with the result that their opinions are always thoroughly wrong and unsound. (La 93)

The foundations of social life can therefore be systematized. The root is self-love—the "dung." The structure that keeps social life whole is made up of "reciprocal deceit," the "solder" that keeps the very precarious and fragile human institutions and relationships together. Self-love, concupiscence, treasons, envy, and other emotions would, were it not for this solder, dissolve the social body. The last foundation of social life noted by Brás Cubas is the "formalidade" ("formality"). He introduces this element when he refers to the sadness of Damasceno, the father of Nhan-loló. His sadness is, however, due not to his daughter's death but to the insignificant number of people that came to her funeral. Cotrim tries to comfort him:

> —Vieram os que deveras se interessam por você e por nós. Os oitenta [convidados] viriam por formalidade, fala- riam da inércia do governo, das panacéias dos boticários, do preço das casas, ou uns dos outros . . . (OC 1: 620; see Appendix 83)

To this Damasceno replies: "—Mas viessem!" (OC 1: 620) (" 'But they should . . . have come' " [E 195]).

Appearance rules over essence. Brás Cubas philosophizes about the episode in the following chapter. He notes that in Damasceno's case, as in others,

> surge aí a orelha de uma rígida e meiga companheira do homem social . . .
>
> Amável Formalidade, tu és, sim, o bordão da vida, o bálsamo dos corações, a medianeira entre os homens. . . . tu enxugas as lágrimas de um pai. . . . Se a dor adormece, e a consciência se acomada, a quem, senão a ti, devem esse imenso benefício? A estima que passa de chapéu na cabeça não diz nada à alma; mas a indiferença que corteja deixa-lhe uma deleitosa impressão. A razão é que, ao contrário de uma

velha fórmula absurda, não é a letra que mata; a letra dá vida;
o espírito é que é objeto de controvérsia, de dúvida, de
interpretação, e conseguintemente de luta e de morte. Vive
tu, amável Formalidade, para sossego do Damasceno. (OC
1: 620; see Appendix 84)

"Formality" complements "opinion" in the configuration of
social life because it is a motivational force for acting. This
function is Pascalian. Formality fills the emptiness that has
been the human predicament since Adam's fall. It "diverts"
human beings from themselves, from their fragility, and mitigates the consciousness of death. For Damasceno, it mitigates
his consciousness of the cruel and absurd death of his daughter. The evolution in Machado's fiction is remarkable: from the
mere condemnation of social life in "Women's preference for
tolos," to the philosophical understanding of its existential
function in *Epitaph.* (Compare Brás Cubas's view of formality
with one of Machado's earliest short stories, "The country of
chimeras"—see Chapter Four above.)

Brás Cubas's criticism of "the absurd old saying" is Pyrrhonian. The nonmanifest (the "spirit") is that which brings
controversy, disturbance, and death. Damasceno could find
ataraxia in conforming himself to (social) appearance. This is
not possible, however, for Brás Cubas. He does not find peace
of mind in appearances, so he directs his inquiry toward essences ("spirit"). But his inquiry brings him melancholy and,
as indicated in the passage, death. Dom Casmurro is the next
character of Machado's novels to experience the skeptical crisis and to exemplify the Pyrrhonian conclusion that essences,
not appearances, are the source of controversy and doubt.

Chapter Six

Dom Casmurro

The *Casmurro* Writer

Pascal says that the imagination is "all the more deceptive for not being invariably so; for it would be an infallible criterion of truth if it were infallibly that of lies" (La 44). This deceptive feature of the imagination is crucial in *Dom Casmurro*. In the Machadian fiction up to and including *Epitaph*, social appearances are infallible criteria of lies, the disguise of vicious motivations and dispositions. The view of social life becomes more skeptical in *Dom Casmurro*, where the imagination is one of the grounds of the environment of uncertainty that characterizes the novel.

There are several formal and thematic similarities between *Epitaph* and *Dom Casmurro*, but there is also a natural development toward skepticism from the first to the second. We have seen in the previous chapter that Brás Cubas's investigation (*zetesis*) shows—starting with himself when he was still alive—the duality of subjectivity and external behavior, thereby destroying the supposition of a continuity between social appearance and subjectivity. Thus it is logical that the observer, in a second stage of his constitution, loses access to the subjectivity of the other characters. This situation is more Pyrrhonian than that in *Epitaph* (which represents the first stage) because in this second stage, it can be neither affirmed nor denied that the performed behavior corresponds to the correlate subjective dispositions of the actor. Subjectivity becomes, therefore, opaque and uncertain.

The thesis presented in this chapter is that Dom Casmurro's position with regard to Capitu (the world) corresponds to this Pyrrhonian second stage, and that this is the main cause of his being a "casmurro" author. Dom Casmurro, the narrator of the novel, cannot make statements grounded on certain evidence. He explains that the nickname "casmurro" comes from his "hábitos reclusos e calados" ("taciturn, recluse-like habits") and that in his case, it designates a "homem calado e metido consigo" (OC 1: 807) ("tight-lipped man withdrawn within himself" [DC 3–4]). We suggest that *casmurro* in *Dom Casmurro* has the philosophical meaning of *aphasic* in Sextus's sense of being unable to make statements (PH 1.192–93).

There is a skeptical intensification in *Dom Casmurro* on both the thematic and formal levels. As in *Epitaph,* the narrative point of view is that of the character functioning as an observer. The disposition of the chapters is also analogous to that of *Epitaph.* Like *Epitaph, Dom Casmurro* begins with prolego-menous chapters that set out the status of the work and the posi-tion of the author. Only then does the narration of the memoir begin. In both novels one sees the trajectory of the narrator-character whose final position is that of a withdrawn author. Bento Santiago, the author, is Dom Casmurro, a narrator who does not enjoy the enlarged (broad) point of view available to the deceased writer. Less radically withdrawn, he occupies a position that frames a more restricted point of view. Dom Casmurro's assertions do not have the positive philosophical import that we see in those of Brás Cubas. On the contrary, Dom Casmurro is fully aware that the main assertion he utters in his book—namely, that Capitu, his former wife, was unfaith-ful to him—is totally unsupported, that is, completely deprived of epistemological justification. This is the main difference between my interpretation and most other interpretations of the novel. Scholars acknowledge this awareness but claim that it is Machado's and not Dom Casmurro's. When they do recog-nize that Dom Casmurro knows that his belief is unsupported, they interpret his narrative as meant to convince the reader— and even himself—that his position is justified.[1] However, rather than trying to persuade the reader that his evidence for the adultery justifies his belief, Dom Casmurro, in writing his memoir, shows how unsupported his belief really is, that is, he makes the skeptical philosophical point—as in the case of Brás Cubas, who starts from himself—that beliefs crucial to one's life lack objective (epistemological) certainty.

This interpretation of *Dom Casmurro* sets the novel in a developmental line with *Epitaph*. It is shown in the previous chapter that Brás Cubas argues that, contrary to the opinion of the moral philosophers, it is harmful to hold beliefs about the nature of goodness. Dom Casmurro broadens the point by showing that this is so not only with respect to moral beliefs, but also for ordinary beliefs, which may be harmful as well. Note that the claim is not that Dom Casmurro is insincere in his belief that Capitu was unfaithful, for he truly holds this belief despite his awareness of the lack of conclusive evidence to support it. This is neither an inconsistent nor a psychologically untenable position. Most ordinary beliefs lack conclusive epistemic ground. Skeptical fideists read by Machado, such as Montaigne, claim that the most crucial beliefs lack rational or empirical support. Moreover, they claim that the believer must be aware of this hopeless epistemological situation so that he or she can be open and well disposed to accept divine revelation. Dom Casmurro's belief is Machado's correlate to the fideist faith proclaimed by skeptical fideists who believe that skepticism is irrefutable and that only an act of faith can rescue the individual from the despair of doubt. It is precisely to avoid this despair that Dom Casmurro believes in his wife's infidelity. To be sure, to avoid the despair of doubt, he could as well believe in his wife's fidelity (some *pragmatic* reasons for his believing in the infidelity are suggested below). The interpretation proposed is that Dom Casmurro is not only aware that he could do that, but indeed wants to stress this possibility, for it shows the fragility of human life (human life depends on crucial beliefs that are utterly gratuitous). Dom Casmurro is therefore not, strictly speaking, a Pyrrhonian skeptic, since he believes his wife to be guilty of adultery. But he is as much a skeptic as are the skeptical fideists because he is aware that his belief is not supported by epistemological grounds.

Dom Casmurro exhibits a sharp consciousness of the frailty of judgments or beliefs in general: they are relative to particular and precarious (changeable) situations and dispositions—age, time, mood, place. The main theme of the novel is the difficulty or even impossibility of making statements. This Pyrrhonian standpoint is the narrative point of view of the novel. In the novel, Dom Casmurro presents a sincere account of the conflicting appearances that affected him before becoming an author, that disturbed him and made him oscillate between contradictory beliefs until he retired from social life.

It is worthwhile to pause here to indicate the development toward skepticism of the Machadian character's mental disturbances. They begin in the very first short stories as the spiritual grief suffered by the *homens de espírito* as a result of women's fortuitous variations of mood. Disturbances arise in Brás Cubas as a result of his failures experienced in pursuit of fame and in attempts at social projects such as marrying and having children. The disturbance results therefore from the incongruity between his "fixed ideas" (projects nurtured by belief in fame as the *summum bonum*) and the precarious social reality where these fixed ideas must be actualized. Bentinho oscillates between contrary mental dispositions because his *judgment* oscillates with varying circumstances.

Another contrast between the narrators of *Epitaph* and *Dom Casmurro* is related to the *aphasia* of Dom Casmurro. Philosophical commentaries, so frequent in *Epitaph,* are rare in *Dom Casmurro.* Brás Cubas-author explains the metaphysical meaning of the events that he lived and now narrates. Dom Casmurro typically just records the events that affected him from childhood to divorce.

Distance from time, symbolized by distance from women, is an element indicative of Dom Casmurro's rupture from social life.

> Os amigos que me restam são de data recente; todos os antigos foram estudar a geologia dos campos-santos. Quanto às amigas, algumas datam de quinze anos, outras de menos, e quase todas crêem na mocidade. Duas ou três fariam crer nela aos outros, mas a língua que falam obriga muita vez a consultar os dicionários, e tal freqüência é cansativa. (OC 1: 808; see Appendix 85)

Dom Casmurro's temporal divorce from the world appears in his reduced contact with women, representatives of life and the world in Machado. They are always associated with the predicaments of life, and temporality is a major predicament. Bento Santiago, the *casmurro* author, stands as if he were outside the dimension of time. In the passage just cited, he shows lack of interest in bringing his vocabulary up to date, which would be a necessary precondition to engaging in social relationships with women. His claim that this updating would require wearisome consultation of a dictionary points to another of his features: the tedium or boredom he feels with respect to taking action. His practical life is weak, although more developed than that of Brás Cubas-author, who has no practical life at all. The fact that active life is suppressed or highly reduced in these authors (Brás Cubas and Dom Casmurro as well as Counselor Aires) sheds light on the meaning of writing for them: it is the activity that makes possible, as Brás Cubas puts it, "distraction from eternity" (DC 131), in which all, *stricto* or *lato sensu,* more or less intensely, are situated as authors.

> Ora, como tudo cansa, esta monotonia acabou por exaurir-me também. Quis variar, e lembrou-me escrever um livro. Jurisprudência, filosofia e política acudiram-me, mas não me acudiram as forças necessárias. Depois, pensei em fazer uma "História dos Subúrbios" . . . era obra modesta, mas exigia documentos e datas, como preliminares, tudo árido e longo. Foi então que os bustos pintados nas paredes entraram a falar-me e a dizer-me que, uma vez que eles não alcançavam reconstituir-me os tempos idos, pegasse da pena e contasse alguns. Talvez a narração me desse a ilusão, e as sombras viessem perpassar ligeiras, como ao poeta . . . *Aí vindes outra vez, inquietas sombras?* . . . e vou deitar ao papel as reminiscências que me vierem vindo. Deste modo, viverei o que vivi, e assentarei a mão para alguma obra de maior tomo. (OC 1: 808–09; see Appendix 86)

Like the cellist of "The little guitar" (see Chapter Two), Dom Casmurro needs to be affected by the appearances of outward life, which, nonetheless, given their ambiguity and opacity, he cannot bear. In order to enjoy them without being disturbed by them, he indulges in memories: "Também se goza por influição dos lábios que narram" (OC 1: 831) ("Pleasure may also be sipped from lips that narrate" [DC 48]).

Dom Casmurro's search for the impressions of outward life is clear from the verbs and expressions he uses indicating the passivity of being affected by appearances: "the walls spoke to me and said . . . ," "restless shades" (that is, restless appearances), "memories that come crowding" (DC 6). *Epitaph,* Brás

Cubas's narrative, is not characterized—at least to this degree—by this nostalgia. The deceased writer does not let himself be affected by the conflicting appearances that affected him while still alive. On the contrary, his procedure is to uncover the emptiness that these appearances attempt to hide. Dom Casmurro's attitude is quite different. His narration remains on the phenomenal level. Even when he asserts that Capitu is guilty of adultery, he does so on the bases of appearances and impressions, not grounded proofs and evidences (as Sextus says, not on the bases of the "non-evident").

Dom Casmurro's valuation of appearances should not obscure the fact that authorship is the alternative to disturbing and uncertain social life. The passage quoted below is similar to another from *Epitaph,* quoted in Chapter Five, in which the deceased writer talks about the advantages of withdrawn authorship. It is worth citing the passage again to compare it with Dom Casmurro's. The first passage is Brás Cubas's, the second Dom Casmurro's.

> Creiam-me, o menos mau é recordar. . . . Corrido o tempo e cessado o espasmo, então sim, então talvez se pode gozar deveras, porque entre uma e outra dessas duas ilusões, melhor é a que se gosta sem doer. (OC 1: 516; see Appendix 87)

> Entretanto, vida diferente não quer dizer vida pior; é outra coisa. A certos respeitos, aquela vida antiga aparece-me despida de muitos encantos que lhe achei; mas é também exato que perdeu muito espinho que a fez molesta, e, de memória, conservo alguma recordação doce e feiticeira. (OC 1: 808; see Appendix 88)

To Dom Casmurro the "substance of life" is no longer reduced—at least during his adolescence—to grief, as it is for Brás Cubas. Also, life is not for him a "spasm"—an accurate description of Brás Cubas's life. Like Brás Cubas, Dom Casmurro does see his adolescence as an illusion. From his present skeptical life-view, he is aware that the positivity that he experienced when he was young was the result of the naive life-view he had then. Still, he desires to have the illusion that he can recover this life, because his present skeptical perspective tells him that his present perspective, which denounces the naive one, is precarious as well. Since they are relative to specific contexts, both life-views are circumstantial. The naive life-view he had before becoming an author does not bring him closer to, nor leave him farther from, the truth than his present one does. He wants to recapture the old view because, unlike the present one, it is a life-view that offered him emotions, even if those emotions arose out of illusions.

Finally, the memoir is relevant not only to the aforementioned recovery, but also because it makes a philosophical claim about the fragility of the human condition. "Agora que penso naqueles dias de Andaraí e da Glória, sinto que a vida e o resto não sejam tão rijos como as Pirâmides" (OC 1: 908) ("Now when I think of those days at Andarahy and Gloria, I feel a regret that life and all the rest are not as rugged as the Pyramids" [DC 196]).

The literary form of a memoir is crucial for the apprehension of the dimension and effect of time in life and all the rest. Brás Cubas utilizes the same metaphor to emphasize the rigidity of the "fixed ideas," which are problematic because they contrast with the fragility of being. In this more skeptical stage that characterizes *Dom Casmurro,* the fragility of the "fixed ideas" (such as Dom Casmurro's belief in the existence of the adultery) represents the fragility of life. The distance that Dom Casmurro notes between his present life and the one he lived in Andaraí and Glória is not so much the result of deaths and miseries (fragility of being) as of the radical inversion of *meaning* determined by his shift of perspective and by his belief—a belief not grounded in objective evidence, possibly true, possibly false—in Capitu's unfaithfulness.

Whereas the theme of finiteness in *Epitaph* appears in the destructive action of time—miserable deaths of things (the newspaper, the project of being Minister, etc.) and people (Marcela, Quincas Borba, Dona Plácida, etc.)—this same theme in *Dom Casmurro* appears in the alteration of perspectives, each perspective attributing distinct meaning to experience. Dom Casmurro does not recover the impressions he had when young. He fails to "tie together the two ends of [his] life" (DC 5), not because of the chronological distance that lies between them, but because of the distance between the naive life-view he had at the time and the present skeptical one. So, with respect to the theme of time, the objective finiteness of being in *Epitaph* is replaced in *Dom Casmurro* by the subjective finiteness of meaning and belief.

The precariousness of life is portrayed in *Epitaph* as death, pain, and misery, while in *Dom Casmurro,* it appears as the fragility of man's spirit, completely dependent upon precarious judgments that change according to gratuitous circumstances. Fragility appears, above all, as absence of solid grounds for belief. Thus, whereas Brás Cubas's rejection of life is due to objective causes, Dom Casmurro's is due to the impossibility of bearing the uncertainty of conflicting appearances that cannot be grasped by the understanding. Unlike Brás Cubas's case, there are no objective reasons for Dom Casmurro's unhappiness. He moves from happiness to unhappiness, from hope to despair, from active to contemplative life, only because he changes his opinion about Capitu, an opinion that, like any other opinion, lacks epistemological foundation. Human misery now results from man's dependence on precarious beliefs.

This modification is reflected in the form of the novel. In his autobiography, Brás Cubas refers to a large diversity of characters and situations. His pessimistic diagnosis, which refutes the optimistic philosophies of his time, requires the accumulation of many examples of misery and grief. In *Dom Casmurro,* the attack on judgment requires only Bento's relationship with Capitu. Capitu concentrates the conflicting and opaque appearances that render beliefs problematic. So the problem posed to human beings by their dependence on and attachment to beliefs is presented in *Epitaph* and developed and intensified in *Dom Casmurro*. The solution—to be presented with Counselor Aires—is Pyrrhonian: the definition of a life that can be lived without beliefs.

The Opera

The chapter "The Opera" in *Dom Casmurro* has a function and meaning similar to that of the chapter "The Delirium" in *Epitaph*. Appearing at the beginning of the narrative, it summarizes and intensifies the reflective dimension to be presented in the novel. In this chapter, Dom Casmurro describes a Manichean theory about the Creation held by an Italian tenor, according to whom life is like an opera. God is the poet and Satan the composer. Having banned Satan from the celestial conservatory, God created a "special theater" (the earth) and "a whole company" to stage the opera. Because God refused the work, the stage of the opera was done without "divine corrections."

> Foi talvez um mal esta recusa; dela resultaram alguns desconcertos que a audiência prévia e a colaboração amiga teriam evitado. Com efeito, há lugares em que o verso vai para a direita e a música para a esquerda. Não falta quem diga que nisso mesmo está a beleza da composição, fugindo à monotonia, e assim explicam o terceto do Éden, a ária de Abel, os coros da guilhotina e da escravidão. Não é raro que os mesmos lances se reproduzam, sem razão suficiente. Certos motivos cansam à força de repetição. Também há obscuridades; o maestro abusa das massas corais, encobrindo muita vez o sentido por um modo confuso. . . .
>
> Os amigos do maestro querem que dificilmente se possa achar obra tão bem acabada. . . . Já . . . os amigos [do poeta] [j]uram . . . que a partitura corrompeu o sentido da letra, e, posto seja bonita em alguns lugares, e trabalhada com arte em outros, é absolutamente diversa e até contrária ao drama. . . .
>
> —Esta peça, concluiu o velho tenor, durará enquanto durar o teatro, não se podendo calcular em que tempo será ele demolido por utilidade astronômica. (OC 1: 816–17; see Appendix 89)

The theory (DC 19–20) indicates a skeptical philosophy that Bento Santiago's life corroborates (see the following sections of this chapter).

1. The music/libretto duality expresses the fundamental duality in social life of external behavior and subjectivity.

2. With duality goes "incongruity." The novelty here is that both the duality and the incongruity—up to this point in Machadian fiction, major reasons for the condemnation and rejection of social life—now appear, at least to some people, as having positive value, precisely, an aesthetic value: "and there are those who say that this is the beauty of the composition."

3. The theme of Ecclesiastes—"not infrequently the same plot situation is used over again"—and that of the ultimate irrationality of the world—"without sufficient reason"—are also present.

4. The theory alludes to the main theme of the novel. Because of the opacity of social life, subjectivity is in the dark—it is, after all, an opera. Since the theater is the whole earth, one can be either a spectator (Dom Casmurro) or an actor (Bento). The metaphor does not allow one to conceive of the actor as having some identity other than that of the role being performed: "there are obscure passages; the maestro makes too much use of the choral masses, which often drown out the words with their confused harmony."

5. Finally, note the skeptical conclusion in the passage. There are different views about the value of the opera, that is, of life. Unlike Brás Cubas, Dom Casmurro explicitly avoids taking the side of the "friends of the [poet]," although the centrality of the themes of precariousness of beliefs and of life reveals his pessimism; he is surely not one of the "friends of Satan." Although Dom Casmurro retains Brás Cubas's view—rooted in Machado's first published work—that evil preponderates in the world, he does discover a positive value in the world that the tenor's theory highlights: aesthetic value. This aesthetic value is developed, we shall see, by Counselor Aires.

Dom Casmurro begins his memoir by telling of his realization—when he was an adolescent—that he loved his neighbor/friend Capitu. It is at this moment that he begins acting in "the opera." He notes that during the childhood friendship, he and Capitu were rehearsing backstage. Dom Casmurro accepts the theory (ch. 10, "I Accept the Theory") and the substantial part of the narrative focus on his performance: "Cantei um *duo* terníssimo, depois um *trio,* depois um *quatuor*" (OC 1: 817) ("I sang a tender *duo,* then a *trio,* then a *quatuor*" [DC 21]).

Dom Casmurro's performance in the opera centers around his interaction with Capitu. It is Capitu whom Dom Casmurro wants to recollect, to enjoy again, now without the prickles, and she also is what he tries to understand. A problematic understanding, given that the role obscures the actor. It is a quite revealing fact that the narrative begins with José Dias's denunciation of the love between Bento and Capitu. This sets a framework (a stage) that demands duplicity and dissembling, since Bento's mother had other plans for him: the confirmation of the denunciation could destroy the couple's sentimental aspirations and plans. It provides a situation in which Capitu's skill as an actress becomes crucial and is for the first time utilized and tested. It means the transition from the transparent and spontaneous world of childhood to the immoral social world, the outward world in which the realization of the matrimonial project requires sophisticated strategies. (Remember that marriage was once the last bastion of morality and truth in Machadian fiction!) It marks the beginning of life as an opera.

The deceased author Brás Cubas is somebody who left the "theater," "tardy and jaded" (E 20). Dom Casmurro, the author, is also an outsider. At the moment he writes, "the opera" is already over for him, yet, he admires its beautiful parts. Only Counselor Aires finally discovers the alternative place that affords direct aesthetic experience free from the prickles that harmed Bento. This is the standpoint of the spectator.

Naive vs. Strategic Life-view

Dona Glória's promise to make her son a priest defines the framework of Bento's relationship with Capitu: it must be disguised under the appearance of mere friendship, and the action must be strategic in order to remove this obstacle to their future marriage. This context offers the conditions for the distinction of the two life-views. The woman's is the strategic one: "[Capitu] era mulher por dentro e por fora, mulher à direita e à esquerda, mulher por todos os lados, e desde os pés até a cabeça" (OC 1: 890) ("[Capitu] was a woman within and without, a woman to the right and to the left, woman on every side and from head to foot" [DC 161]). In contrast to the woman is the *homem de espírito,* who adopts the naive life-view. Bento exhibits characteristics of the *homem de espírito* as described in "Women's preference for *tolos*" (see Chapter One). He is intimately attached to (identified with) his feelings: "Eu, que era muito chorão por esse tempo, sentia os olhos molhados. . . . Era amor puro, era efeito dos padecimentos da amiguinha" (OC 1: 857) ("I, who was easily moved to tears in those days, felt my eyes grow moist. . . . It was pure love, it was the effect of my darling's sufferings" [DC 97]). Like the *homem de espírito* of Machado's early first phase, young Bento despises the "outward life" of society, which he opposes to "domestic peace."

> Eu prometia à minha esposa [fazendo planos para o futuro] uma vida sossegada e bela, na roça ou fora da cidade. Viríamos aqui uma vez por ano. Se fosse em arrabalde, seria

longe, onde ninguém nos fosse aborrecer. (OC 1: 858; see Appendix 90)

The necessity, existing from the very beginning of the relationship, of using strategies establishes a context in which the woman exhibits skill and flexibility, and the *homem de espírito,* perplexity and immobility.

In the passage that describes Capitu's writing her and Bento's names on the wall, the two young neighbors look at one another, holding hands, completely in love. Capitu's father (Pádua) comes upon them suddenly and, noting that they are staring at each other, asks if they were playing *siso* (a game in which two people stare fixedly at one another, the game being won by the one who resists smiling the longest).

> Olhei para um pé de sabugueiro . . . ; Capitu respondeu por ambos.
> —Estávamos, sim, senhor, mas Bentinho ri logo, não agüenta. . . .
> E séria, fitou em mim os olhos, convidando-me ao jogo, . . . eu estava ainda sob a ação do que trouxe a entrada de Pádua [a censura à Capitu por ter riscado o muro], e não fui capaz de rir, por mais que devesse fazê-lo, para legitimar a resposta de Capitu. . . . Há coisas que só se aprendem tarde; é mister nascer com elas para fazê-las cedo. E melhor é naturalmente cedo que artificialmente tarde. (OC 1: 822; see Appendix 91)

Later they experience their first kiss. This time it is Capitu's mother who appears suddenly. Capitu quickly composes herself; Bento is completely embarrassed. "Assim, apanhados pela mãe, éramos dois e contrários, ela encobrindo com a palavra o que eu publicava pelo silêncio" (OC 1: 843) ("Thus, caught by her mother, we were two and contrary: she covered over with words what I published with my silence" [DC 71]).

Another kiss: now it is again Pádua who comes upon them unexpectedly. "Capitu não se dominava só em presença da mãe; o pai não lhe meteu mais medo. No meio de uma situação que me atava a língua, usava da palavra com a maior ingenuidade deste mundo" (OC 1: 848) ("Capitu was mistress of herself not only in the presence of her mother; her father did not frighten her a bit more. In the midst of a situation which left me tongue-tied, she talked away with the greatest ingenuousness in the world" [DC 80]).

On another occasion, the young couple quarrels. Bento provokes Capitu, talking about the advantages of being a priest. She replies by inviting him to baptize her first child. "[N]ão achei palavra . . . fiquei estúpido. Capitu sorria; eu via o primeiro filho brincando no chão . . ." (OC 1: 856) ("I found neither word nor gesture, but sat stupefied. Capitu smiled; I saw her first-born playing on the ground . . ." [DC 96]).

Another quarrel, now a more serious one. This time Bento suspects that Capitu is interested in another young man.

> [Capitu] disse-me que era grande injúria que lhe fazia; não podia crer que depois da nossa troca de juramentos, tão leviana a julgasse que pudesse crer . . . E aqui romperam-lhe lágrimas, e fez um gesto de separação; mas eu acudi de pronto, peguei-lhe das mãos e beijei-as com . . . calor. . . . Enxugou os olhos com os dedos. . . . Confessou-me que não conhecia o rapaz, senão como os outros que ali passavam às tardes. . . . Se olhara para ele, era prova exatamente de não haver nada entre ambos; se houvesse, era natural dissimular. (OC 1: 884; see Appendix 92)

These passages show the tremendous evolution that has taken place in Machado's treatment of the opposition between woman and the *homem de espírito*. There is a similar resolution to the quarrel between the naive Ernesto and the strategic Rosina in "Ernesto Doe" (see the end of Chapter Two). Despite the evident culpability of Rosina, her skill, combined with Ernesto's naïveté, allows her to manipulate the situation and turn it around, shifting from the position of defendant to that of victim thanks to her decisive appeal to tears. Note the evolution in the strategic perspective that takes place during the twenty-eight years that separate "Ernesto Doe" from *Dom Casmurro*. There is no doubt that Rosina deceives Ernesto, for she feigns appearances that are false. It is the weakness of Ernesto that keeps him from seeing that appearances do not correspond to reality. In Capitu's case, nothing can be said about correspondence to reality. While Rosina's tears are deceitful appearances, Capitu's tears may be sincere or insincere, there being no way to decide the matter.

The improved characterization of the strategic life-view appears in the construction of the character. Rosina is coquettish; Capitu is mysterious. Rosina is just affected; Capitu is delightfully imponderable. Rosina wants to marry at all cost no matter whom; Capitu designs subtle and sophisticated strategies to marry Bento.

Corresponding to this development is another: the new sophistication of the narrative point of view. In *Dom Casmurro,* the story is told by the character involved in the action, expressing the *homem de espírito*'s perplexity when faced with woman's opacity. The skeptical-cognitive relationship can therefore be established. In "Ernesto Doe," on the contrary, the omniscient narrator states Rosina's hypocrisy outright, for he has unlimited access to the subjectivity of his characters. In *Dom Casmurro,* one notes a skeptical elaboration of the object (the woman) and of the subject (point of view) in the cognitive relationship.

Bentinho, unlike the skeptic Dom Casmurro, is a naive man, while Capitu is a prime example of Machado's female characters. The naive man identifies himself with emotions. The woman exhibits a distance from emotions that allows her to control and manipulate situations. In Machado, this ability is a central factor in women's vocation for the outward life, since social life remains the place of strategies and dissembling. One of the main instruments of such strategic action is rhetoric. This view of rhetoric is present in Machadian fiction beginning in 1861 in the *tolo*'s letters and speeches. In the case of the *tolo,* it is clearly a false appearance denounced by the narrator. The situation is far more complex in *Dom Casmurro.* The words uttered by the *tolo* of the first phase, although deceitful, reveal subjective states because they are infallible signs of falsehood. Now the words just conceal. They contain no information at all about Capitu's real intentions and dispositions.

The naive man's divorce from social life is expressed in his transparency and silence: "she covered over with words what I published with my silence," "[the] situation . . . left me tongue-tied" (DC 71, 80). Recall the suggestion that *casmurro* means the impossibility of making statements. The disqualification of speech is an avenue that leads to skepticism. It renders Bento a Dom Casmurro. The main reason why the subjectivity of the other is opaque is that speech covers over instead of revealing.

There is discontinuity between Capitu's visible behavior and audible discourse and her subjectivity. It cannot be affirmed that her subjectivity is inconsistent with what is visible and audible, nor is there sufficient information to claim that Capitu's behavior is motivated by mere interest in contracting an advantageous marriage. The argument she uses in response to Bento's suspicion—"if there had been [anything between them], it would be natural to dissemble" (DC 150)—wipes out the informative content of a whole class of external behavior. Meaningful interactions—at least those concerning love affairs—are all hidden. As long as Bento is Capitu's accomplice—both are engaged in the project of their future marriage—the problem of this strategic logic does not appear. Once married, they leave backstage and begin performing (recall that marriage is already the center of outward life). Given the disqualification of visible behavior as a sign of subjective states, and given that the only available means of communication is that very visible behavior that is so unreliable, the context of uncertainty and opacity that problematizes marriage—formerly presented as domestic peace whose basic feature was transparency—becomes apparent. (Bento's marriage is discussed in the next section.)

The opposition between Bento's naive life-view and Capitu's strategic one can also be indicated by comparing their relationship with that of the couple in the short story "Straight line and curved line" (see Chapter One).

Bento's and Capitu's differing approaches to a problem clash again over his mother's decision to send him to the seminary.

> Capitu, aos quatorze anos, tinha já idéias atrevidas . . . [que] na prática faziam-se hábeis, sinuosas, surdas, e alcançavam o fim proposto, não de salto, mas aos saltinhos. . . . Tal era a feição particular do caráter da minha amiga . . . combatendo os meus projetos de resistência franca [ao seminário], fosse antes pelos meios brandos, pela ação do empenho, da palavra, da persuasão lenta e diuturna, e examinasse antes as pessoas com quem podíamos contar. (OC 1: 827; see Appendix 93)

Bento inclines toward direct and frank action: he would just let his mother know that he has matrimonial plans. Capitu designs strategies. Her action is instrumental. She exhibits an intuitive knowledge (more developed than Guiomar's in *The Hand and the Glove*) of the logic of interaction. Capitu is aware of the necessity of employing persuasive rhetoric, planning actions carefully, and fitting means to ends. That this necessity is real can be verified by the fact that things go her way instead of Bento's.

Before concluding this section, it must be emphasized that the heterogeneity of life-views constitutes the terms of the skeptical-cognitive relationship essential in the novel. Woman appears unintelligible to the observer not only because of her opacity but also because of the conflicting appearances that she exhibits. "De manhã, ela derreou a cabeça [para que a beijasse], agora fugia-me" (OC 1: 847) ("In the morning she bent back her head [so that Bento could kiss her]; now, she shrank from me" [DC 78]).

Bento attempts to kiss Capitu, who refuses. In the middle of the confusion they hear a noise that indicates that somebody is coming.

> Eu . . . não tive tempo de soltar as mãos da minha amiga; pensei nisso, cheguei a tentá-lo, mas Capitu, antes que o pai acabasse de entrar, fez um gesto inesperado, pousou a boca na minha boca, e deu de vontade o que estava a recusar à força. Repito, a alma é cheia de mistérios. (OC 1: 847; see Appendix 94)

Bento experiences the same perplexity—although in a more elaborate way—referred to by Machado in his first published work ("Women's preference for *tolos*"):

> É possível que ela tenha mudado tão de repente? Pois não foi ainda ontem que de volta de um passeio ao bosque, lhe enxugou o suor da testa? . . .
> Hoje, nem mais doçuras, nem mais apertos de mão. (OC 3: 970; see Appendix 95)

On an earlier occasion, Bento tells Capitu of his mother's plan to send him to the seminary. The violence of Capitu's reaction stupefies him. "Fiquei aturdido. Capitu gostava tanto de minha mãe, e minha mãe dela, que eu não podia entender tamanha explosão" (OC 1: 825) ("I was stunned. Capitu was so fond of my mother, and my mother of her, that I could not understand such an explosion" [DC 37]). The paradox is even stronger because Capitu calls Bento's mother a "pew warmer," "popeholy," and "church louse." Bento wonders how he can

"understand" "que lhe chamasse nomes tão feios, e princi-
palmente para deprimir costumes religiosos, que eram os
seus?" (OC 1: 825) ("the abusive epithets, to call her such ugly
names, and especially to revile religious customs which were
her own" [DC 37]).

Conflicting appearances—Capitu likes Dona Glória but
speaks badly of her, she is religious but reviles religious customs, denies and gives the kiss—exhibited by Capitu make her
a paradoxical object. Although these paradoxes are already
present in previous characters of Machadian fiction, they are
intensified and qualified as cognitive objects only in *Dom
Casmurro*. This is one component of the constitution of the
skeptical life-view. These are some of the contradictions that
make Dom Casmurro say that the "soul is full of mysteries"
(DC 79). Recall that for Brás Cubas, once deprived of social
appearances, the soul is revealed as fundamentally vicious.
Dom Casmurro does not extract the soul from social appearances nor does he hold Brás Cubas's anthropology. The restric-
tion to his own point of view allows him just to record these
conflicting appearances, disqualifying any epistemological
status they may have.

When Capitu visits Dona Glória, Bento earnestly wants her
glance, but it is refused. At the conclusion of the visit, Dona
Glória asks Bento to accompany Capitu to her house. Capitu
replies that this is not necessary and insists that Bento stay.
"Novamente me intimou que ficasse, e retirou-se; eu deixei-me
estar parado, pregado, agarrado ao chão" (OC 1: 850) ("Once
more she intimated to me that I should remain, and began to
move away. I remained motionless, fixed, rooted to the ground"
[DC 84]).

Bento's relationship with Capitu is one of problematic intelligibility. His perplexity signifies the *homem de espírito*'s divorce from the external world. This divorce becomes dramatic
precisely where it was resolved during the early first phase of
Machado's fiction, namely, in the domestic sphere of marriage.[2]

Dom Casmurro's *Zetesis* and *Epoche*

The contrast between the naive and the strategic life-views does
not change with Bento and Capitu's marriage. Their honeymoon is spent in Tijuca. (Recall that Brás Cubas withdraws
from social life by moving to Tijuca.) Bento then has a brief

experience—it lasts no longer than seven days—of the domestic peace that reigns in marriages of Machado's first phase.

> S. Pedro, que tem as chaves do céu, abriu-nos as portas dele. . . . Em seguida, fez sinal aos anjos, e eles entoaram um trecho do *Cântico,* tão concertadamente, que desmentiriam a hipótese do tenor italiano, se a execução fosse na terra; mas era no céu. A música ia com o texto. . . . Descansa que não farei descrição alguma, nem a língua humana possui formas idôneas para tanto. (OC 1: 906; see Appendix 96)

The narrator is aware of the accuracy of the Italian tenor's hypothesis. This heaven, a reclusive domestic peace, is not the theater in which the opera of life is staged. Language cannot describe it because language is the deceitful rhetoric employed in the real theater: social life. "Domestic happiness" is no longer woman's main aspiration; she wants to perform in the opera.

> Não obstante, achei que Capitu estava um tanto impaciente por descer. . . .
> A alegria com que pôs o seu chapéu de casada, e o ar de casada com que me deu a mão para entrar e sair do carro, e o braço para andar na rua, tudo me mostrou que a causa da impaciência de Capitu eram os sinais exteriores do novo estado. Não lhe bastava ser casada entre quatro paredes e algumas árvores; precisava do resto do mundo também. (OC 1: 907; see Appendix 97)

To Capitu, as to Guiomar (*The Hand and the Glove*) and to Iaiá Garcia (see Chapter Two), marriage means entrance into the outward life. The condition of being married is equivalent to Jacobina's uniform ("The looking glass") and to the new pair of boots of the unlucky man of "Final Chapter." Capitu's complexity is transferred to the social life with which she is identified. With Capitu, the outward life, concentrated in marriage during Machado's second phase, becomes opaque, ambiguous, and uncertain.

I point out in the previous chapter that marriage is analyzed by Brás Cubas. While still alive, Brás Cubas observes marriage from the outside, from a position (that of lover) that allows marriage to be seen as hypocritical and immoral. In *Dom Casmurro,* the view of marriage becomes Pyrrhonian. Presented as neither the moral institution of the beginning of Machado's first phase, nor the immoral one of *Epitaph,* marriage now becomes the *locus* of irresolvable doubts. Opacity precludes the evaluation of the morality of the actions that take place within it. This Pyrrhonian context is grounded in the characterization of the protagonists. Capitu is opaque. The narrator is not a former lover but the former husband. He is not critical like Brás Cubas, but *aphasic.*

The naive Bento becomes the skeptic Dom Casmurro when he withdraws from social life and becomes an author. While still a naive or dogmatic (in Sextus's sense) character, he experiences the oscillations and perturbations resulting from his yearning to find the truth beyond the appearances of social interaction. This yearning is symbolized by and intensified in his search for certainty about the possible unfaithfulness of his wife. The ambiguity of appearances precludes a grounded judgment and makes him often shift from a belief to its contrary. This instability causes him deep disturbance and distress that are overcome only when Bento earnestly believes his wife to be guilty of adultery. This belief is, however, not properly an epistemological position that follows from evidential premises, but a psychological view he is left with because of the strong impression some appearances make on him. This kind of assent does not necessarily involve epistemic commitment to the truth of the belief. Dom Casmurro is aware that epistemic grounds are lacking. Some contemporary scholars of ancient skepticism (Frede, Bett, and Pereira) have argued that this kind of assent is not inconsistent with the Pyrrhonian position, whose *epoche* concerns only a stronger, epistemic, kind of assent. Although Bento's assent is not epistemologically strong, it is strong psychologically.

The sincerity required by the literary form of a memoir is repeatedly pledged by the author. Dom Casmurro does not try to convince the reader to believe that Capitu was unfaithful. He argues both ways. His procedure is *zetetic:* he disqualifies the evidence both against and in favor of the hypothesis of adultery. He does this deliberately by putting pro and con evidences side by side. It has been noted that Brás Cubas's criterion of what is to be included in his autobiography is philosophical— he includes that which reveals the misery of life. Dom Casmurro's criterion is the relevance of the episode to the establishment of equipollence. Also worth noting is Dom Casmurro's procedure of putting the objectivity of his observations in doubt. After mentioning some evidence in favor of or against the adultery, Dom Casmurro often refers to the particular and arbitrary disposition under which he observed or inferred the evidence. He thereby casts doubt upon the objectivity of his judgment. Rather than trying to convince the reader that Capitu was unfaithful, Dom Casmurro is trying to show the groundlessness of any belief whatsoever.

While still a naive character, Bento, like the character Brás Cubas, is "shaken like a baby's rattle." As suggested above, the difference between Brás Cubas's and Bento's oscillations is that Bento's oscillation results from the shaking of his beliefs and not from the objective fragility of things and persons. Objectively, nothing changes during Bento's marriage. Unlike *Epitaph,* there are no passions that extinguish, deaths, failures in the realization of projects, social constraints to the free enjoyment of passions, nor is there any necessity to engage in immoral actions to enjoy them. In chapter 104, after two years of marriage, Dom Casmurro says that he was then completely happy with Capitu despite their immersion in the outward life (parties, theaters, visits, etc.). This does not mean that the main theme of the novel is not that of *Epitaph*—viz., human misery. But this misery is now placed elsewhere. Social life is not objectively miserable. It is miserable because it is uncertain. Human beings are miserable because they are completely dependent on utterly uncertain beliefs. The cause of the destruction of Bento's marriage—the cause of the destruction of his happiness—is not only a mere belief, but worse, a belief that is precarious and ungrounded.

The strongest evidence that Ezequiel is not Bento's son but Escobar's is the physical resemblance. The question, therefore, is: can nature—that is, external reality—determine the truth or falsehood of beliefs? Is there correspondence between impressions and external reality? *Dom Casmurro,* like the short story "A question of husbands" discussed in Chapter Three, is a skeptical narrative. The answer is negative. The remaining part of this chapter is devoted to the verification of this interpretation through textual analysis of the novel. Dom Casmurro's use of the Pyrrhonian *tropoi,* both those concerning the subject who examines a state of affairs and those concerning the state of affairs themselves, will be pointed out. The analysis concludes with the indication of the passages and circumstances that most clearly show Dom Casmurro's construction of equipollence.

First, the episodes that show the opacity of the cognitive object will be examined.

Bento goes alone to an opera because Capitu is slightly ill. He tells his wife that he would prefer not to go and to stay with her instead, but Capitu insists that he go and enjoy himself. Worried about his wife's health, he returns early and encounters Escobar.

> Capitu estava melhor e até boa. Confessou-me que apenas tivera uma dor de cabeça de nada, mas agravara o padecimento para que eu fosse divertir-me. Não falava alegre, o que me fez desconfiar que mentia, para me não meter medo, mas jurou que era a verdade pura. (OC 1: 917; see Appendix 98)

Dissembling aimed at not worrying one's husband is a behavior quite permissible in the ethics of marriage. Therefore, Capitu's behavior is consistent with this standard if her purpose is that imagined by Bento. *If* her purpose is that *possibly* being suggested by Dom Casmurro, it *may* indicate a hidden relationship with Escobar. Now that marriage does not contain only transparent actions, now that both the legitimate purpose and the immoral one are equally covered by the *same* external signs, how can one judge? Note that Dom Casmurro *does not* assert the immoral hypothesis. He only implies its possibility. He does that not because he wants to convince the reader subtly to come to believe infidelity occurred, but simply because he is *unable* to assert. His report is confined to his remembrance of Capitu's appearances—"she did not speak cheerfully, etc." (DC 214). His point of view allows only the record of these impressions. He cannot transcend them to make claims about independent external reality.

Escobar justifies his late visit by indicating the necessity of informing Bento of new circumstances in a legal proceeding of his (Bento is Escobar's lawyer). He mentions "third party claim proceedings." Bento replies that there is no reason to worry because such claims have no juridical relevance.

> Escobar olhava para mim desconfiado, como se cuidasse que
> eu recusava a circunstância nova por forrar-me a escrevê-la;
> mas tal suspeita não ia com a nossa amizade.
>
> Quando ele saiu, referi as minhas dúvidas a Capitu; ela
> as desfez com a arte fina que possuía. (OC 1: 918; see
> Appendix 99)

One notes again the opacity and ambiguity of the interactions. Escobar's suspicion *may* be due to the reason Bento thought at the time, but *may* also result from his *possible* worry that Bento is suspicious of his relationship with Capitu (in this hypothesis Bento would not have been convinced by the reason given for the late visit). In fact, other possible reasons for Escobar's visible behavior may be conceived; or there may be no ulterior reason at all, and Bento may be just imagining things. Whatever is Escobar's motivation, the external appearance is again the same, the point being that sincerity, transparency, and frankness—those enemies of peace and order (E 152)—have no place in Bento's domestic intimacy.

The perplexity that strikes Bento on the occasion reveals his then naive life-view. He was expecting transparency in his intimate circle of friends. That is, he was expecting domestic peace. But because at this point that which used to be domestic peace has also become part of the outward life, both hypotheses are possible. Uncertainty is at the core of domestic intimacy.

Capitu's motivation is also uncertain: it may result from the concern of a wife worried about her husband's doubts of his best friend—a quite legitimate attitude—or it may be part of her effort to annihilate what she might think is the beginning of her husband's suspicion. Thus Capitu's "oath," her "sickness," and the easing of Bento's doubts are all ambiguous signs, but the only available ones. After Escobar's death, Bento observes Capitu.

> Ao passar pelo espelho, concertou os cabelos tão demora-
> damente que pareceria afetação, se não soubéssemos que ela
> era muito amiga de si. Quando tornou, trazia os olhos ver-
> melhos; disse-nos que, ao mirar o filho dormindo, pensara
> na filhinha de Sancha, e na aflição da viúva. E, sem se lhe
> dar das visitas, nem reparar se havia algum criado, abraçou-
> me e disse-me que, se quisesse pensar nela, era preciso pensar
> primeiro em minha vida. (OC 1: 928; see Appendix 100)

Because affectation is one of Capitu's natural characteristics, she remains veiled behind legitimate external appearances (words, gestures, attitudes). Given that she frequently arranges her hair in passing mirrors before presenting herself on the stage (living room) where the opera takes place (interactions with husband, visitors, and servants), how can one interpret her gesture as concealing the grief she feels for the death of her lover, since it may well be just concern with her appearance? Moreover, given the consistency and legitimacy of what she says, how can one assert that her red eyes correspond to the pain of the lover rather than to the sorrow for Sancha's daughter?

But the situation is even more complex than that. Even assuming her infidelity, Capitu's gesture and words may still be sincere. We have already seen that Machado's women are skillful in reconciling apparent incongruities. In *Epitaph,* Virgília reconciles the "little house" with being a "wife," sheds sincere tears at her husband's death despite the fact that she was unfaithful to him, and at Brás Cubas's death bed, speaks with sincere indignation of the adulterous love of acquaintances. Even if Escobar was Capitu's lover, this does not mean that she does not love Bento or that Bento's life is not crucial to her own. Those dispositions are contradictory only from the naive point of view then adopted by Bento. The result is that not only is the correspondence between sign and reality discontinued, but also the whole semantic system is relative to a particular life-view.

In the climax of the novel, Bento tells Capitu that Ezequiel is not his son.

> Grande foi a estupefação de Capitu, e não menor a indignação que lhe sucedeu, tão naturais ambas que fariam duvidar as primeiras testemunhas de vista do nosso foro. Já ouvi que as há para vários casos, questão de preço; eu não creio. . . . Mas, haja ou não testemunhas alugadas, a minha era verdadeira; a própria natureza jurava por si, e eu não queria duvidar dela. Assim que, sem atender à linguagem de Capitu, aos seus gestos, à dor que a retorcia, a coisa nenhuma, repeti as palavras ditas duas vezes com tal resolução que a fizeram afrouxar. (OC 1: 935; see Appendix 101)

We have noticed in the previous section that before marrying, Bento had many opportunities to witness the contrast between

Capitu's external behavior and her real intention or disposition. For example, on one occasion Capitu agreed with conviction with Dona Glória's remark that Bento had a vocation for the priesthood. These dissimulations appeared to be natural, thanks to Capitu's skill in presenting them. Bento could be reassured of her real feelings only because he knew that the act was part of the plan to free him from the seminary. Now Bento and Capitu are no longer backstage. They are no longer accomplices but are on the stage, performing the opera. Bento no longer has access to Capitu's subjectivity. His witnessing of her previous performances, such as the one mentioned above, makes him realize the ambiguity of the informative content of the signs he sees in her. In this final confrontation, Bento ignores what his perceptive organs tell him in order not to feel inclined to believe in her innocence, a hypothesis that the present appearances would suggest. The epistemic value of sense perception is annulled. In order to overcome the uncertainty of the situation, Bento tries to substitute his will for his perception, attempting to hold fast to some evidence independent of the subject's perceptual faculties. He wants to ground his belief on intrinsic, independent, external reality. In a word, Bento dogmatizes in Sextus's sense (belief in a non-evident proposition, that is, a proposition independent of appearances). The skeptical Dom Casmurro, however, rules out this possibility. In this very chapter and in others he makes remarks that point to the hypothesis of fidelity and that cast doubt on the validity of appealing to nature or external independent reality. "[E]u ... não pedia outra coisa mais que a plena justificação dela" (OC 1: 936) ("I ... would have liked nothing better than her complete justification" [DC 249]). But more on that later. Here it is important to note that given the lack of reasons to sustain his belief, and given that the psychological state determined by such crucial doubt is unbearable, Bento takes an authoritarian attitude: he repeats the charge twice with resoluteness. The will steps in where reason is insufficient. This step is similar to that pointed out by some skeptical fideists: doubt about the existence of God and the immortality of the soul is so distressing and unbearable that it must be overcome by an act of the will. In one way or another, skeptical fideists usually give pragmatic reasons for believing instead of disbelieving (see, for example, Pascal's "wager argument" [La 418]). Pragmatic reasons may also explain why

Dom Casmurro believed that Capitu was unfaithful instead of innocent and, accordingly, decided to exile her and the child. For example, the undeniable physical resemblance of his son to Escobar would constitute an ever-existing discomfort and would make the reappearance of distressing doubt an always-present possibility.

Not only is the cognitive object enveloped in the Pyrrhonian net, but the cognitive subject is also located in a skeptical framework. Dom Casmurro points out "circumstances, conditions or dispositions" (PH 1.100) that qualify his opinions. He repeatedly refers to his jealousy:

> Os meus ciúmes eram intensos, mas curtos; com pouco derrubaria tudo, mas com o mesmo pouco ou menos reconstruiria o céu, a terra e as estrelas. (OC 1: 911; also 916 and 927; see Appendix 102)

Sextus Empiricus notes that one's judgment varies according to such predispositions as "hate or love, . . . trust or fear, sadness or happiness" (PH 1.100). These predispositions affect the subject's perception of an object, thereby precluding assertions about its external reality (independent of perception). Persuaded of Capitu's unfaithfulness, Bento decides to kill himself. But before attempting suicide, he goes to his mother's home and

> [o]u de verdade ou por ilusão, tudo ali me pareceu melhor nesse dia, minha mãe menos triste, tio Cosme esquecido do coração. . . . Passei uma hora em paz. Cheguei a abrir mão do projeto. Que era preciso para viver? Nunca mais deixar aquela casa, ou prender aquela hora a mim mesmo . . . (OC 1: 932; see Appendix 103)

Back home, Bento runs across Escobar's portrait and faces Ezequiel's insistence on staying in sight, increasingly *resembling* Escobar. He then feels assured of Capitu's infidelity and thinks again about committing suicide.

Bento's impressions change according to the place and position he occupies. Sextus says that one of Aenesidemus's *tropoi* is "based on positions, distances, locations; for owing to each of these the same objects appear different" (PH 1.118). Bento's mother's house is associated with his happy childhood, an experience full of positivity, given that he then had direct and open communication with Capitu (life). His living room is associated with the problematic marriage in which life (Capitu) has become opaque and distressing. Because the object (Capitu) is ambiguous, its perception is determined by the location of the observer.

Besides jealousy and places, Dom Casmurro mentions other factors, such as self-love, modesty, and moral respect, that shape judgments. Bento visits Escobar and Sancha in their house, where Escobar tells Bento that he has a project for the two couples but that he will reveal it only the next day. Demanding secrecy from Bento, Sancha then tells him what her husband has in mind. The project, in which she appears to be very interested, is a trip to Europe. At this point, according to the recollection of the memorialist, a prolonged exchange of glances took place between him and Sancha, whose hand "apertou muito a minha, e demorou-se mais que de costume" (OC 1: 922) "pressed mine, and lingered there longer than usual" [DC 223]) when Bento was leaving.

> A modéstia pedia então, como agora, que eu visse naquele gesto de Sancha uma sanção ao projeto do marido e um agradecimento. Assim devia ser, mas o fluido particular que me correu todo o corpo desviou de mim a conclusão que deixo escrita. . . .
> O retrato de Escobar, que eu tinha ali . . . falou-me como se fosse a própria pessoa. Combati sinceramente os impulsos que trazia do Flamengo. (OC 1: 922–23; see Appendix 104)

Not only the conclusion about the meaning of the gesture but its very perception is relative to the subjective disposition of the observer when he perceives and concludes. Dom Casmurro highlights this relativity of judgment by pointing out contrary principles that operate in his readings of the gesture. The principles of modesty and loyalty, which finally prevailed, made him see and conclude Sancha's thankfulness. Sexual desire and self-love made him see and conclude Sancha's adulterous impulses. The fact that Escobar's photograph determines the context in which the judgment of *his own and Sancha's fidelity* is made is quite revealing of Dom Casmurro's deliberate attack on the rationality of beliefs—that is, his Pyrrhonian point that beliefs do not necessarily correspond to actual objective states of affairs, being instead mere products of casual circumstances. It is shown below that this very same picture of Escobar determines the context in which the judgment is made of *Escobar's and Capitu's betrayal.*

To return to Sancha's episode, note that Dom Casmurro is again indicating the ambiguity of the signs through which interaction takes place: "Demais, quem me afirmava que houvesse alguma intenção daquela espécie no gesto da despedida e nos anteriores? Tudo podia ligar-se ao interesse da nossa viagem" (OC 1: 923) ("Besides, who could say there had been any intention of that sort in her goodbye gesture and in the previous ones? It could all be ascribed to her interest in our trip" [DC 224]). Social life is neither transparent nor unambiguous. The same gesture may mean different things. Because Escobar wanted to reveal the project only the next day, no matter what Sancha had in mind at the moment of the gesture, she had to act in the dissembling way she did. Ambiguity is inherent to interaction, leaving Bento with "doubts upon doubts" (the title of a previous chapter in which Escobar's late and unexpected visit—another ambiguous situation—is reported). A later chapter ("Cismando" ["Musing"]) is similar to "Doubts upon Doubts." Dom Casmurro narrates the disturbance caused by his doubts concerning Sancha and concerning the meaning of Capitu's glance at the deceased Escobar. Uncertainty prevails everywhere because of, as Pyrrho is reported to have said (Long and Sedley 14–15), the "equally . . . unmeasurable and inarbitrable" nature of—in *Dom Casmurro,* social—things.

Dom Casmurro's procedure is most Pyrrhonian when he establishes equipollence. Two instances of this procedure are indicated in what follows.

Dom Casmurro inverts the chronological order of the events narrated in chapters 130, 131, and 132. After the jealousy he feels at Capitu's reaction to Escobar's death, Bento attributes his suspicion of Capitu's infidelity to his excessive jealousy and dismisses the possibility. In chapter 130, he tells of his deep weariness of Capitu. In chapter 131, entitled "Anterior ao anterior" ("Prior to the Prior"), he says that before the weariness alluded to in the previous chapter, his "vida era outra vez doce e plácida, a banca do advogado rendia-me bastante, Capitu estava mais bela, Ezequiel ia crescendo" (OC 1: 929) ("life was once again sweet and placid. The law paid me well enough.

Capitu was more beautiful. Ezekiel was growing up" [DC 237]). During this occasion Capitu herself points out to Bento that Ezequiel's expression is similar to that of the deceased Escobar (Bento had not told her his suspicions on the occasion of Escobar's death).

> Aproximei-me de Ezequiel, achei que Capitu tinha razão; eram os olhos de Escobar, mas não me pareceram esquisitos por isso. Afinal não haveria mais que meia dúzia de expressões no mundo, e muitas semelhanças se dariam naturalmente. (OC 1: 929–30; see Appendix 105)

In the very same chapter, when referring to his love for Capitu, Dom Casmurro says that "[a]s pessoas valem o que vale a afeição da gente" (OC 1: 930) ("[p]eople are worth the value that our affection sets on them" [DC 238]). In the following chapter, Dom Casmurro reveals the reason for the weariness alluded to in chapter 130.

> Nem só os olhos, mas as restantes feições, a cara, o corpo, a pessoa inteira, iam-se apurando com o tempo. . . .
> Escobar vinha assim surgindo da sepultura, do seminário e do Flamengo para se sentar comigo à mesa, receber-me na escada, beijar-me no gabinete de manhã, ou pedir-me à noite a bênção do costume. (OC 1: 930; see Appendix 106)

Were the events presented in chronological order, we would have: (1) the reference to domestic peace and Capitu's remark on the physical resemblance (evidence that works in her favor); (2) with the passing of time, Bento's increasing perception of the extent of the resemblance until reaching the conclusion that Ezequiel is not his son; and finally (3) the reference to his weariness. Were the events narrated in this order, Bento's belief in the adultery would appear more plausible. The state of affairs described in (1) changes to that described in (3) because of (2), which occurs over an extended period of time. In the order that Dom Casmurro chose to narrate the events, however, the weariness arises suddenly and gratuitously, and chapters that suggest contrary hypotheses are juxtaposed (on the one hand, Capitu's remark suggests her innocence; on the other, the perception of accentuated physical resemblance suggests the adultery). Add to this Dom Casmurro's skeptical remark that "people are worth the value that our affection sets on them." That, together with his emphasis on the subjective force of his perception—"Escobar emerged from the grave, etc."—brings uncertainty about the objectivity of his perception.

The conclusion is that Dom Casmurro's insertion of the chapter "Prior to the Prior" just before the chapter "The Sketch and the Color" is meant to establish equipollence at a moment in which the degree of physical resemblance indicated in "The Sketch and the Color" could decide the matter for the infidelity hypothesis.[3] Besides establishing equipollence, with this procedure Dom Casmurro also shows the quick (from one chapter to the next), radical (from a certain belief to its contrary), and groundless oscillation of Bento's judgment. Considering that this shift means to Bento the transition from happiness to unhappiness, it becomes clear that with *Dom Casmurro,* the Machadian theme of human precariousness is now understood in terms of the frailty of beliefs.

The chapter in which Bento tells Capitu that Ezequiel is not his son is entitled "The Photograph." The title refers to Escobar's photograph, which was instrumental in making Bento disbelieve in Capitu's faithfulness.

> Palavra que estive a pique de crer que era vítima de uma grande ilusão, uma fantasmagoria de alucinado; mas a entrada repentina de Ezequiel, gritando . . . restituiu-me à consciência da realidade. Capitu e eu, involuntariamente, olhamos para a fotografia de Escobar, e depois um para o outro. Desta vez a confusão dela fez-se confissão pura. Este era aquele. (OC 1: 936; see Appendix 107)

The photograph here tips the scales that were balanced up to this point, for if on the one hand Bento perceives an extreme physical resemblance, on the other hand he admits that he might be hallucinating. The photograph corroborates the adultery hypothesis because it allows empirical verification of correspondence—presumably verified by them both—to external reality, that is, it eliminates the possibility of Bento's hallucinating. But as he does in the succession of events mentioned earlier, Dom Casmurro mitigates the strength of this objective piece of evidence by bringing in other evidence *equally* strong against the adultery.

Right after the chapter just mentioned, Dom Casmurro recalls a previous chapter, entitled "The Portrait." It deals with an episode that took place during the author's youth that has no relevance to the plot except as a contraposition to "The Photograph." "The Portrait" is that of Sancha's mother, who had an extraordinary physical resemblance to Capitu (although there is no kinship between them). The inclusion of this chapter in his memoirs and the explicit reference to it—Dom Casmurro even asks the reader to read the chapter again—clearly shows that *Dom Casmurro* constructs his narrative so as to build equipollence.[4] The choice of interchangeable titles is quite revealing. In "The Portrait," physical resemblance appears as coincidence. In "The Photograph," physical resemblance appears as verification of kinship. The same thing (portrait/photograph) is "evidence" of contrary theses in different contexts. The conclusion is that beliefs are unavoidably biased by particular and circumstantial contexts. One can say that "casual resemblance" and "genetic resemblance" are equipollent theses since they are "grounded" on the same "evidence." Dom Casmurro proceeds exactly as does the Pyrrhonian. He establishes equipollence that forces suspension (*epoche*) of dogmatic judgment.

***

To conclude this chapter, we indicate in *Dom Casmurro* the primacy of nonrational factors in determining not only beliefs but perception itself. The point is Augustinian and was held by Pascal and the Jansenists in the seventeenth century. It sets some of Aenesidemus's *tropoi* indicated above in a Christian context. This is important because it shows the Christian appropriation of Pyrrhonism to ground a Christian anthropology that emphasizes the fragility of fallen man. As indicated above, Machado was not directly acquainted with the Greek skeptics. His main source was the Christian Pyrrhonism of Montaigne and Pascal.[5] This Christian mediation is one of the reasons for the pessimistic nature of Brás Cubas's, Dom Casmurro's, and Aires's skepticism. Because of the Fall of Man, reason has become the slave of the passions. Skepticism is an epistemological consequence of Original Sin. Passions, prejudices, and preconceptions play major roles in determining beliefs. Pascal claims that

> [t]he will is one of the chief organs of belief, not because it creates belief, but because things are true or false according to the aspect by which we judge them. When the will likes one aspect more than another, it deflects the mind from considering the qualities of the one it does not care to see. Thus the mind, keeping in step with the will, remains looking at the aspect preferred by the will and so judges by what it sees there. (La 539)

Dom Casmurro is aware that the eventual belief or life-view he happens to have on a certain occasion, together with his momentary inclination on this occasion, are the determining factors in his perception and judgment. "Pelo dia adiante, e nos outros dias, Ezequiel ia ter comigo ao gabinete, e as feições do pequeno davam idéia clara das do outro, *ou eu ia atentando mais nelas*" (OC 1: 937; emphasis added) ("Later in the day, and on the other days, Ezekiel came to see me in the study, and the child's features were a clear image of him who was dead, *or perhaps I was paying more attention to them*" [DC 251; emphasis added]).

Once persuaded of the unfaithfulness, Bento reinterprets past situations from a standpoint that presupposes that hypothesis.

> De envolta, lembravam-me episódios vagos e remotos, palavras, encontros e incidentes, tudo em que a minha cegueira não pôs malícia, e a que faltou o meu velho ciúme. Uma vez em que os fui achar sozinhos e calados, um segredo que me fez rir, uma palavra dela sonhando, todas essas reminiscências vieram vindo agora, em tal atropêlo que me atordoaram . . . (OC 1: 937; see Appendix 108)

In a chapter from the first half of the narrative, referring to a period during which Bento was a typical naive young man, Dom Casmurro reports the jealousy he then felt when he saw the glance exchanged between Capitu and a passing man on horseback. The jealousy he felt on that occasion was even stronger because José Dias had insinuated that Capitu was flirting with a neighbor.

> Era certamente alusão ao cavaleiro. Tal recordação agravou a impressão que eu trazia da rua; mas não seria essa palavra, inconscientemente guardada, que me dispôs a crer na malícia dos seus olhares? (OC 1: 883; see Appendix 109)

It is the same author who writes the two passages above. Taking them together, it follows that it is possible to perceive social interactions—in themselves so ambiguous—only with naïveté or with malice. There is no objective access to social phenomena. Every perception is conditioned by one or another subjective disposition. Recall that this is precisely the theme of the short story "A question of husbands" (Chapter Three). Moraes Pancada's conclusion is that "each [husband], in passing through [his wife's] spirit, was transformed completely."

Dom Casmurro says that he failed to "atar as duas pontas da vida, e restaurar na velhice a adolescência" (OC 1: 808) ("tie together the two ends of [his] life, to restore adolescence in old age" [DC 5]). What precludes the tying is the change of perspective or life-view he went through, from the naive life-view of adolescence to the skeptical life-view of old age. Each life-view not only assigns different meanings to experience but even construes reality differently. The very same experiences, from the objective point of view, that were positive to the naive Bento become dubious to the skeptical *casmurro*. This reinterpretation is crucial because it concerns the final question of the novel: "se a Capitu da Praia da Glória já estava dentro da de Mata-cavalos" (OC 1: 942) ("whether the Capitu of Gloria was already within the Capitu of Matacavallos" [DC 262]), that is, if the Capitu of marriage was already within the Capitu of Bento's childhood and adolescence. Dom Casmurro's answer is affirmative, and this last chapter resembles the last chapter of *Epitaph* ("Negatives"). There Brás Cubas presents his redefinition of the value of the main experiences of his life. Adopting the skeptical life-view, that which was experienced as negative is now seen as positive, above all, the fact that he did not have children. A similar redefinition occurs in the last chapter of *Dom Casmurro*. Although also pessimistic, Dom Casmurro's redefinition is more skeptical than Brás Cubas's. There are no independent, unbiased reasons supporting the conclusion that the Capitu of adolescence was already the Capitu of marriage, and even if she was, this does not mean that she was then hypocritical and vicious (like the characters in *Epitaph*), but that she was already opaque and uncertain. Dom Casmurro's situation is as miserable as Brás Cubas's because he is aware that the happiness he enjoyed as an adolescent (and there is not the least certainty about this possibility) may have been the mere fruit of his naïveté. Moreover—and this makes his situation far more tragic than that of Brás Cubas—Dom Casmurro is aware that his present unhappiness may be the mere fruit of his current *casmurro* perspective.

Note that Dom Casmurro's skeptical life-view has two axes: one dogmatic and the other Pyrrhonian. (Brás Cubas's skeptical life-view has only the dogmatic axis, although there are relevant Pyrrhonian elements in it.) The dogmatic axis accounts for his pessimistic beliefs about life (Capitu). The Pyrrhonian axis appears in his suspicion (evident in the way he composes his narrative) about beliefs in general. Dom Casmurro must be located in an intermediary position, between Brás Cubas and Counselor Aires, in the process of constitution of the Pyrrhonian character.

Compared with *Epitaph, Dom Casmurro* presents a more Pyrrhonian treatment of the theme of human frailty. Like Brás Cubas at the end of his life, Dom Casmurro is alone, withdrawn, far from the woman he loved, and childless. Brás Cubas ends up in this condition for objective reasons: the misery and finiteness of being. Dom Casmurro ends up in this condition because of a belief not grounded in the objective reality of things. Had he adopted another belief (not grounded as well), he could have kept Capitu, a child, and the domestic peace that we find in the beginning of Machado's fiction. Dom Casmurro is aware that this is the case. "Se o rapaz tem saído à mãe" ("If the young man had taken after his mother"), he confesses towards the end of his memoir, "eu acabava crendo tudo" (OC 1: 940) ("I would have ended by believing everything" [DC 258]). Beliefs gratuitously generated, and not a solid reality, determine the fate of human beings. Chance circumstances insignificant in themselves (to look like one's father instead of like one's mother) generate beliefs that can never be verified.

Chapter Seven

Counselor Aires and His "Memorial"

The Spectator Writer

José da Costa Marcondes Aires, Counselor Aires, is the third and last character of Machado's novels that exhibits the skeptical life-view. He is the fictional author of and a central character in Machado de Assis's last two novels: *Esaú e Jacó (Esau and Jacob)* of 1904 and *Memorial de Aires (Counselor Ayres' Memorial)* of 1908. In Aires, the definition and elaboration of the skeptical life-view are concluded. With Aires, Machado solves basic problems that we have been following from the very beginning of his fiction: (1) definition of a place for the *homem de espírito* divorced from women and social life, (2) expression of the kind of knowledge possible after the suspension of judgment observed in *Dom Casmurro* (a main issue dealt with in this chapter concerns the kind of skeptical knowledge consistent with Pyrrhonism that is presented by Aires), and (3) achievement of Pyrrhonian *ataraxia* without sacrifice of the practical life.

There are relevant modifications in Aires's spectator stance as compared with that of his predecessors but without breach of continuity. Like Brás Cubas and Dom Casmurro, Aires is not bound by the main links that tie individuals to social reality. He is not married—"tinha o feitio do solteirão" (OC 1: 963) ("he was a bachelor by nature" [EJ 39])—does not have children, and does not work. However, unlike Brás Cubas, Aires is not radically severed from the world, nor is he, unlike Dom Casmurro, completely divorced from it. The novelty of the character is that although withdrawn and detached, Aires is a live character, interacting with other characters *at the same time that he is an author.* (Remember that when they become writers, Brás

Cubas's practical life is eliminated and Dom Casmurro's is drastically reduced.) So, one of the solutions devised by Aires is the attainment of a psychological inward distance from social life in place of a physical spatial distance. This is a crucial achievement because now distance from the agitations of social life that disturbed previous characters can be obtained without going into reclusion. Within Machado's fiction, this is a practical solution to the problem of heterogeneity between *homem de espírito* and outward social life. Machado solves the problem by adding an aesthetic component to the skeptical life-view. The aesthetic solution is not completely new in Machadian fiction previous to 1904. Its first sign appears in Machado's first published work—"Women's preference for *tolos*" (see Chapter One)—and it becomes progressively stronger from Brás Cubas to Dom Casmurro (remember the theory of the "opera," according to which the positive value of life is the aesthetic one).

From the point of view of Pyrrhonism, the characterization of Aires is a positive Machadian solution to the problem of whether the skeptic can live his skepticism.[1] One of the traditional objections to Pyrrhonism is that it is not a philosophy one can live by. This objection was raised by Pyrrho's contemporaries, repeated by modern philosophers such as Pascal and Hume, and recently discussed by Burnyeat. The latter argues that the skeptic cannot live his skepticism because a life without beliefs would require a humanly unfeasible self-detachment, or, more precisely, detachment from oneself. Sextus Empiricus claims that the skeptic assents to appearances without claiming that these appearances correspond to some external reality, that they are true. The skeptic's own impressions and thoughts have to the skeptic the same epistemic status of anyone else's impressions and thoughts. According to Burnyeat, this kind of assent presupposes total indifference and annihilation of emotions, which, if ever possible, would make life meaningless.

> [I]f [the skeptic] refuses to identify with his assent, he is as it were detaching himself from the person (namely, himself) who was convinced by the argument, and he is treating his own thought as if it were the thought of someone else, someone thinking thoughts within him. . . . When one has seen how radically the sceptic must detach himself from himself,

one will agree that the supposed life without belief is not, after all, a possible life for man. (Burnyeat 53)

Aires's aesthetic attitude makes this detachment possible. As Kant points out, the aesthetic attitude is neither an interested nor a pragmatic one. Since Aires has no projects or aspirations to be realized in the world, he is in a condition to establish an external relationship with appearances. Their truth value does not affect his personal existence, so Aires is not interested in or concerned with them. He is not under pressure to adopt beliefs nor to become emotionally involved, because these are demands of an active life, not of a contemplative one. The claim is not, of course, that Aires has no belief at all. He is free, however, from basic beliefs capable of disturbing one's life, such as conceptions of goodness (Brás Cubas) and belief in one's wife's infidelity (Dom Casmurro). According to Jonathan Barnes, the Pyrrhonian is not bound to suspend all beliefs because not all the beliefs he holds are sources of concern and intranquility. The Pyrrhonian must suspend only those beliefs that keep him from attaining *ataraxia*. These beliefs are those concerning matters in which he is interested. The key to Pyrrhonian tranquility is therefore to cancel interest. A way of annulling interest without doing away with one's life (Brás Cubas) or becoming a recluse (Dom Casmurro) is to adopt an aesthetic attitude. The following analysis shows that the main factor in Aires's interaction with Fidélia—related in *Counselor Ayres' Memorial*—is the progressive transformation of the initially interested character (who falls in love, desires, and entertains matrimonial projects) into an aesthete.

Aires is a retired diplomat who, after living abroad most of his life, comes back to Brazil upon retirement. The way he arranges his life can be illuminated by comparing it with the lives of Brás Cubas and Dom Casmurro. Although his sister Rita invites him to live with her, Aires chooses to live alone. The retired man then has a "program" (EJ, ch. 32) of a reclusive and solitary life.

A princípio, Aires cumpriu a solidão, separou-se da sociedade, meteu-se em casa, não aparecia a ninguém ou a raros e de longe em longe. Em verdade estava cansado de homens e de mulheres, de festas e de vigílias. . . .

> Assim foi a princípio. Às quintas-feiras ia jantar com a
> irmã. Às noites passeava pelas praias, ou pelas ruas do
> bairro. O mais do tempo era gasto em ler e reler, compor o
> *Memorial* ou rever o composto, para relembrar as coisas
> passadas. (OC 1: 986; see Appendix 110)

This nostalgic life withdrawn from the social outward world
resembles the lives of Brás Cubas and Dom Casmurro. Writing
is for them the occupation that distracts from the monotony of
being *sub specie aeternitatis*. In Dom Casmurro's case, his
memoir finishes with his announcement of his next book: a
"History of the Suburbs." Because writing is crucial for him,
having concluded his memoirs, he turns to subject matter
without direct relation to his personal life. Note again in comparison that Dom Casmurro's attempt to experience his past
impressions by means of recollection and writing fails because
of his reinterpretation of his past with Capitu.

Dom Casmurro's failure sheds light on Aires's decision to
give up his program of a reclusive and solitary life. The modification that then occurs defines the character and his point of
view, which become the narrative focus of Machado's last
novel.

> Mas tudo cansa, até a solidão. Aires entrou a sentir uma
> ponta de aborrecimento; bocejava, cochilava, tinha sede de
> gente viva. . . .
> Assim se foi o programa da vida nova. Não é que ele já a
> não entendesse nem amasse, ou que a não praticasse ainda
> alguma vez, a espaços, como se faz uso de um remédio que
> obriga a ficar na cama ou na alcova; mas, sarava depressa e
> tornava ao ar livre. Queria ver a outra gente, ouvi-la, cheirá-
> la, gostá-la, apalpá-la, aplicar todos os sentidos a um mundo
> que podia matar o tempo, o imortal tempo. (OC 1: 986–87;
> see Appendix 111)

Brás Cubas, Dom Casmurro, and Aires are all spectators. But
there is a progressive definition of the spectator stance from the
first to the second to the third. The constitution of the spectator
has three stages: (1) withdrawal from social life, (2) nostalgic
life in exile, and (3) return to social life to observe it directly.
The process of withdrawal experienced by the three observers—Brás Cubas, Dom Casmurro, and Aires—can be seen as a

single process of constitution of the spectator. Brás Cubas stops in the first stage, and Dom Casmurro in the second. Only Aires goes through all three stages. Machado's last two novels, in which Aires is both protagonist and author, focus very briefly on the second stage, and the first stage is only alluded to, not described. The plots of both *Esau and Jacob* and *Counselor Ayres' Memorial* show an Aires returned to social life. Aires has, in fact, a crucial role in both novels: the role of observer. Viewed from the standpoint of Machado's craft, it is as if the first two stages need not be focused on because they were already dealt with in *Epitaph* (first stage) and *Dom Casmurro* (second stage). The point now is the direct, live observation of social life. That this is Machado's achievement of a long-pursued goal is strongly suggested by the fact that Machado's last two novels spring largely from Aires's direct observations. Moreover, Machado alludes to the possibility of using Aires again in a new narrative (unfortunately, Machado died shortly after the publication of *Counselor Ayres' Memorial*). It is as if Aires had gone through the other stages and represented the fulfillment of the Machadian enterprise of constructing his skeptical observer-narrator-character. Before retiring, Aires presumably lived a life as agitated as that of the living Brás Cubas. His work as a diplomat provided him a vantage point for seeing life as a theater. The reference to his being tired of men, women, and parties calls to mind the life experience of Brás Cubas, who "has lingered in the theatre long after the end of the performance" and then leaves it "[t]ardy and jaded" (E 20). The second stage occurs right after retirement, when Aires comes back to Brazil. This period in which he remains in reclusion, almost entirely restricted to recollections and to the writing and reading of his "Memorial," resembles Dom Casmurro's way of life after his break with Capitu. It is therefore correct to say that the spectator-character is constructed throughout Machado's second phase (from Brás Cubas to Aires) by going through these three stages.

It is important to note that in returning to (social) life, the skeptical narrator-character does not take the stance of any of the previous Machadian types that are located in social life. He does not return as a naive man because there is no identification with—not even belief in—such things as values, projects, and feelings. Nor is he like the problematic *homem de espírito*—he is not a madman, a suicidal or suffering character. Even less is he a man reconciled with life in marriage or a *tolo* or strategic man. Aires retains the reflective frame of mind that is characteristic of Brás Cubas and Dom Casmurro—it is as if he had inherited their wisdom. Moreover, the main and unique thing about Aires is that although he is back in social life, he is inwardly detached from it. He keeps the theoretical stance and lets himself be affected by the appearances of social life without being disturbed by them.

Aires exhibits an aesthetic-cognitive attitude, a double feature that is crucial to the solutions that the character represents. The cognitive attitude points to a positive knowledge that is suspended in *Dom Casmurro* and that is more skeptical than the metaphysical knowledge presented by Brás Cubas in *Epitaph*. The aesthetic attitude points to the possibility of enjoyment of the (to quote Dom Casmurro) "beautiful passages of the opera," free from the prickles that hurt the *homens de espírito*.

Aires's return to social life is intimately related to the composition of his "Memorial." One of the reasons the Counselor gives up his program of a reclusive and solitary life is the need to find content (phenomena and appearances) for his "Memorial." As suggested above, Aires begins where Dom Casmurro ends. He leaves the reclusive life in order to go after actual phenomena. This point is functional in Aires's relationship with the other characters and defines his position in the plots of both novels in which he appears. His position is that of spectator. For example, when he accepts Natividade's request to advise her twin sons, Pedro and Paulo, it is suggested that Aires "buscasse somente matéria nova para as páginas nuas de seu *Memorial*" (OC 1: 1000) ("was only looking for new material for the blank pages of his *Memorial*" [EJ 109]).

Aires's cognitive interest leads him to locate himself physically close to the object of observation. Thus his method of observation is different from that of Brás Cubas. As a deceased writer, Brás Cubas captures the misery that is covered by the outward life. Only from a radically distant point of view—the point of view of a deceased writer—can the ultimate meaninglessness and finiteness of life be fully apprehended. Aires's position is consistent with his aesthetic-cognitive attitude.

Observation must be direct, alive, and close. This explains the literary difference between the two novels. In his autobiography, Brás Cubas selects the episodes of his life that show human misery—"the substance of life." Aires writes in his "Memorial" a variety of direct observations and impressions without a philosophical selection of them. Experience and aesthetic enjoyment, not metaphysics, guide the composition of the "Memorial." The diary form facilitates this procedure. Thus the "Memorial" is the place where Aires records the appearances that affect him.

Although Aires's aesthetic-cognitive attitude can be seen in Machado's last two novels, there is a shift of emphasis from cognition to aesthetics when we move from *Esau and Jacob* to *Counselor Ayres' Memorial* (although the cognitive aspect is also very strong in Machado's last novel).

Unlike Brás Cubas and Dom Casmurro, Aires is not one of the vertices of the love triangle that structures the narrative he writes (*Esau and Jacob*). He establishes a skeptical relationship with its components. Flora is "Inexplicável" ("Mysterious"), in the title of chapter 34 of the novel. With respect to the twins, Pedro and Paulo, Aires establishes a cognitive relation that symbolizes Pyrrhonian equipollence. We have seen that moral skepticism is the focus of *Epitaph,* and skepticism about other minds is the focus of *Dom Casmurro.* Beliefs concerning politics are a major target of Aires's skepticism in *Esau and Jacob;* because the twins are identified with their radical and contrary political beliefs, these beliefs are indirectly the object of Aires's *zetesis.* The beliefs are contrary, and the believers are irreconcilable. From the Counselor's skeptical point of view, the twins' opposing beliefs appear as having equal weight. The equipollence of the two men—they are twin brothers—symbolizes the equipollence of their opinions. So, whereas their beliefs are the cause of their conflict and disturbance, Aires suspends judgment about them. During a breakfast Aires offered to Pedro and Paulo, Paulo talked of his political article "with love"; Pedro, who opposed it, talked of it "with disdain."

> Aires estudava os dois rapazes e suas opiniões. . . . Paulo . . .
> se declarou capaz de derribar a monarquia com dez homens,
> e Pedro de extirpar o gérmen republicano com um decreto.

> Mas o ex-ministro, sem mais decreto que uma caçarola, nem
> mais homens que o seu cozinheiro, envolveu os dois regi-
> mens no mesmo salmão delicioso. (OC 1: 1000; see Appen-
> dix 112)

The scene is a neat illustration of Aires's position in contrast
to the other characters, in particular the opinionated twin brothers. His position is that of the Pyrrhonian vis-à-vis the dogmatic
philosopher. Whereas groundless beliefs obsess and disturb the
dogmatic philosophers, the Pyrrhonian suspends judgment and
follows the "normal rules of life," viz.,

> Nature's guidance . . . by which we are naturally capable of
> sensation and thought; constraint of the passions . . . whereby
> hunger drives us to food and thirst to drink; tradition of
> customs and laws, . . . [and] instruction of the arts, that
> whereby we are not inactive in such arts as we adopt.
> (PH 1.23–24)

Aires's mode of life fits squarely with the Pyrrhonian practical rules. The constraint of the passions is symbolized in the
passage cited above. Respect for tradition is a basic feature of
the character. The art adopted by the Counselor is authorship—
the composition of his "Memorial." Finally, the guidance of
nature referred to by Sextus is the basic element of *Counselor
Ayres' Memorial:* Aires basically perceives, has sensations, and
thinks. He makes observations, follows their development,
makes predictions, revises them according to new data, enjoys
the appearances that he observes, and records them in his
"Memorial." That constitutes the narrative. The main object of
Aires's aesthetic cognition is, of course, a woman: Fidélia.

Aires's *Zetesis* and Constructive Skepticism

Besides direct and personal observations, Aires's method in
Counselor Ayres' Memorial includes the collection of data from
informers (Rita and Campos). The knowledge he accumulates
is always provisional, his projections, always tentative, for he
constantly revises his hypotheses and projections according to
new data. The most remarkable thing about Aires's method is
that his inquiry is limited to appearances. If Brás Cubas's
inquiry is metaphysical, Aires's is positivist (although there

is no room in Machado's skeptical phase for an objective and unbiased observer with nonproblematic access to the truth). Instead of Brás Cubas's observation of disguised motives hidden in Virgília's behavior, and unlike Dom Casmurro's failed attempt to observe Capitu's hidden subjectivity, Aires's inquiry does not transcend the external appearances generated by Fidélia.[2] Like the observations by the empirical skeptics of late antiquity discussed by Victor Brochard and those of the "constructive" skeptics of the seventeenth century discussed by Richard H. Popkin (*History of Scepticism*), Aires's observations concern appearances, not essences. It is an empirical inquiry about the manner of concatenation of phenomena.

Before discussing Aires's method, a few comments must be made about the novel. Like Machado's previous novels, *Counselor Ayres' Memorial* presents the triangular structure indicated in "Women's preference for *tolos*." There is a separation of Aires (*homem de espírito* in the first phase, skeptical character in the second) from Fidélia (woman), who prefers Tristão— a descendant of the *tolos* of the first phase who adopts the strategic life-view. The life-views, although clearly distinguished, are not as polarized as they are in the previous novels. Fidélia and, to a lesser degree, Tristão do not appear to Aires to be as negative as do Lobo Neves and Virgília to Brás Cubas, or Capitu and Escobar to Dom Casmurro. Unlike Brás Cubas while still alive, and unlike Bento, Aires is not sentimentally interested in the female character, or more precisely, his initial sentimental interest is replaced by an aesthetic-cognitive one. This attitude saves him from the failures, pain, and mental disturbance that arise from the heterogeneity between *homens de espírito* and women (social life). The aesthetic-cognitive attitude is also the substitute for marriage as the *locus* alternative to social life, given that even before *Epitaph,* marriage becomes the core of the corrupted social life. Aires's attitude is therefore an ingenious practical alternative to the absolute hegemony of social life.

The novel is a part of Aires's "Memorial" that deals with a period of his life during which he observes and interacts with Fidélia. The narrative begins on the day he first saw her, beautiful, young, and, paradoxically, a widow, in a cemetery. It ends with Fidélia's departure with her husband, Tristão, for Lisbon.

In the second entry of the novel, 10 January 1888, Aires reports his and his sister's visit to their parents' grave in celebration of the first anniversary of his return to Brazil. But his attention is not attracted by the dead. He notes the figure

> de uma senhora . . . ao pé de outra sepultura. . . . Era moça, vestia de preto, e parecia rezar também, com as mãos cruzadas e pendentes. . . . E bonita, e gentilíssima. (OC 1: 1096; see Appendix 113)

In the first place, Fidélia is pretty. Analysis of *Dom Casmurro* has indicated the narrator's esteem for beauty and his search for its enjoyment. Second, the Counselor's attention is called to the fact that the woman is outside her natural place. Fidélia's fidelity to her deceased husband puts her outside the spheres of outward social life and of time that are characteristic of Machado's women from 1872 onward. This anachronism poses a question to the observer-narrator-character, namely, whether Fidélia will remain an outsider or marry again, thereby returning to (social) life. In other words, the question is: has the *homem de espírito* (Aires) finally found—after thirty-six years of strategic women—a woman hostile to the outward life?

On this same day, Rita, an acquaintance of the widow, tells her brother the circumstances surrounding Fidélia's marriage (opposition from the parents, passion she felt for her husband, intense pain when he died, etc.) that make her think that Fidélia will remain single. To remain a widow means, besides remaining outside the outward life, to refuse the dimension of time, to refuse finiteness, to refuse to face the fact of the death of her husband: "Fidélia . . . não vai a teatros, nem a festas públicas" (OC 1: 1140) ("Fidelia . . . does not go to the theater nor to large parties" [CAM 88]). Aires—as if he had the experience of Brás Cubas and Dom Casmurro—thinks that she is likely to remarry. His opinion is, however, only tentative. Aires will change it according to what he is told and observes himself.

The strict notation of time in the novel is fundamental to the assessment of the question of whether or not Fidélia will rejoin outward social life. During the first part of the narrative, which lasts one year, the widow takes the first step in this direction: she falls in love with Tristão and decides to marry him. The notation of the dates in the "Memorial" shows Aires's procedure for monitoring Fidélia's movement toward this decision. The image (appearance) of the contrite widow at the foot of her husband's grave contrasts with that of the fiancée that she is one year later. Aires more than once juxtaposes these contrary appearances.

Assuming the hypothesis of Fidélia's marriage, there arises a second question. Given that a woman who apparently has no preference for the *tolo* meets a genuine descendant of the *homens de espírito,* would Aires be Fidélia's second husband? They are in an identical position: outside temporality—"Tudo serão modas neste mundo, exceto as estrelas e eu, que sou o mesmo antigo sujeito" (OC 1: 1111) ("Everything is fashion in this world—except the stars and me, who am the same old fellow as always" [CAM 36]). In the Counselor's case, this is a feature that he shares with the previous narrator-characters. Fidélia, on the contrary, is, as it were, outside her natural place. Thus, Fidélia's return to matrimonial life indicates her identification with Machado's women's vocation (first question raised above). In the same way, the definition of Aires as a detached spectator instead of as a husband indicates his identification with Machado's skeptical characters (second question raised above). While Fidélia moves toward marriage and outward social life during the year of 1888, Aires "[reconcilia-se] com [suas] cãs" (OC 1: 1137) ("[is] reconciled to [his] white hair" [CAM 83]). The initial sexual impulses he felt blended with aesthetic admiration and cognitive curiosity are progressively suppressed.[3]

On January 25, Aires is introduced to Fidélia at the Aguiar household. The impression he had at the cemetery is confirmed. The widow excites the sense organs with which Aires wants to taste life. Aires finds her "saborosa" ("tasty") and "vistosa" ("eye-catching"). But on the same occasion that he enjoys Fidélia's beauty, Aires thinks of one of Shelley's verses, which he adopts as his *motto.* The verse reminds him of his withdrawn position: "I can give not what men call love" (CAM 19). This position halts the initial sexual and matrimonial interest, redirecting it toward aesthetics. During this same party at the Aguiar home, Aires indicates his place as spectator.

> Eu deixei-me estar na sala, a mirar aquela porção de homens alegres e de mulheres verdes e maduras, dominando a todas

> pelo aspecto particular da velhice D. Carmo, e pela graça
> apetitosa da mocidade de Fidélia. . . . Shelley continuava a
> murmurar ao meu ouvido para que eu repetisse a mim
> mesmo: *I can give not what men call love.* (OC 1: 1103; see
> Appendix 114)

The passage shows the character's attempt to sublimate desire by defining himself as a contemplative spectator. The aesthetic is gradually strengthened until August 17—six months later—when Aires announces in his "Memorial" the victory of the aesthetic attitude.

> Fidélia chegou, Tristão e a madrinha chegaram, tudo chegou;
> eu mesmo cheguei a mim mesmo,—por outras palavras,
> estou reconciliado com as minhas cãs. Os olhos que pus na
> viúva Noronha foram de admiração pura, sem a mínima
> intenção de outra espécie, como nos primeiros dias deste
> ano. . . . A admiração basta. (OC 1: 1137; see Appendix 115)

Aires's insistence upon the aesthetic attitude is consistent with the conditions of his return to Brazil as a retired diplomat. He returns tired of and bored with active life. As he points out to Batista in *Esau and Jacob,* he no longer belongs to the world: he has no duties, no projects, ambitions, or interests. Aires has retired from life. Nonetheless, he feels the need to be in touch—in the full enjoyment of his senses—with the appearances of the world. This double disposition of his—willingness to withdraw from the world but desire to enjoy its appearances—is reconciled in his aesthetic attitude. Because in Machado's fiction woman represents life, Fidélia is the object of Aires's enjoyment. The aesthetic nature of Aires's enjoyment of Fidélia is indicated in its association with the aesthetic perception of works of art. Fidélia plays the piano (OC 1: 1140; CAM 89) and paints landscapes (OC 1: 1165; CAM 132–33). Aires wants to *hear her* playing, to *see her* painting, and he orients his interaction with her "de modo que mais ouvisse que falasse" (OC 1: 1121) ("in such a way as to hear more and speak less" [CAM 53]).

Because the aesthetic attitude is detached, it is quite consistent with the skeptical attitude. Suspension of judgment, to the Pyrrhonian, is basically related to beliefs in ethical values. Abrogation of interest is a precondition of *ataraxia* because objects of interest are potential sources of disquiet. Besides, there is no room in aesthetic contemplation for an inquiry, such as Brás Cubas's, into what lies behind appearances. The external appearances themselves are the object of contemplation. The attention of the observer is focused on appearances, not on some hidden subjectivity. This kind of observation allows a more positive attitude by the narrator-character with respect to woman and life. Fidélia appears to Counselor Aires as modest and circumspect, without affectation of any kind—she makes no use of rhetoric; her letters have no "frases feitas, nem frases rebuscadas; [são] simplesmente simples" (OC 1: 1128) ("conventional phrases, nor high-flown phrases: [they are] simply simple" [CAM 67]). These features seem to distinguish Fidélia from other Machadian women who exhibit a duality of external behavior and subjectivity. The interesting point here is that there is no evidence that Fidélia is *objectively* different from Virgília and Capitu. As Gledson ("Last Betrayal") has suggested, she might be as strategic and deceitful as the worst Machadian women. But the crucial thing in *Counselor Ayres' Memorial* is that this possibility is completely *beside* the point, for a more faithful interpretation of the novel focuses elsewhere. The most interesting relation in this novel, as in most novels of Machado's second phase, is the cognitive one between narrators and women. The issue is how the narrators see them. Brás Cubas indicates their duplicity. Dom Casmurro assumes a duplicity that he cannot show or prove. Aires is just not concerned with or interested in possible hidden dispositions of Fidélia. Note the development of the narrator's point of view toward skepticism—from the statement of an essence to the impossibility of positing it to the acquiescence in appearances. With Fidélia as viewed by the observer-narrator-character Aires (Capitu or Virgília, being equally beautiful and interesting, might do as well), the issue of duplicity is not raised—does not appear—nor does visible behavior appear as covering subjectivity, for this very behavior is the appearance that Aires observes and wants to enjoy.[4] By marrying, Fidélia transports her positivity—beauty and morality—to the sphere of social life. An example of this can be found in Aires's entry of June 11, 1889. Aires watches Fidélia and Tristão, already married, walking on Ouvidor Street. He explicitly refers to the wifely walk of Fidélia, whom he finds even more beautiful than on other occasions when he had observed her walking on Ouvidor Street. Now contrast Aires's attitude toward Fidélia with Dom Casmurro's toward Capitu (see Chapter Six). The situation is exactly the same: after the honeymoon the couple walks on Ouvidor Street, the heart of Rio at the time. Bento regrets that the honeymoon is over. He complains that domestic peace was not enough for Capitu, for she was impatient for "the outward display of her new state" (DC 194). The outward display of Fidélia's new state is precisely what Aires enjoys. He is not the husband but the aesthetic observer.

So far the focus has been on the aesthetic side of Aires's aesthetic-cognitive attitude. It is now time to turn to its cognitive side. Aires refers to Fidélia as his "objeto de estudo" (OC 1: 1115) ("the object of my study" [CAM 42]).

> Escuta, papel. O que naquela dama Fidélia me atrai é principalmente certa feição de espírito, algo parecida com o sorriso fugitivo, que já lhe vi algumas vezes. Quero estudá-la se tiver ocasião. (OC 1: 1114; see Appendix 116)

Aires's opinion that Fidélia will remarry is not definitive. He reviews the hypothesis according to new data. On June 16 he notes that "Já me parece que realmente Fidélia acaba sem casar. Não é só a piedade conjugal que lhe perdura, é a tendência a coisas de ordem intelectual e artística" (OC 1: 1125) ("I really believe that Fidelia will never marry. It is not only her wifely devotion that endures, there is also her tendency toward things of an intellectual and artistic order" [CAM 60]).

Aires's perception that Fidélia has a "tendency toward things of an intellectual and artistic order" suggests to him that she will remain single because it is a feature of a spiritual sphere alien to that of the outward life in which marriage is situated. The issue is, however, still open, and Aires continues his study. On October 17, when analyzing Rita's information that Fidélia was making arrangements for flowers to take to the cemetery on All Souls' Day, he makes an explicit reference to his cognitive interest. On this occasion Aires asks his sister if Fidélia had dined at the Aguiar household with Tristão. The answer is no.

> Ouvi todas essas minúcias e ainda outras com interesse.
> Sempre me sucedeu apreciar a maneira por que os caracteres

> se exprimem e se compõem, e muita vez não me desgosta o
> arranjo dos próprios fatos. Gosto de ver e antever, e também
> de concluir. Esta Fidélia foge a alguma coisa, se não foge a
> si mesma. (OC 1: 1160; see Appendix 117)

Aires's method consists of seeing (attention to facts and aesthetic enjoyment), drawing conclusions (formulation of a
theory about the current state of affairs), and foreseeing (hypothetical projections on the bases of past and present patterns).
The issue is whether or not Fidélia will marry. There are signs
that Tristão is a candidate. The question of whether Fidélia
dined with Tristão raises the hypothesis of marriage. The attention with which Aires listens to Rita's report of Fidélia's
arrangements for All Souls' Day shows him exploring the plausibility of the contrary hypothesis. Aires examines both and
returns to his initial opinion that she will marry. Aires's perception of Fidélia is oriented by a "theory," namely, that the natural place of woman is in social life, the entrance to which is
marriage. He then interprets Fidélia's effort to remain a widow
as an attempt to "run away from herself."

Aires's source of information is not limited to informants.
He subtly approaches Fidélia herself to grasp something of her
feelings and tries to capture all relevant signs. On Novem-
ber 12, he writes in his "Memorial" his impression that Tristão
is in love with Fidélia. He then announces his intention:
"[q]uando lá for . . . hei de abrir todas as velas à minha saga-
cidade, a ver se confirmo ou desminto estas duas impressões.
Pode ser engano, mas pode ser verdade" (OC 1: 1166) ("[w]hen
I go there now [to the Aguiar house] I must unfurl all the sails
of my sagacity to see if I can confirm or disprove these two
impressions. I could be mistaken, but I could be right" [CAM
135]). It is remarkable that Aires's impressions, unlike those of
Brás Cubas, do not lead to assertive and confident claims about
reality. Aires's statements are provisional and tentative, always
in need of further verification.

Aires's method is fundamental to his less negative and more
sympathetic perspective of social life as compared to the views
of his predecessors. The key point, alluded to by the diplomat
at least four times, is *understanding*. Understanding here means
both comprehension and acceptance of woman's immersion in
the dimension of time that Fidélia's willingness to marry

represents. The circumstance of Aires being just a spectator and
not an interested party, as Brás Cubas and Dom Casmurro are,
is a relevant factor in this understanding. It is no longer a cognitive paradox, nor is it in tension with morality, that Fidélia,
faithful to and loving her deceased husband, falls in love with
and marries Tristão. This solves the cognitive problem—a
source of disturbance—of women's variation. And once the
cognitive problem is solved, the moral problem is also solved:
Aires does not condemn Fidélia's action.

January 9, 1889, marks the second anniversary of Aires's
return to Brazil. Fidélia already is Tristão's fiancée. In his
"Memorial," Aires recollects his visit a year before to the cemetery with his sister, when he saw a sorrowful Fidélia at her
husband's grave. Note the relevance of the chronological form
of the diary. In precisely one year Aires can measure and assess
the change in Fidélia's condition from widow to fiancée. Aires
juxtaposes the two conditions and notes, in the tradition of the
preceding narrators, woman's variation over time. Contemplating his return with Rita to the cemetery, he muses:

> Quem sabe se não iríamos dar com a viúva Noronha ao pé
> da sepultura do marido, as mãos cruzadas, rezando, como há
> um ano? Se eu tivesse ainda agora a impressão que me levou
> a apostar com Rita o casamento da moça, poderia crer que
> tal presença e tal atitude me dariam gosto. Acharia nelas o
> sinal de que não ama a Tristão, e, não podendo eu desposá-la,
> preferia que amasse o defunto. Mas não, não é isso; é o que
> vou dizer. (OC 1: 1175; see Appendix 118)

Aires indicates in this paragraph what his position would be in
case he shared the framework of his predecessors. As for the
initial question, supposing that Fidélia were at the grave, he
points to the incongruity of appearances and suggests the duality
of external behavior and subjectivity. In this framework, her
presence in the cemetery would mean the fiancée's hypocrisy,
in the same way that her presence at the Aguiar house with
Tristão would mean the widow's dissembling. This would
match the characterization of the main women of the previous
novels as seen by their narrators. Aires then indicates how he
would have evaluated the situation if his initial desire had prevailed. Not being able to marry her, he would have preferred

that she remain a widow—for in this case Fidélia would be taking a stand against the finiteness of things. Aires alludes to these possibilities, however, only to reject them.

> Mas não, não é isso; é o que vou dizer.
> Se eu a visse no mesmo lugar e postura, não duvidaria ainda assim do amor que Tristão lhe inspira. Tudo poderia existir na mesma pessoa, sem hipocrisia da viúva nem infidelidade da próxima esposa. . . . A recordação do finado vive nela, sem embargo da ação do pretendente; vive com todas as doçuras e melancolias antigas. (OC 1: 1175; see Appendix 119)

Aires no longer considers the contrast of appearances as a contradiction. Both attitudes are understood within the different, but equally acceptable, contexts in which each occurs. The result is that what were seen as women's contradictory attitudes are now reconciled. The theme of woman's ability to reconcile contrary attitudes is already present in *Epitaph*. However, to Aires this reconciliation is neither a contradiction on the cognitive level nor hypocrisy on the moral level. The understanding of woman from Aires's point of view is a result of his method: the close witnessing of Fidélia's attitudes and emotions; the relatively unbiased nature of his observation given that he is not an interested party concerning Fidélia; knowledge of the history of Fidélia and her dead husband, her faithfulness, and her simple and unaffected interaction with the Aguiar couple and himself; and his monitoring of the evolution of Fidélia's feelings toward Tristão.

On February 26, Aires goes to a funeral and sees fresh flowers on Noronha's grave. He is informed by the gravedigger that the flowers were deposited by Fidélia. Thus the situation he imagined on January 9 has been realized. Aires seems to insist that, although a fact, the contrast widow/fiancée does not imply immoral duplicity on Fidélia's part. That the spectator attentive to particular circumstances and restricted to phenomena is quite relevant in making this understanding possible is clear from the following passage:

> Em caminho pensei que a viúva Noronha, se efetivamente ainda leva flores ao túmulo do marido, é que lhe ficou este costume, se lhe não ficou essa afeição. Escolha quem quiser;

> eu estudei a questão por ambos os lados, e . . . [cheguei a
> uma] terceira solução. . . . [I]maginei poder encontrá-la
> diante da pessoa extinta, como se fosse a pessoa futura,
> fazendo de ambas uma só criatura presente. (OC 1: 1183; see
> Appendix 120)

Aires's understanding is that Fidélia unifies and makes compatible the two people—the dead and the living—thereby overcoming the contradiction of two fidelities. Two Fidélias exist without duality. The widow, defined in relation to Noronha, and the wife, defined in relation to Tristão, are reconciled in a harmonious whole. There is no reference to an essential subjectivity that is independent of each relation, defined *a priori* and absolutely, determining behavior and dispositions appropriate to wife and widow.

Some scholars such as Oswaldo P. Pereira argue that the scope of the beliefs suspended by the Pyrrhonian does not include appearances. The Pyrrhonian's *epoche* is restricted to beliefs about essences understood as the real nature of the perceived appearances. The passage from Sextus most cited in support of this interpretation is the following:

> We do not overthrow the affective sense-impressions which
> induce our assent involuntarily; and these impressions are
> "the appearances." And when we question whether the
> underlying object is such as it appears, we grant the fact that
> it appears, and our doubt does not concern the appearance
> itself but the account given of that appearance. (PH 1.19)

The skeptic's doubt concerns, therefore, the passage from appearance to essence. So, when the dogmatist draws the conclusion, for example, from the sweetness he tastes in the honey that honey *is* sweet, the skeptic presents circumstances in which honey appears sour. He juxtaposes the two theses—"honey is sweet" and "honey is sour"—establishing equipollence and forcing the suspension of judgment about the essential reality of honey, independent of impressions—"not more this than that." According to this view, rather than denying, the skeptic "defends" the reality of the contrary impressions of sweet and sour, denying the legitimacy of singling out one of them as the only real attribute of the external thing (honey).

Françoise Caujolle-Zaslawsky emphasizes the constructive aspect of this position that, together with the empirical method (direct observation of the phenomenon, attention to the historical circumstances in which it appeared, and inductive reasoning), makes possible a nondogmatic knowledge that avoids the aporetic fate of absolute judgments. The negative expression "not more this than that" has a positive counterpoint: "this *and* that." One moves from the negative to the positive expression when one's investigation withdraws from the realm of essences to that of appearances. In claiming that honey is essentially no more sweet than it is sour, the skeptic implies a positive empirical description of honey: it appears sweet in such and such circumstances and sour in such and such circumstances. Caujolle-Zaslawsky argues that the skeptic's perspectivism "avoids the logical impossibility that would obtain in simultaneous assertion of two contradictory propositions, and allows the indication of the particular meaning, manner, and limits within which each proposition is asserted."[5]

The passage from negative skepticism ("neither one nor the other") to constructive skepticism ("one and the other," according to each specific context) sheds light on the modification from Dom Casmurro's to Aires's skeptical life-view (or even from Aires's skeptical life-view in *Esau and Jacob* to his view in *Counselor Ayres' Memorial*). Dom Casmurro establishes equipollence—"neither one nor the other"—with respect to Capitu's infidelity (see Chapter Six). This leads him to the following contradiction: Capitu is no more unfaithful than she is faithful. Dom Casmurro is trapped by conflicting appearances that point to two Capitus. He attempts to find the truth of the matter concerning the real Capitu. Who essentially was Capitu? The faithful wife? The deceitful and adulterous woman? Dom Casmurro wants, but fails, to come to a judgment independent of the changeable and contrary appearances exhibited by Capitu. Capitu *appears* to him as faithful and as loving him in some circumstances and she *appears* as unfaithful and as loving Escobar under other circumstances. Because Dom Casmurro seeks the true subjectivity of Capitu, he is paralyzed by contradiction. Aires overcomes the contradiction thanks to his skeptical-empirical method. When Tristão and Fidélia marry, Aires has an idea.

> A idéia é saber se Fidélia terá voltado ao cemitério depois de casada. Possivelmente, sim; possivelmente não. Não a censurarei, se não; a alma de uma pessoa pode ser estreita para duas afeições grandes. Se sim, não lhe ficarei querendo mal, ao contrário. Os mortos podem muito bem combater os vivos, sem os vencer inteiramente. (OC 1: 1194; see Appendix 121)

The observer-narrator-character no longer searches for an absolute and uniquely subjective state in the female character. Her going to the cemetery would indicate her condition as the widow Noronha; her not going, that of Tristão's wife. Aires could say that Fidélia is neither the widow nor the wife, absolutely speaking. She is widow from one point of view, wife from another. Because Aires employs "la méthode des sceptiques grecs" (according to Caujolle-Zaslawsky's interpretation of it), one can say that Aires overcomes the dogmatic framework in which the conflicting appearances exhibited by women (that is, exhibited by the world) are contradictions, and thereby he attains a higher level (nondogmatic) of understanding. Virgília cries sincere tears at her husband's death. Ezequiel may be Escobar's son, and nonetheless Capitu may have been faithful to Bento. Each behavior and disposition is consistent with the particular context in which it occurs. The conception of truth in place is no longer correspondence (with external reality) but coherence (of appearances in given circumstances). This epistemological shift allows a less pessimistic view of the morality that prevails in social life. By accepting moral relativism, the *homem de espírito* realizes that he must accept this less than perfect world in which he lives.

***

During the year of 1888, Aires witnesses Fidélia's first step toward social life. During 1889, he sees her second and final step in this direction: her and Tristão's decision to live in Lisbon. Politics and fame (remember Lobo Neves)await Tristão in Lisbon. The strong ties between Fidélia and the Aguiar couple pose a second question to the Counselor: would the couple give up the project of an amusing outward life abroad to stay in their familiar domestic peace? Aires's sister Rita thinks they will stay; the Counselor believes they will go. As if Aires possessed the wisdom accumulated by his predecessors, he again bets on woman's variation and vocation for social outward life—destruction of the Aguiars' domestic peace, whose soul is the lovely and beautiful Fidélia.

At the end of the narrative, Aires makes a remark that summarizes the philosophical conclusion he draws from his study. He tells Campos—Fidélia's uncle—that "se os mortos vão depressa, os velhos ainda vão mais depressa que os mortos" (OC 1: 1198) ("if the dead go quickly, old people go even more quickly than the dead" [CAM 195]). Indeed, Aires notes that Noronha "went" in one year—1888 (Aires followed the widow's resistance to a second marriage). Fidélia's resistance to abandoning the Aguiar couple is more quickly overcome ("old people go even more quickly than the dead"). This, the second part of the narrative, lasts only eight months—in 1889.

Despite Aires's view that "a mocidade tem o direito de viver e amar, e separar-se alegremente do extinto e do caduco" (OC 1: 1198) ("youth has the right to live and love, and lightly part from the dead and the dying" [CAM 195]), the conclusion is ironical and melancholic. Dona Carmo suffered very much when, years before, she lost Tristão—her "filho postiço" (OC 1: 1111) ("foster son" [CAM 35])—who moved to Portugal, where he finally forgot his godmother. Later, Dona Carmo's affections are transferred to Fidélia—her "foster daughter." Then this same Tristão comes back, revives Dona Carmo's maternal feelings, and, to the great happiness of the Aguiar couple, marries Fidélia—taken by them as an indication that he will settle in Brazil. However, not only does Tristão return to Portugal, but worse, he carries off with him the "foster daughter" that replaced him when he first left. So, although more subtle, the plot corroborates Brás Cubas's pessimistic view that while happiness is short, unhappiness always comes back and intensifies. At one point, Aires writes in the "Memorial" that he would like to write a modern version of Ecclesiastes,

> posto nada deva haver moderno depois daquele livro. Já dizia ele que nada era novo debaixo do sol, e se o não era então, não o foi nem será nunca mais. Tudo é assim contraditório e vago também. (OC 1: 1139; see Appendix 122)

The reference to Ecclesiastes shows that despite Aires's understanding and acceptance of the temporal predicament of life, he holds a philosophy of finiteness and vanity. To be sure, he is not assertive and metaphysical as is Brás Cubas. After the Pyrrhonian impasse noted in *Dom Casmurro,* a nondogmatic, melancholic philosophy develops, grounded in an empirical "study" of Fidélia that recognizes the beauty and exhibits understanding of the temporal predicament of humankind.

The reader will recall a discussion of the short story "Happiness through marriage" (1866) presented in the first chapter. The narrator of this story sets Ecclesiastes aside—together with authorship and pessimistic philosophy—when he establishes domestic peace with a woman who does not prefer the *tolo*. He then leaves the agitated life of the court for the tranquil life of the countryside, taking with him, together with his wife, his wife's old father and uncle. Tristão carries Fidélia to the agitation and diversion of the Portuguese court, leaving their "foster parents" and Fidélia's uncle behind. The symmetrically opposite situations well illuminate the consciousness of finiteness built into Machado's fiction from 1866 to 1908. Despite Aires's recognition and acceptance of the outward life, some negative features of social life are still noted by him. In the first place it is clear that to marry Tristão means to Fidélia the taking up of an important role in the "opera" (to cite Dom Casmurro), where fame may be achieved. This aspect is not without relevance to Fidélia, who refuses the courtship of Osório—an honest but modest man from the Aguiars' domestic circle. The alienating function of *divertissement* (Pascal) provided by social life is also underlined. Aires notes that although "Fidélia ia realmente triste; o mar não tardaria em espancar as sombras, e depois a outra terra, que a receberia com a outra gente" (OC 1: 1196) ("Fidelia was truly sad; the sea would soon drive away the dark shadows and, after the sea, that other land, where that other family waited to receive her" [CAM 192–93]). *Divertissement* would obscure for her the perspective of human finiteness. Finally, Aires wonders if Fidélia was aware that she would not return. Because he thinks she was and nothing is said to the Aguiar couple, the wife Fidélia is no longer seen by the observer to be as transparent as was the widow Fidélia. Aires accepts Fidélia's return to marriage, to social life, to life. But if it is true that social life no longer has the strong negative meaning it has in Machado's previous fiction, it is also true that marriage is far from having the positive ethical meaning it has in the first phase.

Aires's *Ataraxia*

If Aires's method resembles that of the empirical skeptics, the main features of the character resemble those that are known of Pyrrho. Like Socrates, Pyrrho opposed the Sophists. Victor Brochard's distinction between Pyrrho and the Sophists also obtains between the skeptical and the strategic life-views. Brochard says that "[Greek] sophistry is above all a doctrine of action whereas Pyrrho is completely indifferent or apathetic; . . . He just let himself live. [Pyrrhonism] is a doctrine of old age."[6]

Like Dom Casmurro, Aires dislikes activity. Furthermore, as we have seen, a major definition of the character is the process at the end of which he is "reconciled to [his] white hair" (CAM 83). Retirement from public office for Aires, as for Montaigne, means repose and tranquility. The few diplomatic assignments he receives cause him displeasure and boredom. Dinner with a young Belgian diplomat brings him weariness. In commenting on this meeting, he says that he would prefer the company of the Aguiar couple, who "vão com a minha velhice" (OC 1: 1179–80) ("are in keeping with my old age" [CAM 163]).

The fact that Aires was a diplomat is not without relevance for his skepticism. His work demanded a lot of traveling. Referring to Pyrrho, who traveled with Alexander to the East, Brochard says that "voyages are a school of skepticism."[7] The contact with foreign cultures provides an occasion to realize the relativity of customs, practices, and beliefs. Besides, diplomacy helped to develop Aires's habit of staying away from political parties and opinions, which leads him to be very cautious about opinions in general. Batista, a character in *Esau and Jacob* who is a member of the conservative party, receives an invitation to occupy a position in the government then ruled by the liberals. Uncertain about taking it, he asks Aires if he would accept the job were he in Batista's place, to which Aires responds:

> —Comigo não podia ser. Sabe que eu já não sou deste mundo, e politicamente nunca figurei em nada. A diplomacia tem este efeito que separa o funcionário dos partidos e o deixa tão alheio a eles, que fica impossível de opinar com

verdade, ou, quando menos, com certeza. (OC 1: 1016; see Appendix 123)

Distance from the political parties reveals inward distance from the world, that is, distance from convictions and beliefs that engage and mobilize the individual to action, political or otherwise.

The most remarkable resemblance to Pyrrho is Aires's famous "tédio à controvérsia" (OC 1: 963) ("argument bored him" [EJ 39]). This is characteristic of early ancient Pyrrhonism, a feature that contrasts Pyrrho and his immediate followers both with their contemporary Academic skeptics and with the late Pyrrhonians of Sextus's time. Brochard notes that

> Timon describes Pyrrho as avoiding discussions. Pyrrho's immediate successors exhibit this same feature. One often perceives in Timon's fragments his disgust for vain and endless discussions. He frequently condemns [the dogmatic philosophers'] outcries, disputes, and, in particular, their pretension and arrogance.[8]

The reason Aires refuses to engage in discussions resembles that of Pyrrho.

> Tinha observado que as convicções, quando contrariadas, descompõem o rosto à gente, e não queria ver a cara dos outros assim, nem dar à sua um aspecto abominável. . . . Daí o arranjo de gestos e frases afirmativas que deixavam os partidos quietos, e mais quieto a si mesmo. (OC 1: 1055; see Appendix 124)

When a belief is a strong conviction, avoiding opposing it may be an alternative path to tranquility. The psychological distress caused by opinions is, as we have seen, a crucial theme in *Epitaph* and *Dom Casmurro*. Brás Cubas curses the "fixed ideas"—the direct cause of his distress and depression and the indirect cause of his death. Bento is tortured by the continuous and radical oscillation of his judgment concerning Capitu. Aires presents a remedy to the harm caused by opinions: a weaker kind of assent.

> [E]ste Aires . . . tinha que nas controvérsias uma opinião dúbia ou média pode trazer a oportunidade de uma pílula, e

compunha as suas de tal jeito, que o enfermo, se não sarava, não morria, e é o mais que fazem pílulas. (OC 1: 963; see Appendix 125)

As Martha Nussbaum has recently emphasized, the therapeutic metaphor of the skeptic's procedure and the reference to dogmatism as a disease is frequently found in the ancient sources of Greek skepticism. Aires, like Pyrrho, having gone a long way through philosophies and human agitations, does not think it worthwhile to defend, dispute, or argue for any opinion whatsoever. Philo, referring to Pyrrho's admiration for Homer, says that Pyrrho "used to cite . . . all the lines which point to the inconsistency of men and their futility and childishness" (Long and Sedley 14). Aires does not exhibit a questioning attitude toward this futility and childishness. If we take Machado's creation of characters from Brás Cubas through Dom Casmurro to Aires as a single construction of the spectator, we can apply to the Counselor, Brochard's explanation of Pyrrho's nonargumentative attitude.

> Only after having made a journey through philosophical doctrines—as he did around the world—does Pyrrho find repose in indifference and apathy. Not because he is ignorant of man's sciences, but because he knows them well.[9]

The reference to the journey around the world is directly applicable to Aires's past life not covered in the novels. This part of Aires's life is not narrated because it is equivalent to Brás Cubas's, who, according to Machado, "viajou à roda da vida" (OC 1: 510) ("traveled around life"). The indication of acquaintance with philosophies is also consistent with the character, but is not presented in the novel because, again, it brings to mind Brás Cubas's struggle with philosophical systems symbolized by Humanitism. In Aires, one finds, therefore, the final point of the Pyrrhonian's journey: the moment when, after Brás Cubas's painful *zetesis* and Dom Casmurro's distressing *epoche, ataraxia* and indifference is fully achieved.

To be sure, the Pyrrhonian journey from *zetesis* to *ataraxia* occurs in one single movement. And we have seen that these three stages are present in each of the three Machadian skeptics. The point here is that each stage is progressively developed and defined in the sequence of the novels. This development can be seen in the titles of the sections of the last three chapters of this study: *zetesis* is the strongest element in *Epitaph; zetesis* and *epoche* predominate in *Dom Casmurro;* and *zetesis* and *ataraxia* in *Counselor Ayres' Memorial* (Aires exhibits a nondogmatic knowledge of appearances, so *epoche* can be avoided). Note also that philosophical doctrines are present in the beginning of the first two novels—"The Delirium" in *Epitaph* and "The Opera" in *Dom Casmurro*—but absent in the more skeptical *Counselor Ayres' Memorial*. Finally, unlike the narrators of *Epitaph* and *Dom Casmurro,* the narrator of *Esau and Jacob* and *Counselor Ayres' Memorial* does not go through the naive and strategic life-views, but adopts the skeptical life-view from the outset.

Aires's Relevance in Machadian Fiction

Aires is the only character who is a major protagonist in two Machadian novels. It is quite significant that these novels are Machado's last. With Aires, Machado finally achieves the elaboration of a character he has pursued since his first narrative—"Women's preference for *tolos*"—in 1861. His use of Aires again in *Counselor Ayres' Memorial* is an exploration of the aesthetic, cognitive, and literary possibilities opened by the creation of the character in *Esau and Jacob*. Machado's last novel differs from *Esau and Jacob* in emphasizing the Counselor's point of view as determined by his characterization and position in the plot and in social life. Aires, Machado's last creation, is also his most skeptical character. Machado's development is toward the intensification of the skeptical life-view. This becomes clear when we note from *Esau and Jacob* to *Counselor Ayres' Memorial* the increased relevance of Aires's perception of the other characters (appearances that cause him impressions, which he thinks about and writes down in his "Memorial"). The increased relevance of Aires's point of view is proportionate to the decreased relevance of the plot's objectivity. This is a general pattern of Machado's fiction. We saw this pattern in the short stories he revised for a second publication (Chapter Four), in his preface to *Resurrection* and *The Hand and the Glove,* and in the progression that occurs from *Epitaph* through *Dom Casmurro* and *Esau and Jacob* to *Counselor Ayres' Memorial.*

In the preface to *Esau and Jacob,* we are told that although the narrative was found enclosed with the manuscript notebooks of the Counselor,

> não fazia parte do *Memorial,* diário de lembranças que o conselheiro escrevia desde muitos anos e era a matéria dos seis [outros volumes]. . . . Era uma narrativa; e, posto figure aqui o próprio Aires, com o seu nome e título de conselho, e, por alusão, algumas aventuras, nem assim deixava de ser a narrativa estranha à matéria dos seis cadernos. (OC 1: 944; see Appendix 126)

So, the content proper of the notebooks—"descobertas, observações, reflexões, críticas e anedotas" (OC 1: 963) ("discoveries, observations, reflections, criticisms, and anecdotes" [EJ 40]) with "ordem de datas, com indicação da hora e do minuto" (OC 1: 944) ("arrangement by dates, with indication of hour and minute" [EJ 3])—appears rarely in *Esau and Jacob* and only in the background of the plot. On the other hand, although the narration is in the third person, there are indications of Aires's authorship in some commentaries by the narrator and in Aires's position as observer in the plot. Moreover, Aires makes several observations and writes them down in his "Memorial" throughout the novel. Finally, still in the preface to *Esau and Jacob,* it is indicated that only the narrative was published because in the other six notebooks, that is, in the "Memorial" itself, Aires "tratava de si" (OC 1: 944) ("wrote about himself" [EJ 3]), that is, about his impressions and recollections.

In the foreword to his last novel—*Counselor Ayres' Memorial*—Machado describes the work as the publication of a section of these six notebooks that constitute the "Memorial," "relativa a uns dois anos (1888–1889)" ("relating to the two years 1888–1889"), which, "se for decotada de algumas circunstâncias, anedotas, descrições e reflexões,—pode dar uma narração seguida, que talvez interesse, apesar da forma de diário que tem" (OC 1: 1094) ("if pruned of certain incidents, descriptions, and reflections, could present a connected narrative that might hold some interest in spite of the diary form in which it is written" [CAM 5]). These explanations indicate that Machado is moving further away from connected narrative, from objective plots, toward the free form of a diary. Although the material has been edited, descriptions and reflections that constitute the content of the "Memorial" itself appear much more frequently in this than in the previous novel. Besides, the passages that have been pruned are described as only those not directly related to Fidélia and the Aguiar couple, and many reflections completely unrelated to the plot are preserved in the book.

Machado's changes in literary form from *Esau and Jacob* to *Counselor Ayres' Memorial* reflect his intention to explore the diary form. The diary makes possible the expression of subjective impressions without commitment to the external reality and truth of the events narrated. So, besides the practical solution to the problem of how a skeptic can live his skepticism, Aires also presents a solution to another traditional charge raised against the Pyrrhonians: how can the Pyrrhonians utter propositions against the dogmatic philosophers without asserting them, that is, without being committed to their truth value?

Sextus addresses this problem in many chapters of his *Outlines of Pyrrhonism*. He notes that all skeptical formulae contain, implicitly, qualification of the type "*it appears to me* that such and such is the case." This qualification means that the skeptic is merely reporting an impression that is presently affecting him instead of making a claim about the external reality. "[O]f none of our future statements," claims Sextus, "do we positively affirm that the fact is exactly as we state it, but we simply record each fact, like a chronicler, as it appears to us at the moment" (PH 1.4).

During his second phase, Machado de Assis—who was a chronicler during most of his life—worked out a literary form in which the narrator's impressions could be increasingly more relevant in the narratives and increasingly less committed to the external reality of the events narrated. An autobiography such as Brás Cubas's binds its author to criteria of relevance and real facts. A memoir such as Dom Casmurro's restricts its author to the experiences which—however reinterpreted they may be— he actually had. Only a diary of impressions does not require any commitment to the reality or the truth value of what is written. In his last novel, Machado finds the literary form most consistent with a skeptical life-view.[10]

Machado's final note in his foreword to *Counselor Ayres'
Memorial* is intriguing. Publishing only the Counselor's descriptions and reflections that "liga o mesmo assunto" ("a single
theme ties together"), Machado announces that "[o] resto
aparecerá um dia, se aparecer algum dia" (OC 1: 1094) ("[t]he
rest will appear some day, if some day comes" [CAM 5]). Taking this announcement together with the preface to *Esau and
Jacob,* we note the shift of emphasis from the plot to the
narrator's impressions. Given this pattern, I suggest that Aires
would have been used again in a new book had Machado not
died soon after the publication of *Counselor Ayres' Memorial.*
The book (note that I am not assuming that it would be a novel)
would contain the descriptions, reflections, and anecdotes that
make up most of the six volumes of the "Memorial" and were
left out of *Counselor Ayres' Memorial* because they did not "tie
together a single theme." It would be an impressionistic account
of appearances that affected or affect Aires. The appearance/
reality dualism that is presupposed in the Pyrrhonians' attack
on the dogmatic philosophers would finally be overcome in
Machado's fiction.

This brings me to a final note concerning Aires and the broader
historical implications of Machado's treatment of skepticism.

***

Machado probably never read Sextus Empiricus. His major
sources for skepticism are two early modern authors who were
fundamental in the configuration of the modern intellectual
world, viz., Pascal and Montaigne. Now whereas Pascal is the
key thinker in the arrival of skepticism in Machado's fiction that
marks the beginning of his second phase (*Epitaph*), Montaigne
is the key one in the final solution to skepticism as found in the
character of Aires. As Cohen points out,

> Montaigne's description of Pyrrho is very sympathetic;
> Pyrrho, for Montaigne, is a symbol of a *libertine thinker.*
> Montaigne's Pyrrho does not give up thinking as he is often
> described; he is a different *type* of thinker. According to
> Montaigne, "Pyrrho wants to make himself a living, think-
> ing, reasoning man, enjoying all natural pleasures and
> comforts, employing and using his bodily and spiritual
> faculties in regular and upright fashion. (424)

There are interesting similarities between Aires and Montaigne. Aires's "tédio à controvérsia" is one of them. Montaigne wonders, "[i]s it not better to remain in suspense than to entangle yourself in the many errors that human fancy has produced? Is it not better to suspend your conviction, than to get mixed up in these seditious and quarrelsome divisions?" (Montaigne 373). Another is the retirement from public affairs, seen by both as an obstacle to tranquility. Remember finally that Aires gives up his project of a completely reclusive life because "he wanted," like Pyrrho (according to Montaigne) and like Montaigne himself, "to see other people, hear them, smell them, taste them, feel them, apply all his senses [and mind, one shall add] to a world that could kill time, deathless time" (EJ 84–85). Besides, Aires says: "Gosto de ver e antever, e também de concluir" (OC 1: 1160) ("I enjoy seeing and foreseeing, and drawing conclusions" [EJ 124]).

But the most remarkable similarity between Montaigne and Aires concerns the role of writing in Western modern secularization. Michael O'Loughlin cites Erich Auerbach on Montaigne's rupture with the Christian *Weltanschauung*:

> Life on earth is no longer the figure of the world beyond; he can no longer permit himself to scorn the here for the sake of a there. Life on earth is the only one he has. He wants to savor it to the last day; *car enfin c'est nostre estre, c'est nostre tout.* (O'Loughlin 238)

Commenting on the passage, O'Loughlin claims that

> even though [Montaigne] may regard this life as *nostre estre, nostre tout,* Montaigne does not contemplate it the way angels enjoy the beatific vision or Christian contemplatives find intimations of "paradise." They do not contemplate themselves contemplating their object. And they do not write "essays." . . . the "personal" quality of the essays . . . resides in the extraordinary extent to which their subject is their own composition. The essays not only enact the process of Montaigne's contemplative leisure but are themselves the objects of his contemplation. The essays are assays of themselves. (280)

O'Loughlin understands the evolution of Montaigne's essays as a movement from a religious (one could also add metaphysical) kind of contemplation of the eternal being to the contemplation of one's own changeable self in time, in which the experience of writing is an important feature. It gives expression to the humanistic realization that this temporal and precarious world is the only world available and that we must conform to it.

The evolution of Machado's second phase also presents a pattern similar to that perceived by O'Loughlin in Montaigne's *Essays*. Brás Cubas's contemplation has both something anti-Christian and something Christian in it: the narcissistic self-love exhibited by the living character, the deceased writer's reluctance to accept the human fallen predicament, his pessimistic view of human depravity, and his despair over his incapacity to follow Pascal all the way and have faith. The contemplation Brás Cubas experiences in the "delirium" is terrifying: it is the converse of the angelic kind of beatific contemplation. But already in *Epitaph*, and even more so in *Dom Casmurro*, there is a possibility of an alternative kind of contemplation. This possibility is fully explored by Counselor Aires: aesthetic contemplation of the world (enjoyment of Fidélia) and of his own contemplative stance (composition of the "Memorial").

The skepticism Machado deals with is the revived skepticism of early modern history. His theme is essentially modern and has to do with the impact of the revival of ancient skepticism on the shaping of the modern human condition. Richard H. Popkin, evaluating this impact, notes that

> when ancient scepticism was introduced into the debates about rationalizing the world . . . too much was cast in doubt. . . . The exploration of what assurance we could have after sceptically challenging the previously nicely ordered world showed all innocence was gone, and we could only rely on ourselves and our feelings as guides. The modern sceptic has been in the forefront of delineating what this entails, and in so doing has sought for some naturalistically explicable values, or some kind of blind faith. ("Scepticism" 244–45)

Machado de Assis is the Brazilian author most in touch with the impact that the revival of skepticism caused in Judeo-Christianity. He presents a solution that is neither the positivistic one—which arises from the mitigated or constructive skepticism of Mersenne, Gassendi, and Hume (although features of this solution are exhibited in Aires's method)—nor the fideistic one of Pascal and Kierkegaard (although an antithesis of this solution is exhibited by Brás Cubas and Dom Casmurro). Machado's final response is unique: ancient Pyrrhonism and modern aestheticism, ingeniously blended in literary form.

Appendix

English Translations

These English translations for the longer Portuguese quotations are keyed to the text by the number in brackets. All translations are mine unless otherwise indicated.

1 "I know that, from the point of view of worldly wisdom, diamonds are precious. But suppose . . . all the coal mines become diamond mines. All of a sudden the world would become poor. Coal [would become] precious, diamonds superfluous."

2 lets himself be affected by strange illusions. . . . He thinks that special qualities are required to please women. Shy by nature, he exaggerates his own insufficiency even more when close to them.

3 Because everything is superficial and a matter of external appearance for the *tolos,* love is not for them something that changes their lives: they continue, as usual, dissipating their lives in games, salons, and trips.

4 considers love something quite important and serious. He regards love as the most serious thing in his life. [He commits himself] without any distraction or reserve.

5 Because it is not he who loves, it is he who dominates. In order to conquer a woman, he feigns, for a few moments, despair and passion. But this is just a strategy of war, tactics to deceive and seduce the enemy.

6 the *homem de espírito,* given his personality, rouses a secret repulsion in the women. They wonder about his shyness, are made uneasy by his sensitivity, and are intimidated by his character, [but] . . . the *tolo* does not disturb or intimidate women. From the first date, he cheers them up and fraternizes with them. He praises himself, shamelessly, in the most insipid conversations. He chatters and waddles with them. He understands them, and

they understand him. Far from feeling uncomfortable in his company, they seek it because they shine in it. With the *tolo* they can bring up any subject and talk innocently and frivolously about everything.

7   Pedro Alves: The string that you have played has been out of tune for a while and does not produce sound. Love, respect, dedication! If I did not know you, I would say that you have just arrived from another world.

     Luiz: Indeed, I belong to a world absolutely different from yours.

     Pedro Alves: I see, you belong to the realm of the dreamers and visionaries. . . . it is a tribe that never ends.

     Luiz: That's what it seems, isn't it?

     Pedro Alves: But it is evident that it will perish.

8 Is it possible that she might have changed so suddenly? For wasn't it just yesterday that . . . she dried the sweat off his forehead? . . .

     Today, no more sweetness, no more handshakes.

9 might come to feel a love as pure, intense, and *naive* as he used to feel during the fresh years of his adolescence. *Far from having been relieved from the disturbance* [emphasis added], . . . here he is obliged to fall on his knees before a woman.

10 Given that there is no other solution available, to try to take the beautiful sex from the *tolo*'s rule, by revealing the perversity of their taste, is something out of the question: it would be the equivalent of trying to change nature or to contradict fate.

11 Deep and magnetic eyes, elegant and delicate manners, a peculiar and distinct look quite different from the affected and prosaically restrained one of the other men. . . . He showed himself to be such an admirer of good taste and such a discreet and pertinent talker . . . [that] by the end of the evening everyone was captivated by him.

12 unaware of the nullity of his spirit, acted as though he were witty, so that he could achieve that which no self-conscious man could. . . . He knew how to utter a statement with three periods and two tropes, which already stank, because spoken by so many mouths, but which Fernanda heard with delight, for it was a new language to her.

13 For five years I have enjoyed the happiness of having Angela as my wife; and each day I find in her new qualities. . . .

     For a long time I searched for happiness in loneliness; this is wrong; I found it in marriage, the moral gathering of two wills, two minds, and two hearts.

14 no one, at least in their circle, was more elegant in the manner of lifting his arms, of fixing his hair, or simply of offering a cup of tea.

15 Rosina smothered a cry; . . . two heavy tears dropped from her eyes. Ernesto could not bear watching her cry; although the reasons were all on his side, . . . he quickly submitted and apologized. . . .

The girl listened to many things Ernesto said to her, and to all of them she answered with such a contrite air, and with words impregnated with such bitterness, that our boyfriend almost felt tears dropping from his own eyes. Meanwhile, Rosina's eyes were already quieter.

16 Angela was a whirlwind.

Life lay for her outside home. . . . She did not miss a single ball, or spectacle, or walk, or famous party, and did all this costumed in many laces, jewels, and silks, which she bought every day, as though there were no end to the money.

17 What! The morality? My story is just this. . . . I am not out to punish anyone. . . . Clemente Soares suffered no punishment, and I won't make up on a sheet of paper what does not happen in life. Clemente Soares lived beloved and celebrated by all until he died of apoplexy, amid many tears that were not more sincere than he was during his life.

18 Inácio enjoyed *hearing* and *seeing* her; he loved her a lot, and *besides*, it was as if he sometimes needed that expression of *outward life* in order to give himself completely to the speculations of his spirit. (Emphasis added)

19 His whole body followed the gradation and variation of the tunes; he bent himself over the instrument, stretched his body, turned his head now to one side, then to another, lifted his leg, smiled, looked around or closed his eyes in the moments that appeared to him most pathetic. The point was not so much to hear but to watch him. One who could only hear him would not be able to understand him.

20 due entirely to my manner of presentation: the graceful bending of my arms to pick up the shawm, which was brought to me on a silver tray, my proud and stiff posture, the unction with which I raised my eyes skyward and the disdainful pride with which I lowered them again to look at the crowd. At that point there broke out such a concert of enthusiastic outcries and applause that I was almost convinced that I merited this response. (DV 13)

21 He was a flatterer by temperament and method; . . . Nobody knew better than he how to flatter feminine self-love: nobody could more enthusiastically provide the little social arrangements that often constitute a man's whole reputation. He used to organize the picnics, buy the latest fashionable novel or musical score, . . . take pianists to evening parties, all this in such a serviceable manner, that one would end up being willing to die for him.

22 soul became arid and dry. I was then overwhelmed by a cruel misanthropy, at first violent and full of anger, later melancholic and resigned. My soul slowly hardened, and my heart literally died.

23 a sagacious observer, and at the same time deprived of scruples and passions, had perceived . . . that the more Félix's love became suspicious and tyrannical, the larger the ground he would lose in the widow's heart, so that, once her enchantment with Félix was gone, the time of generous reparations would come, with which he was willing to comfort the girl in her tardy change of mind.

24 The difficulty was certainly bigger and subtler [for Iago lies about Desdemona directly to Othello], but [Luís Batista] had the required skills for the task. He had to pretend a mysterious intimacy with the girl, but it had to be discreet, without pomp; it had to be surrounded with infinite cautions, veiled enough so she would not perceive it, but it would be so clearly dissembling that it would strike squarely into Félix's heart.

25 [Unlike Lívia], Félix would not end up in a cloister. . . . True, [the outcome] depressed him deeply, but he quickly forgot it. His love went out like a lamp that had run out of fuel.

26 Furthermore, he had taken his first step toward becoming a public figure; he was going to enter squarely on the road which carries the strong to victory. He was going to be surrounded by light, which was the girl's ambition, the atmosphere she wanted to breathe. . . . in Luís Alves she could envision domestic warmth combined with the bustle of noise outside. (HG 91)

27 But why did Jorge's name pass her lips? The girl didn't want to deceive the baroness but to convey unfaithfully the voice of her heart in order that her godmother would, on her own, compare the translation against the original. There was in this a bit of the circuitous, a bit of tactic, of affectation, I'm almost saying of hypocrisy, if you don't misunderstand my use of the term. There was, but this itself will tell you that this Guiomar, without forfeiting the excellences of her heart, was of the ordinary clay that God

made our seldom sincere humanity, and will tell you that in spite of her tender years, she already knew that the appearance of a sacrifice is ofttimes worth more than the sacrifice itself. (HG 109)

28 the drawing of such characters—that of Guiomar, especially—was my principal objective, if not my exclusive one, the action serving only as canvas upon which I cast the contour of the profiles. Although they are incomplete, I wonder if they might have come out natural and true. (HG 3)

29 found untold happiness in marriage. . . . If, before she married, Iaiá already knew the rudiments of elegance, she quickly learned its development and rules; she acquainted herself with all the refinements of society with the speed of a sagacious and penetrating spirit. (IG 165)

30 Oh cruel mother, who does not honor your children's death with a tear of pain and a sigh of resentment. . . . It seems that you enjoy creating them to kill them, producing them with an illusion, and in absorbing them with a disenchantment—a true condemnation of those who hoped for this disenchantment and believed in this illusion.

31 When Valério considered the conditions of his existence, his unhappy youth, his hopeless future, he threw a melancholic look at suicide, as the reasonable solution to life's problem. He then asked himself if the morality that disarms man's arms was not just a conventional morality.

32 was nevertheless happily walking along contemplating his feet, or rather his shoes. They were new, of patent leather, very well cut, and probably sewn with great care. He looked up toward the windows and toward people but always looked back down at his shoes. . . . He was happy—one could see the expression of bliss on his face. He was obviously happy, even though he might not have eaten any breakfast and didn't have a cent in his pockets. (DV 64)

33 [he] treads along with them upon the soil of a planet that belongs to him. Hence, the pride in his stance, the firmness of his steps, and a certain air of Olympic tranquillity . . . Yes, happiness is a pair of boots. (DV 64)

34 There is no other explanation for my will. The superficial readers will say I'm insane, that my delirium is evident in every clause of the testament, but I'm speaking to the wise and the unfortunate. . . . Cheer up, unlucky people of the world! May my final wish be granted! Good night, and put your shoes on! (DV 64–65)

35 Nothing was lacking in the letter; the infinite, the abyss, the eternal were all there. One of the *eternals,* written in the fold of the sheet, could not be clearly read, but it could be guessed. The sentence was this: "[Give me] just one minute of your love, and I am ready to suffer an et . . ." A moth had eaten the remainder of the word; it ate the *eternal* and left the *minute.* One does not know to what to attribute this preference, whether to the moth's philosophy or to its voracity.

36 The *Genius of trifles* . . . was seated on a paper-thin throne, surrounded by two peacocks, one on each side. . . . All those peacocks, minute after minute, puffed themselves up and uttered the usual shrieks. . . . The most insignificant act in that country does not take place without the observation of this formality.

37 Many chimerical people around the table were discussing the different methods of inspiring the diplomats and managers of this our world to develop ways of occupying people's time with futilities and scaring them with scarecrows. These men had the air of experts and gentlemen. There was an order from the king not to let anybody in that room during work hours, and there was a soldier at the door. The slightest distraction of these men would be regarded as a public calamity.

38 When I was about to speak, I noticed that both (hearers) had become thin and vaporous . . . volatilizing as if they were made of fog. . . . I soon felt that support was lacking for my feet and I realized that I was adrift in space.

39 However, despite the strange ways observed by our traveler, despite the guides he had and the spectacle he saw, one must recognize that on a deeper level, what he observed is the most natural and possible thing in our world.

40 At this point the author stops talking so the protagonist may speak. I don't want to deprive you of the natural enchantment of the poet's reporting his own impressions.

41 He had witnessed the death of all his affections. . . . Other affections of his, and not a few of them, had betrayed him; and this one and that one, the good and the evil, the sincere and the treacherous, he was bound to go through them over and over again, without a break, without even a breath, *for experience could not help him against his need to hold fast to something amid that quick flow of men and generations.* He had a desire for eternal life; without it, he would go mad. He had tasted everything, exhausted

everything; now all was repetition, monotony, deprived of all hope, deprived of everything. (Emphasis added)

42 Each century, my dear Alcibíades, changes its modes of dancing as it changes its ideas.

43 It is, in truth, a diffuse work, in which I, Braz Cubas, if indeed I have adopted the free form of a Sterne or of a Xavier de Maistre, have possibly added a certain peevish pessimism of my own. Quite possibly. The work of a man already dead. I wrote it with the pen of Mirth and the ink of Melancholy. . . . Moreover, solemn people will find in the book an aspect of pure romance, while frivolous folk will not find in it the sort of romance to which they have become accustomed. (E 17)

44 it is a work supinely philosophical, but of a philosophy wanting in uniformity, now austere, now playful, a thing that neither edifies nor destroys, neither inflames, nor chills, and that is at once more than pastime and less than preachment. (E 24)

45 prologue to a life of delight, of remorse, of pleasures ending in grief, of troubles blossoming into joy, of patient, systematic hypocrisy, the only restraint upon an otherwise unbridled love— a life of nervousness, of anger, of despair, of jealousy, all of them paid for in full by one hour; but another hour would come and would swallow up the first and everything that went with it, leaving only the nervousness and the dregs, and the dregs of the dregs, which are satiety and disgust: such was to be the book of which this kiss was the prologue. (E 108–09)

46 You want to live fast, to get to the end, and the book ambles along slowly; you like straight, solid narrative and a smooth style, but this book and my style are like a pair of drunks: they stagger to the right and to the left, they start and they stop, they mutter, they roar, they guffaw, they threaten the sky, they slip and fall . . . (E 131–32)

47 I am beginning to be sorry that I ever undertook to write this book. Not that it bores me; I have nothing else to do; indeed, it is a welcome distraction from eternity. But the book is tedious, it smells of the tomb, it has a rigor mortis about it. (E 131)

48 Perhaps you noted that my literary style is less gay, less spirited than in the early years. . . . I do not mean . . . to suggest that I am older than when I began to write the book. Death does not age one. The meaning of the sentence rests upon the fact that in writing

each phase of the story of my life I feel the corresponding emotion or attitude, which is of course reflected in my style. (E 200, 204)

49 Believe me, remembrance is the lesser evil. Let no one trust the happiness of the moment; there is in it a drop of gall. When time has gone by and the spasm has ended, then, if ever, one can truly enjoy the event; for, of these two illusions, the better is the one that can be experienced without pain. (E 28)

50 Perhaps the reader is astonished by the frankness with which I expose and emphasize my mediocrity; let him remember that frankness is the virtue most appropriate to a defunct. In life, the watchful eye of public opinion, the conflict of interests, the struggle of greed against greed oblige a man to hide his old rags, to conceal the rips and patches, to withhold from the world the revelations that he makes to his own conscience. . . . But in death, what a difference! what relief! what freedom! How glorious to throw away your cloak, to dump your spangles in a ditch, to unfold yourself, to strip off all your paint and ornaments, to confess plainly what you were and what you failed to be! For, after all, you have no neighbors, no friends, no enemies, no acquaintances, no strangers, no audience at all. The sharp and judicial eye of public opinion loses its power as soon as we enter the territory of death. I do not deny that it sometimes glances this way and examines and judges us, but we dead folk are not concerned about its judgment. You who still live, believe me, there is nothing in the world so monstrously vast as our indifference. (E 71)

51 Did it fall from the air? Did it rise from the earth? I do not know. I know only that an immense shape, the figure of woman, then appeared before me. . . . Everything about this figure . . . was indeed all too much for human perception, for its contours were lost in the surroundings, and what appeared at first to be dense turned out, in many cases to be diaphanous. Stupefied, I said nothing. (E 32)

52 look down and to see the ages continuing to go by, fast and turbulent; . . . Each age brought its share of light and shade, of apathy and struggle, of truth and error, and its parade of systems, of new ideas, of new illusions; in each of them the verdure of spring burst forth, grew yellow with age, and then, young once more, burst forth again. While life thus moved with the regularity of a calendar, history and civilization developed; and man, at first naked and unarmed, clothed and armed himself, . . . created science that scrutinizes and art that elevates, made himself an orator, a mechanic, a philosopher, ran all over the face of the globe, went down into

the earth and up to the clouds, performing the mysterious work through which he satisfied the necessities of life and tried to forget his loneliness. (E 35–36)

53 because the eyes of delirium have a virtue of their own, I was able to distinguish everything that passed before me, afflictions and joys, glory and misery, and I saw love augmenting misery, and misery aggravating human debility. Along came voracious greed, fiery anger, drooling envy, and the hoe and the pen, both wet with sweat, and ambition, hunger, vanity, melancholy, affluence, love, and all of them were shaking man like a baby's rattle until they transformed him into something not unlike an old rag. (E 34)

54 My tired eyes finally saw the present age go by. . . . [It] was agile, skilful, vibrant, proud, a little verbose, audacious, learned, but in the end it was as miserable as the earlier ones. (E 36)

55 The naturalists, reshaping history, called the outside world to the attention of a young generation that cannot understand Job's curses; on the contrary, it seems that one of the features of the new intellectual direction is a triumphant optimism, . . . the general design of the universe is seen as perfection itself. The humanity that it sings in its verses . . . is a god. Justice . . . is announced in enthusiastic verses. . . . It is the inverse of the biblical tradition: paradise is at the end. . . . In summary, let the new generation of poets come and sing something new—to sing this justice, for example, and that it may some day falsify Pascal's concept.

56 Three days later, downcast and silent, I crossed the bar. I did not even cry; I had a fixed idea. Accursed fixed ideas! On this occasion, my idea was to repeat the name of Marcella as I leaped into the ocean. (E 59)

57 [A]mbition was replacing Marcella. A great future? Perhaps I would be a naturalist, a man of letters, an archeologist, a banker, a statesman, or even a bishop—any profession, provided that it entailed preeminence, reputation, a status of superiority. . . . I studied [the disciplines] with profound mediocrity, which did not prevent my acquiring a bachelor's degree; they gave it to me with all the customary solemnity. . . . I was a harebrained scholar, superficial, tumultuous, and capricious, fond of adventures of all kinds, engaging in practical romanticism and theoretical liberalism, with complete faith in dark eyes and written constitutions . . . with an impulse, a curiosity, a desire to elbow other people out of the way, to exert influence, to enjoy, to live—to prolong my college days throughout my life. (E 65)

199

58 I renounced everything; my spirit was stunned. I believe that it was then that the flower of melancholy in me began to open. . . . Nobody visited me; I had expressly requested that people let me alone. (E 72–73)

59 Part of me said yes, that political office and a beautiful wife were advantages not to be scorned; another part said no, and the death of my mother loomed in my mind as an example of the fragility of the things of this world, of the things to which we become attached, of the family . . . (E 75)

60 "Fear obscurity, Braz; flee everything that isn't big. Look here, there are different ways for a man to amount to something, but the surest of all is to amount to something in other men's opinions." (E 78)

61 Eyes so clear, lips so fresh, composure so ladylike . . . and lame! This contrast made me suspect that nature is sometimes an immense mockery. Why pretty, if lame? Why lame, if pretty? These were my thoughts as I walked home in the evening, but I found no answer to the enigma. (E 84)

62 I lived as a sort of recluse; once in a great while I went to a ball, or the theatre, or a speech, but I spent most of the time alone. I existed; I let myself drift with the ebb and flow of the days, now restless, now apathetic, oscillating between ambition and discouragement. I wrote on politics and dabbled in literature. . . . Whenever I thought of Lobo Neves, who was already a deputy, and of Virgilia, the future marchioness, I asked myself why I would not be a better deputy and a better marquis than Lobo Neves. (E 101)

63 I shuddered, I searched her face, I saw that her indignation was sincere. Then it occurred to me that perhaps at one time I had provoked that same expression on her face, and I understood how great had been my evolution. I had come all the way from importunity to opportunity. (E 111)

64 One afternoon the castle of my paternal fantasies crumbled to dust. The embryo went away. . . . I leaned against the window and looked out at the grounds behind the house, where the orange trees were turning green. . . . Where are they now, the blossoms of yesteryear? (E 162)

65 I said nothing. It would have been idle to explain that a little despair and terror might have restored to our situation the

delightfully caustic flavor it had once had. Yet, if I had told her, it is by no means impossible that, by patient artifice, she would have achieved the desiderated touch of despair and terror. (E 164)

66 I was past forty and amounted to nothing, not even an alderman. I had to accomplish something soon—for Virgilia's sake if for no other reason; it would make her proud to see my name in headlines . . . (E 166)

67 Virgilia's departure gave me a taste of what it is like to be a widower. I spent most of my time at home. . . . This was all: memories, a little boredom, and much day-dreaming.
   During this period my uncle the canon died; item, two cousins. . . . Some died, others were born; I went on harpooning flies. (E 182–83)

68 Between the cheese and the coffee, Quincas Borba showed me that his system would destroy pain. According to Humanitism, pain is pure illusion. . . . Intellectual acceptance of the system will not, of itself, immediately expel pain; it is, however, an indispensable beginning. Natural evolution will take care of the rest. Once man is fully convinced that he is Humanitas[1] itself, he has only to make his thoughts revert to the original substance in order to avoid every painful sensation or sentiment. (E 186)

69 Quincas Borba . . . was serenely gnawing a chicken wing. . . . "Hunger (and he sucked the chicken wing philosophically), hunger is a discipline to which Humanitas subjects its own viscera. But the sublimity of my system really requires no better documentation than this very chicken. It was fed on corn that was planted, let us say, by an African imported from Angola. This African was born, grew up, was sold; a ship brought him here, a ship built of wood cut in the forest by ten or twelve men and driven by sails that eight or ten men wove, not to mention the rope and the rest of the nautical apparatus. Thus, this chicken, on which I have just lunched, is the result of a multitude of efforts and struggles carried on for the sole ultimate purpose of satisfying my appetite." (E 185–86)

70 Yes, I was really meant to be a father. A bachelor's life had certain advantages, to be sure, but they were unsubstantial and cost too much in loneliness. Childless! No, it was something to avoid at all costs. . . . The philosopher [Quincas Borba] listened and beamed. He declared that Humanitas was stirring in my breast; he encouraged me to marry; he informed me that additional fellows were knocking at the door. (E 188–89)[2]

71 The first issue of my newspaper filled my soul with a vast dawn, crowned me with laurel, gave me back the lightness of youth. Six months later the hour of old age struck, and two weeks later the hour of death, which was as clandestine as Dona Placida's. On the morning following the night in which it died in its sleep, I breathed heavily, like a man who has walked a long road. (E 215–16)

72 I did not understand the need for the epidemic, much less the need for that particular death. I even think that this death seemed more absurd to me than all the others together. However, Quincas Borba explained to me that epidemics are useful to the species although fatal to a certain number of individuals. . . . He went so far as to ask me whether, in the midst of the turmoil, I did not feel a secret joy at having escaped the claws of the pestilence; but this question was so absurd that I did not dignify it with a reply. (E 195)

73 The sea of life had brought us to the same shore like two bottles from a shipwreck, he managing to contain his resentment, I containing, one would perhaps expect, my remorse; and I use this provisional, problematic, suspensive form of expression in order to be able to point out that in truth I contained nothing whatever except an ambition to become a minister of state. (E 197)

74 "What the devil, you have to be a man! Be strong! Fight! Conquer! Shine! Influence! Dominate! . . . Try to taste life, to enjoy it; and try to understand that the worst philosophy of all is that of the cry-baby who lies down at the edge of the river and bewails the incessant flow of the water. The function of the river is to flow on; adjust yourself to this law of nature and try to take advantage of it." (E 202)

75 If she is worthy of herself, . . . she will not seek in today's glance the same warmth that she found in yesterday's, when other persons, nimble and hearty, were starting on the great parade. *Tempora mutantur.* She understands what this whirlwind is about, she knows that it is sweeping the leaves from the grove and old rags from the road, with neither exception nor pity, and if she has a little philosophy she will not envy but will feel compassion for those who took her carriage, for they too will have to alight and will find the faithful footman OBLIVION at the door. A spectacle whose purpose is to divert the planet Saturn, which would otherwise . . . be utterly bored. (E 201–02)

76 An uncle of mine, a canon . . . , used to say that the love of temporal glory was the perdition of the soul, which should covet only eternal glory. To which my other uncle, an officer in one of the old infantry regiments, would reply that the love of glory was the

most truly human thing about a man and, consequently, his most genuine characteristic.

Let the reader decide between the soldier and the canon; I shall return to the plaster. (E 22)

77 While I was developing and perfecting my invention, a draught of air caught me full on; I fell ill and took no steps to cure myself. I had the plaster on my mind, the fixed idea of supermen and of madmen. I would see myself, at a distance, rising above the common herd and ascending to the sky like an immortal eagle, and it is not before so grand a spectacle that a man can feel pain. . . . I believe I have proved that it was my invention that killed me. . . . I was healthy and strong. Let us suppose that, instead of laying the foundations for a pharmaceutic innovation, I had tried to set up a new political institution or a religious reform. The current of air would have come along just the same and, with its efficacy greater than that of human plans, would have carried everything off with it. On such factors depend the destinies of men. (E 27)

78 Dona Placida would not have to resort to beggary. . . . If it had not been for my illicit love, probably Dona Placida would have faced the same miserable old age as so many other human creatures. From this observation one may reason that vice is often the fertilizing manure of virtue. Which does not prevent virtue from being a fragrant and healthy flower. (E 137)

79 Every man has the need and the ability to contemplate his own nose, in order to see the divine light, and such contemplation, resulting in the subordination of the universe to one nose, establishes social equilibrium. (E 102)

80 Naturally he is chagrined; but he walks on, his eyes looking downward or straight ahead. Then he concentrates, seeking the reasons for the other man's prosperity and his own failure, when he is really a better hatter than the other . . . At this moment, if you look closely, you will see that his eyes are fixed on the tip of his nose. (E 103)

81 I remember that he was constrained but that he made an effort to appear at ease. It seemed to me at the time . . . that he was afraid, not of me, not of himself, not of the law, not of his conscience, but of public opinion. It was this anonymous tribunal, in which every member both prosecutes and judges, that imposed limits upon the exercise of Lobo Neves' free will. Very probably he no longer loved his wife. . . . I believe that he would have been quite ready to leave her had it not been for public opinion, which would have dragged his life through every street in the city. It would have

conducted a minute and thorough inquest, would have collected all the circumstances, antecedents, and surmises, and would have repeated them wherever idle people met. This terrifying public opinion, with its bedroom curiosity, alone prevented a separation. At the same time, it made revenge wholly impossible, for revenge would have meant divulgation. He could not even appear resentful toward me without being compelled to seek a separation. He had to simulate the very ignorance that he had once really enjoyed and, consequently, the old sentiments consistent with such ignorance. (E 179–80)

82 If there is any point to the preceding chapter, it is that public opinion serves as an excellent solder of domestic institutions . . . [and of] politics as well. Some bilious metaphysicians have taken the extreme position that public opinion issues from the irresponsible minds of the dull and the mediocre [this is precisely the view exhibited in "The angel Rafael"]; but obviously, even if so radical a concept did not carry with it its own refutation, the most superficial consideration of the salutary effects of public opinion would suffice to establish it as the supremely superfine product of the flower of mankind, namely, the greater number. (E 180–81)

83 "Those came who had a genuine interest in you and in us. The eighty [that were invited] would have come only as a formality, would have talked about the inertia of the government, about patent medicines, about the price of real estate, or about each other . . ." (E 195)

84 there may be discerned a constant and tender companion of social man . . .
    Sweet Formality, you are the true staff of life, the balsam that heals the heart, the tie that binds man to man and earth to heaven. You dry a father's tears. . . . If . . . grief is assuaged, . . . to whom but you do they owe these benefits? High esteem, passing by with a mere nod, does not speak to the soul; but indifference, bowing and tipping its hat, creates a most delightful impression. The reason is that, contrary to an absurd old saying, it is not the letter that kills; the letter gives life; it is the spirit that causes doubt, interpretation, controversy, and therefore struggle and death. So, long live sweet Formality, to the . . . peace of mind of Damasceno. (E 196)

85 The friends I have left are of recent date; the old ones have all gone to study the geology of holy ground. As for my lady friends, some date back fifteen years, others less, and almost all believe in their own youthfulness. Two or three would have others believe in it,

but the language they speak often obliges one to consult a dictionary, and such intercourse is wearisome. (DC 5)

86 But, as everything wearies one, this monotony too finally exhausted me. I wanted change. What if I wrote a book? Jurisprudence, philosophy and politics suggested themselves; but they did not bring with them the necessary energy. Then I thought of writing a *History of the Suburbs* . . . it would be a modest work, but it would demand documents and dates as preliminaries—a long dull business. It was then that the busts painted on the walls spoke to me and said that since they had failed to bring back the days gone by, I should take my pen and tell over those times. Perhaps the act of narration would summon the illusion for me, and the shades would come treading lightly, as with the poet . . . *Ah there, are you come again restless shades?* . . . and I will put on paper the memories that come crowding. In this way I will live what I have lived, and I will strengthen my hand for some work of greater scope. (DC 6)

87 Believe me, remembrance is the lesser evil. Let no one trust the happiness of the moment; there is in it a drop of gall. When time has gone by and the spasm has ended, then, if ever, one can truly enjoy the event; for, of these two illusions, the better is the one that can be experienced without pain. (E 28)

88 Still, a different life does not mean a worse life; it is just not the same. In certain respects, that old life now appears stripped of much of the enchantment I found in it; but it has also lost many a spine that made it painful, and in my memory I keep some sweet and charming recollections. (DC 5–6)

89 "That refusal was probably a mistake: from it resulted certain incongruities which a hearing would have detected and a friendly collaboration prevented. Indeed in some places the words go to the right and the music to the left. And there are those who say that this is the beauty of the composition and keeps it from being monotonous, and in this way they explain the trio of Eden, the aria of Abel, the choruses of the guillotine and of slavery. Not infrequently the same plot situation is used over again without sufficient reason. Certain motifs grow wearisome from repetition. There are obscure passages; the maestro makes too much use of the choral masses, which often drown out the words with their confused harmony. . . .

"The friends of the maestro have it that a better score would be hard to find. . . . The friends of the [poet] . . . claim that . . . the score corrupts the sense of the words and that although it may be fine in some passages and contrived with art in others, it is absolutely unrelated, and even contrary, to the spirit of the drama. . . .

"This piece," concluded the old tenor, "will last as long as the theater lasts—and there's no telling when *it* will be demolished as an act of astronomic expediency." (DC 19–20)

90   I promised my bride [making plans for the future] a tranquil and beautiful life, in the country or just outside the city. We would return here once a year. If it should be on the outskirts of the city, it would be far away where no one would bother us. (DC 100)

91   I looked at an elderberry shoot. . . . Capitu answered for both of us.
"Yes, senhor; but Bentinho laughs right away, he can't keep a straight face." . . .
And with a serious expression, she turned her gaze on me and invited me to the game. . . . I was still under the effect of [the fright] caused by Padua's arrival. I could not laugh, no matter how much I should have, to make Capitu's answer legitimate. . . . There are things that one learns late. One must be born with them to do them early. And, naturally early is better than artificially late. (DC 31)

92   [Capitu] told me I had done her a great injustice. She could not believe that after our exchange of oaths, I could judge her to be so fickle, that I could believe . . . And here she burst into tears, and made a gesture of separation; but I was at her side immediately. I seized her hands and kissed them with . . . fervor. . . . She wiped her eyes with her fingers. . . . She confessed to me that she did not know the young man—no more than others who passed by in the afternoons. . . . If she had looked at him, that in itself was proof there was nothing between them; if there had been, it would be natural to dissemble. (DC 150)

93   Capitu, at fourteen, already had daring ideas. . . . In practice they were apt, sinuous, unobtrusive, and accomplished the end proposed, not at one leap but by a series of little leaps. . . . Such was the peculiar nature of my little friend's character. It is not to be wondered at that she should oppose my projects of open resistance [to go to the seminary], and resort rather to blander methods—the slow action of intercession, pledges—gentle, daily persuasion— that she should examine beforehand the persons on whom we might count. (DC 40)

94   I did not have time to let go my ladylove's hands. I thought of it. I was on the point of doing it, but Capitu, before her father could come into the room, made an unhoped for gesture, she placed her mouth on mine, and gave willingly what she had refused to yield to force. I repeat: the soul is full of mysteries. (DC 79)

206

95 Is it possible that she might have changed so suddenly? For wasn't it just yesterday that, returning from a walk in the woods, she dried the sweat off his forehead? . . .

Today, no more sweetness, no more handshakes.

96 Saint Peter, who holds the keys of heaven, opened its doors to us . . . he made a sign to the angels and they intoned a passage of the Canticle, in such unison that they would have given the lie to the hypothesis of the Italian tenor if the performance had been on earth; but it was in heaven. The music went with the text. . . . Don't worry, I do not intend to describe it; human language does not possess forms proper to so great a task. (DC 192–93)

97 Nevertheless, I found Capitu a bit impatient to leave. . . .

The joy with which she put on her wifely hat, and the wifely air with which she gave me her hand to get into or out of the carriage, and her arm to walk in the street, all showed me that the cause of Capitu's impatience was the outward display of her new estate. It was not enough to be a wife within four walls and a few trees; she needed the rest of the world too. (DC 194)

98 Capitu was better and even feeling fine. She admitted to me that she had only had a slight headache, but exaggerated her suffering so that I would go out and enjoy myself. She did not speak cheerfully, which made me suspect that she was lying in order not to alarm me, but she swore it was absolutely true. (DC 214)

99 Escobar looked at me suspiciously, as if he thought I rejected the additional claim in order to escape writing it up; but this suspicion conflicted with our friendship.

When he left, I mentioned my doubts to Capitu. She dissolved them into nothing with the fine art she possessed. (DC 216)

100 In passing the mirror, she stopped to arrange her hair, so leisurely that one would have thought it affectation if one had not known she was very fond of herself. When she returned her eyes were red. She told us that when she saw her son sleeping, she thought of Sancha's little daughter, and the widow's sorrow. And, without caring about the visitors or noticing whether a servant happened to be present, she threw her arms around me and told me that if I wished to think of her I should first think of my own life. (DC 234)

101 Capitu's stupefaction, and the succeeding indignation were both so natural they would confuse the finest eye-witnesses of our courts. I have heard that there are such available for all kinds of cases—question of price. I do not believe it. . . . But, whether or

not there are witnesses for hire, mine was genuine. Nature herself took the stand in her own behalf, and I would not care to doubt her. Thus, without marking Capitu's words, her gestures, the pain that racked her, or anything, I repeated the words I had twice spoken, with such resoluteness that she wilted. (DC 248)

102 My fits of jealousy were intense, but brief: in an instant I would tear down everything, but in the same instant I would reconstruct the sky, the earth and the stars. (DC 202; see also 212–13 and 232)

103 [w]hether it was really so or an illusion, everything there seemed better that day: my mother less sad, Uncle Cosme unmindful of his heart. . . . I passed an hour in peace. I even considered relinquishing my project. What would I need in order to live? Never leave that house again, or engrave that hour within myself. . . . (DC 242–43)

104 Modesty demanded then, as now, that I see in Sancha's gesture approval of her husband's project and thankfulness for it. It must have been that, but a strange current passing through my body, forced me to repudiate the conclusion I have just written. . . .
     [But later] [t]he picture of Escobar, that I kept there . . . spoke to me as if it were he *in propria persona*. I struggled sincerely against the impulses I had brought from Flamengo. (DC 223–24)

105 I drew closer to Ezekiel; I found that Capitu was right. They were Escobar's eyes, but they did not seem odd to me for that reason. After all there are probably not more than a half-dozen expressions in the world, and many resemblances occur naturally. (DC 237–38)

106 Not only his eyes, but the remaining features also, face, body, the entire person, were acquiring definition with the passage of time. . . .
     Escobar emerged from the grave, from the seminary, from Flamengo; he sat at table with me, welcomed me on the stairs, kissed me each morning in my study or asked for the customary blessing at night. (DC 238–39)

107 Truthfully, I was on the brink of believing myself victim of a grand illusion, a madman's phantasmagoria; but the sudden entrance of Ezekiel shouting . . . restored me to a sense of reality. Capitu and I, involuntarily, glanced at the photograph of Escobar, and then at each other. This time her confusion was pure confession. They were one. (DC 250)

108 Pell-mell, there rushed to mind vague, remote episodes—words, meetings and incidents, in all of which my blindness saw no wrong

and my old jealousy had been lacking. Once when I found them alone and silent, a secret that made me laugh, a word of hers when she was dreaming, all those recollections now poured upon me in such a rush that they left me dizzy. . . . (DC 251)

109 It was certainly an allusion to the man on horseback. This recollection aggravated the impression that I brought in from the street; but it may have been this phrase, guarded in my unconscious, that had disposed me to believe in the malice of their glances. (DC 147)

110 At first, Ayres stuck by his solitude, cut himself off from society, shut himself up at home, accepted no invitations—or very few, and at rare intervals. He really was tired of men, and of women, of parties and late nights. . . .

This is the way it was in the beginning. On Thursdays he went to take dinner with his sister. At night he walked along the beach, or through the streets of his neighborhood. Most of his time was spent in reading and rereading, or in composing the notebook he called his *Memorial,* or in looking over what he had written, in order to once more call to mind things past. (EJ 82–83)

111 But everything grows wearisome, even solitude. Ayres began to feel a twinge of boredom: he yawned, nodded, got a thirst for live people. . . .

So much for the schedule of the new life! It was not that he no longer believed in it, or no longer found it congenial, or that he did not still practice it at times, once in a great while, as one makes use of a remedy that obliges one to stay in bed or in the bedroom, but he would quickly get well and go outdoors again. He wanted to see other people, hear them, smell them, taste them, feel them, apply all his senses to a world that could kill time, deathless time. (EJ 84–85)

112 Ayres studied the two young men and their opinions. . . . Paulo still maintained that he could overthrow the Monarchy with ten men, and Pedro that he could wipe out the seed of republicanism with a single edict. But the ex-Minister, with no more edict than a stewpan, and with no more men than his cook, wrapped up the two social systems in the same delicious salmon. (EJ 109)

113 of a lady . . . at the foot of another grave to the left of the great cross. She was young, dressed in black, and she too appeared to be praying, with clasped hands pointing downward. . . . She was handsome and most genteel—*gentilissima.* (CAM 11)

114 I stayed in the living room watching that group of happy men, and of women freshly green and summer ripe, all thrown in the shade by Dona Carmo's special air of old age and by the alluring charm

of Fidelia's youthfulness. . . . Shelley kept whispering in my ear, so that I could say it over to myself, "I can give not what men call love." (CAM 21)

115 Fidelia has come, Tristão and his godmother have come, everything is come; I myself have come to myself—in other words—I am reconciled to my white hair. The eyes that I turned upon the widow Noronha were those of pure admiration, without the least notion of another sort as in the first days of this year. . . . Admiration is enough. (CAM 83)

116 Listen, paper, the thing that attracts me about the lady Fidelia is principally a certain aspect of mind, something like the fleeting smile I have detected several times on her lips. This is what I want to study if I get the chance. (CAM 40)

117 I heard all these minutiae, and still others, with interest. It has always been my way to consider the manners through which character is expressed and of which it is composed, and many a time I am not uninterested in the sequence of events themselves. I enjoy seeing and foreseeing, and drawing conclusions. This Fidelia is running away from something, if she is not running away from herself. (CAM 124–25)

118 Who knows if we might not run into the widow Noronha at her husband's grave, her hands clasped in prayer, as we did a year ago? If I should still get the feeling that led me to bet with Rita that the young lady would marry, I am willing to believe that her presence in that place and in that attitude would give me pleasure. I would find in the circumstance a sign that she does not love Tristão, and, not being able to marry her myself, I would prefer that she love the dead man. But no, it is not this. I will say what it is. (CAM 154)

119 But no, it is not this. I will say what it is. If I should see her in the same place, in the same posture, I still would not doubt her love of Tristão. It all could exist in the same person without either hypocrisy on the widow's part or infidelity on the part of the bride to be. . . . The remembrance of her dead husband lives in her, notwithstanding her present suitor's influence; it is there in all its old sweetness and melancholy. (CAM 154)

120 On the way I thought that if the widow Noronha really does still bring flowers to her husband's grave it means that the habit remains if her affection for him does not. Whoever likes may choose. I studied the question from both sides, and . . . [found] a third solution. . . . I imagined I might find her before the deceased

person as if he were the future person, making of both a single present being. (CAM 169)

121 The thought is this: whether Fidelia has returned to the cemetery since her marriage. Possibly yes; possibly no. I will not censure her if she has not; a person's soul may be too narrow for two great affections. If yes, I will not hold it against her—on the contrary. The dead may very well battle the living without entirely vanquishing them. (CAM 189)

122 although there must not be anything modern since that book. He was already saying that there was nothing new under the sun, and if there was nothing new in those days there has been nothing new since, or ever will be. Everything is thus contradictory and unstable also. (CAM 88)

123 "With me it could not happen. As you know, I am no longer of this world, and, politically speaking, I never had a part in anything. Diplomacy has the effect of separating its functionary from the parties and keeping him so far from them that it is impossible to express an opinion with verity, or at least with assurance." (EJ 139)

124 He had observed that when convictions are opposed they discompose a person's looks, and he did not want to see other people's faces like that nor give his own an abominable aspect. . . . Hence his scheme of affirmative gestures and phrases that left the parties calm, and himself still more calm. (EJ 216)

125 [T]his Ayres . . . held that, in arguments, a vague or compromise opinion could have the force of a pill, and he composed his in such a way that the invalid, if he did not get better, at least did not die, and that is the most one can expect of pills. (EJ 39)

126 it was not a part of the *Memorial,* the diary of thoughts and recollections that the Counselor had been writing for many years, and which formed the contents of the first six notebooks. . . . It was a narrative; and, although Ayres himself figured in it, along with his name and title of Counselor, and with hints of several of his love affairs, still, it was a narrative unrelated to the material of the six other notebooks. (EJ 3)

Notes

Part 1
Machado's First Phase
(1861 to 1878)

Introduction

1. The most comprehensive study about the philosophical dimension of Machado's fiction is Coutinho.

2. "Desde cedo, li muito Pascal . . . e afirmo-lhe que não foi por distração" (OC 3: 939) ("From an early age I read much Pascal . . . and I assure you that it was not just as a pastime").

3. The distinction of two phases in Machado helps to clarify the entirety of his fiction. This is justifiable because Machado himself understands his work in terms of two phases (OC 1: 114) and because I do not assert that there is a complete heterogeneity between them. On the contrary, I understand the second phase as containing solutions to problems that arise in the first. Furthermore, I do not suggest that each phase is homogeneous, but distinguish two periods in the first phase and three in the second. (One chapter is devoted to each of these stages: the two periods of the first phase are covered in Chapters One and Two, and the three periods of the second phase are discussed in Chapters Five, Six, and Seven.) While there is change and evolution within each phase, the change that occurs with *Epitaph* is so crucial that it calls for the identification of the two phases.

4. My translation of *tolo* as "vulgar" is not literal. Literally, *tolo* is closer to "stupid," but "vulgar" grasps Machado's meaning better. "Spiritual man" does not quite express Machado's *homem de espírito,* whose meaning—as Chapter One will make clearer—is contrary to that of *tolo.* Because these are crucial technical terms, I leave them in Portuguese.

Chapter One
An Essay of 1861 and the
Short Stories from 1862 to 1871

1. What Paul B. Dixon says of Capitu (*Dom Casmurro*)—"Capitu is the cosmos itself" (102)—is also applicable to most Machadian female characters.

2. Sextus says that, unlike the dogmatist's, the skeptic's investigation—*zetesis*—is endless (PH 1.3).

3. "Este último capítulo é todo de negativas. Não alcancei a celebridade do emplasto, não fui ministro, não fui califa, não conheci o casamento" (OC 1: 637) ("This last chapter consists wholly of negatives.

I did not achieve celebrity, I did not become a minister of state, I did not really become a caliph, I did not marry" [E 223]).

Chapter Two
The Short Stories and First Novels
from 1872 to 1878

1. Machado cites Shakespeare in the epigraph to *Resurrection:* "Our doubts are traitors. / And make us lose the good we oft might win, / By fearing to attempt" (OC 1: 114). The critics who assert Capitu's faithfulness and/or reduce Bento's doubt to mad jealousy reduce *Dom Casmurro* to *Resurrection* and Bento to Félix, virtually taking *Dom Casmurro* as another illustration of these Shakespearean verses. (Cf. Caldwell 117: "*Dom Casmurro* is essentially the same story as *Ressurreição*.")

2. Maria L. Nunes ("Time and Allegory") shows that Flora (*Esau and Jacob*) is an exception.

Chapter Three
Problematic Characters:
The Skeptic's Ancestors

1. "[T]rue on this side of the Pyrenees, false on the other" (La 60).

2. "All their principles are true, sceptics, stoics, atheists, etc. . . . but their conclusions are false, because the contrary principles are also true" (La 619).

3. "Man's greatness comes from knowing he is wretched: a tree does not know it is wretched. / Thus it is wretched to know that one is wretched, but there is greatness in knowing one is wretched" (La 114).

Part 2
Machado's Second Phase
(1879 to 1908)

Chapter Five
Epitaph of a Small Winner

1. Roberto Schwarz contests Brás Cubas's claim that his death is fundamental for the point of view from which he writes his autobiography. Schwarz notes that most critics accepted the distinction, attributing a metaphysical view to the deceased writer as opposed to the ordinary views of the characters, including those of the living Brás Cubas. Schwarz rejects this distinction on the following grounds. "a) Ela desconhece o que há de farsa na situação, e em lugar de sua impertinência, que é parte de um relacionamento mundano e incréu, põe o contraste incaracterístico e 'grave' entre vida e morte, uma daquelas generalidades metafísicas recomendadas na 'Teoria do Medalhão'" ("It misses the farcical of the

situation, and instead of highlighting its impertinence, which is part of a worldly and unlikely relationship, it posits the uncharacteristic and "serious" contrast between life and death, one of those metaphysical generalities recommended in 'Education of a stuffed shirt' "). "b) Não vê que também os vivos têm momentos 'absolutos' de fastio, desilusão, crueldade etc., e que neste ponto não se distinguem do narrador morto" ("It fails to recognize that those alive also have 'absolute' moments of boredom, disillusionment, cruelty, etc., and that on this point those alive are not distinct from the deceased narrator"). "c) Oculta o principal, a saber, que o Brás Cubas 'desafrontado da brevidade do século' é tão mesquinho e perseguido por vaidades sociais quanto a mais lamentável de suas personagens, o que está claro desde a primeira página, onde ele se resigna mal ao número diminuto dos presentes a seu enterro" ("It hides that which is central, namely, that the Brás Cubas 'no longer troubled by the flight of time' [E 24] is as niggardly and pursued by social conceit as the most regretful of his characters, which is clear from the very first page, where he resents the reduced number of people present at his funeral") (Schwarz 57–58). As far as the relevance of the deceased point of view is concerned, I agree with the traditional interpretation of the novel, in particular, Augusto Meyer's. As Meyer notes, deceased authorship is crucial not only in *Epitaph,* but in most of Machado's subsequent fiction (Meyer 27). My analysis of *Epitaph,* in particular the section dealing with the naive and skeptical life-views, shows that Brás Cubas, the living character, and Brás Cubas, the deceased writer, hold different life-views. As to the reasons raised by Schwarz, I shall say here the following. (a.1) The deceased writer is not unaware of what there is of farce in deceased authorship. This feature distinguishes his work from "serious" metaphysical treatises about which he is skeptical, and it is part of the skeptical solution that is being generated in Machado's work. As Brás Cubas puts it, the solution is to transform melancholy into ink for the "pen of Mirth." (a.2) Schwarz is unaware of what there is of seriousness in deceased authorship. It is a solution to problems exhibited in Machado's previous works and an ingenious response to anthropological, epistemological, moral, and religious problems discussed by Pascal. (a.3) The "seriousness" recommended by the "stuffed shirt" is quite different from that found in Brás Cubas. The "stuffed shirt" explicitly recommends that the kind of metaphysical questions that obsess Brás Cubas be avoided because they upset the strategic performance of the "stuffed shirt." (b) The living Brás Cubas surely has moments of melancholy. These moments, whose frequency increases roughly in proportion to his age, lead him to deceased authorship. (c) Nunes also claims that Brás Cubas's reaction to his funeral refutes his claim of sincerity and rupture from the world (Nunes, *Craft* 68). All Brás Cubas writes is this: "fui acompanhado ao cemitério por onze amigos. Onze amigos! Verdade é que não houve cartas nem anúncios" (OC 1: 511) ("[I] was accompanied to the cemetery by eleven friends. Only eleven! True, there had been no invitations and no notices in the newspapers" [E 19]). It is not obvious to me that this reveals resentment. He can be just emphasizing his obscurity. He is doing precisely what he says only a deceased writer can fully do, viz., to speak objectively and frankly of one's own failures. Furthermore, Brás Cubas says that he has a sensation of his past experiences when he writes about them. Now, even if the deceased writer feels resentment, this does not affect the main attributes of deceased authorship: sincerity and rupture from practical/pragmatic life; in particular, active pursuit of what is conceived as the *summum bonum*.

2. I disagree with the view that these interruptions are meant to question the reliability of the narrator and/or as a technique for conveying satire. I also disagree with Schwarz's view that Brás Cubas's style displays caprice that mirrors his ruling class situation. Brás Cubas's life is characterized by impotence, failure, impossibility, and misery. As to the deceased narrator, Schwarz notes that an "atitude filosófica" ("philosophical stance") is one "das mais recorrentes" ("of the most frequent"). "Não obstante, apesar de unificada pela postura reflexiva, esta atitude tampouco é homogênea: nutre-se de Eclesiastes, moralistas franceses, materialismo setecentista, universalismo liberal, cientificismo oitocentista e filosofias do inconsciente. São horizontes incompatíveis, cuja pluralidade é básica para compor o ambiente problemático-apalhaçado do livro" (Schwarz 50) ("Although unified by a reflective stance, this attitude is not homogeneous: it is fed by Ecclesiastes, French moralists, eighteenth-century materialism, liberal universalism, nineteenth-century scientism, and philosophies of the unconscious. These are incompatible horizons, whose plurality is basic in setting the book's problematic and clownish environment"). Schwarz sees incompatibility because he fails to distinguish the deceased narrator from the living character. The narrator exhibits the first two listed positions (which were frequently associated during the seventeenth century), using them to attack the remaining eighteenth- and nineteenth-century philosophies on the list. The latter philosophies are consistent with the position held by Quincas Borba and his disciple, the living Brás Cubas.

3. Schwarz considers the initial chapters of *Epitaph* analyzed in this section as "uma longa brincadeira de mau gosto, destinada a atrasar o começo do romance propriamente dito" (Schwarz 56) ("a play, lengthy and of bad taste, designed to delay the beginning of the novel proper"). It is therefore not surprising that Schwarz totally misses the deceased writer's perspective, being left only with the naive and strategic lifeviews held by the living character.

4. "[I don't know] why the brief span of life allotted to me should be assigned to one moment rather than another of all the eternity which went before me and all that which will come after me" (La 427).

5. The English edition says "Humanity," but the correct translation is "Humanitas."

6. The same kind of metaphor of equipollence appears in "A question of husbands" (see Chapter Three), in the counterposition of "the portrait" with "the photograph" (*Dom Casmurro*), and in the political disagreement of the twin brothers, Pedro and Paulo (*Esau and Jacob*).

7. In "The looking glass," written in the same period as *Epitaph*, although subjugated by the "outward soul," an "inward soul" is still an element in Jacobina's theory.

8. The following are Maxims 78 and 82: "In most men love of justice is only fear of suffering injustice." "Reconciliation with our enemies is nothing more than the desire to improve our position, war-weariness, or fear of some unlucky turn of events" (La Rochefoucauld 47).

Chapter Six
Dom Casmurro

1. Helen Caldwell says that Dom Casmurro, "like Othello . . . tries to delude 'the spectator'—his readers—for if they applaud him more frantically than they did Othello, they exonerate him; his self-delusion will be complete, he will be cleared of guilt in his own eyes, his conscience will be free" (149). John Gledson says that Dom Casmurro "is, of course, a deceiver who is out to persuade us of one version of the facts of his story, but because he is out to persuade himself also (and perhaps because he is a good lawyer) we can trust the facts themselves as given" (*Deceptive Realism* 17). Because Dom Casmurro's narrative is the only available version of the story, note the paradox in which Gledson is trapped in denying Dom Casmurro's reliability: Dom Casmurro is a deceiver, but we can trust the facts that he narrates.

2. Paul Dixon sees the Bento/Capitu interaction as an example of "what C. G. Jung has called the cycle of progression and regression—a sway between extroversion and introversion, expansive hope and frustration, action and quiescence" (62). I emphasize the cognitive aspect of the interaction and would suggest that vis-à-vis Capitu, Bento typically exhibits "regression." His moments of "progression"—Dixon alludes, for example, to the hand holding that follows the wall episode: the "atmosphere . . . of pure nonverbal confession in which sparks of energy seem to sizzle the air as they jump back and forth between the two adolescents" (64)—are controlled by Capitu. Dixon stresses the sea metaphors present in the novel, in particular in association with Capitu—her famous "undertow eyes." He interprets these metaphors as indications of the quest myth narrative that he claims underlies the novel: Bento (the hero) travels through the sea, attempting to conquer the cosmos (Capitu). I think that Bento exhibits more a quest for understanding than a quest for conquering, although these two are not unrelated. I think that the "undertow eyes" stand for Capitu's conflicting and moving appearances (waves) and point to Bento's being adrift in uncertainty. Dixon also emphasizes the epistemological quest. He says that "Capitu is the cosmos itself" (102), "[t]he household is an entire universe, and Bentinho's attempt to fathom his partner's heart is Man's attempt to achieve an understanding of the cosmos" (107).

3. Gledson claims that the inversion is meant to obscure the fact that Bento's "marriage was perfectly contented at this point." "Certainly," Gledson argues, "once the true sequence of events is known, they begin to take on a coherence of their own which argues powerfully that the novel is a study of Bento's pathological obsession, not of Capitu's adultery" (*Deceptive Realism* 31). The inversion is meant to *highlight* the fact that Bento's marriage shifted from contentment to suspicion without objective and proven reasons. The "true sequence of events" would show Bento's increasing perception of the extent of the resemblance. Were the events related in this order, the psychological plausibility of his growing belief that adultery had occurred would obscure its lack of epistemological ground. With the inversion, Dom Casmurro obscures the former and highlights the latter. The novel is a study of skepticism. To ground the interpretation of the novel either on Capitu's objective deed—either adultery or fidelity—or on Bento's "pathological obsession," is to place the interpretation in a dogmatic framework that presupposes nonproblematic cognitive access to a nonproblematic objective truth.

4. Caldwell says that Dom Casmurro requests that the reader go back to the chapter "The Portrait" "if we want to consider such superstitious rubbish. This is the import of his words" (87). I see no such import. Mary L. Pratt claims that because Dom Casmurro mentions the chapter "The Portrait" but says that he does not remember its number, he actually wants to hide from the reader this counterevidence (194 ff.). But, if this is so, why does he recall the event and even ask the reader—in case the reader does not remember the details—to reread the chapter? Besides, the summary he gives of what happened is sufficient to challenge the new evidence for infidelity.

5. Gledson is aware of Pascal's influence in *Dom Casmurro*. He relates Bento's Christianity to Jesuit casuistry, which was attacked by Pascal and the Jansenists. He says that this Christianity is Bento's version of Quincas Borba's Humanitism (*Deception Realism* 186–87). I find this comparison very interesting. In Chapter Four I indicate the Jansenist and Pascalian background of Brás Cubas's attack on Quincas Borba's Humanitism and on the acceptance of it by the living Brás Cubas. I disagree with Gledson in that I think Bento's Jesuit casuistry must be opposed to Dom Casmurro's Jansenist pessimism.

Chapter Seven
Counselor Aires and His "Memorial"

1. Moving from Machadian fiction to intellectual history, I note that a synthesis of an aesthetic with a skeptical life-view was made one generation

earlier by the Danish thinker Sören Kierkegaard (in particular in *Either/ Or*). As in Machado's case, Kierkegaard developed this synthesis as a practical response to the predicament of skepticism. According to Kierkegaard, the treatment of skepticism by modern philosophers is merely intellectual.

2. John Gledson is uneasy about the fact that Aires's point of view is perspectival, relative, and shaped by his subjectivity. Gledson assumes that there *must* be a plain, objective, absolute truth and reality, so Aires's version of the plot is unreliable and must be dismissed by the intelligent reader. A more subtle, political plot must be "allegorically" deduced—this is Machado's point of view (Gledson, "Last Betrayal"). Gledson's interpretation is inappropriate because it is a dogmatic one, whereas the novel is skeptical.

3. *Counselor Ayres' Memorial* has been traditionally interpreted as representing Machado's reconciliation with life (for example, Barreto Filho; Coutinho; and Nunes, *Craft*). I disagree with this view. There is return to life and recognition of its aesthetic value, but not reconciliation. Life is still viewed as miserable and Aires is detached from it. Gledson ("Last Betrayal") presents a dissenting view: Fidélia is as nasty as Virgília and Sofia, Tristão is as nasty as Lobo Neves and Palha (*Philosopher or Dog?*), and the reader should not be deceived by Aires's sympathetic view of them. Gledson's interpretation has merits inasmuch as it indicates the difficulty of *asserting* an *objective* fundamental difference between these characters. What changes is the observer-narrator-character's perspective of them. There is indeed no *substantial* modification in Machado's fiction in his last novel such as the traditional view wants to believe. But Gledson fails to credit the evolution of the life-views and to capture the density of Aires's perspective.

4. Of course, the issue may be raised by a reader such as Gledson. I do not think, however, that it makes the novel more interesting. I think that the skeptical reading is more interesting than the dogmatic one. Furthermore, reading the novel in terms of duality and betrayal is to move backwards to *Epitaph,* losing sight of the evolution of Machadian fiction through *Dom Casmurro* to *Esau and Jacob* and *Counselor Ayres' Memorial.*

5. "[E]vite l'impossibilité logique qu'il y aurait à vouloir affirmer simultanément deux énoncés contradictoires, conduit à préciser en quel sens, de quelle manière, dans quelles limites, chacun d'entre eux peut être affirmé" (Caujolle-Zaslawsky 376).

6. "[L]a sophistique est avant tout une doctrine d'action. . . . Pyrrhon est par-dessus tout indifférent ou apathique; . . . il se laisse vivre. C'est une doctrine de vieillard" (Brochard 46).

7. "Les voyages sont une école de scepticisme" (Brochard 42).

8. "Timon nous représente Pyrrhon comme évitant les discussions. . . . Le même caractère se retrouve d'ailleurs chez les successeurs immédiats de Pyrrhon. Ce qu'on voit reparaître le plus souvent dans les fragments mutilés de Timon, c'est l'horreur des discussions vaines et interminables

... il leur reproche sans cesse leurs criailleries et leurs disputes, surtout leur morgue et leurs prétentions" (Brochard 66).

9. "Ce n'est qu'après avoir fait en quelque sorte le tour des doctrines philosophiques, comme il avait fait le tour du monde, qu'il s'est reposé dans l'indifférence et l'apathie, non parce qu'il ignorait les sciences humaines, mais parce qu'il les connaissait trop" (Brochard 75).

10. I analyze the connections between Machado's skepticism and the literary form of his novels in which skepticism is exhibited in "Machado de Assis."

Appendix

1. The English edition says "Humanity," but the correct translation is "Humanitas."

2. The English translation—"additional converts to Humanitism were knocking at his door" (E 189)—is unacceptable.

Works Cited

Annas, Julia. "Doing without Objective Values: Ancient and Modern Strategies." *The Norms of Nature.* Ed. M. Schofield and G. Striker. Cambridge: Cambridge UP, 1985. 3–29.

Annas, Julia, and Jonathan Barnes. *The Modes of Scepticism.* Cambridge: Cambridge UP, 1985.

Barnes, Jonathan. "The Beliefs of a Pyrrhonist." *Proceedings of the Cambridge Philosophical Society.* Cambridge, Eng.: Cambridge Philosophical Society, 1982. 208: 1–29.

Barreto Filho. *Introdução a Machado de Assis.* Rio de Janeiro: Agir, 1947.

Barros, Roque S. M. de. *A evolução do pensamento de Pereira Barreto.* São Paulo: Grijalbo/USP, 1967.

Berger, Peter, with Hansfried Kellner. "Marriage and the Construction of Reality." *Facing up to Modernity.* By Peter Berger. New York: Basic, 1977. 5–22.

Bett, Richard. "Carneades' Distinction between Assent and Approval." *The Monist* 73 (1990): 3–20.

Bosi, Alfredo. "A máscara e a fenda." *Machado de Assis.* Ed. A. Bosi et al. São Paulo: Ática, 1982. 437–57.

Bouwsma, William J. "The Two Faces of Humanism: Stoicism and Augustinianism in Renaissance Thought." *Itinerarium Italicum.* Leiden: E. J. Brill, 1975. 3–60.

Brochard, Victor. *Les Sceptiques grecs.* Paris: J. Vrin, 1969.

Burnyeat, Myles. "Can the Sceptic Live His Scepticism?" *Doubt and Dogmatism: Studies in Hellenistic Epistemology.* Ed. M. Schofield, M. Burnyeat, and J. Barnes. Oxford: Clarendon, 1980. 20–53.

Caldwell, Helen. *The Brazilian Othello of Machado de Assis: A Study of "Dom Casmurro."* Berkeley and Los Angeles: U of California P, 1960.

Caujolle-Zaslawsky, Françoise. "La Méthode des sceptiques grecs." *Revue Philosophique de la France et de l'Etranger* 172.2 (1982): 371–81.

Cohen, Avner. "Sextus Empiricus: Scepticism as a Therapy." *The Philosophical Forum* 15 (1984): 405–24.

Coutinho, Afrânio. *A filosofia na obra de Machado de Assis.* Rio de Janeiro: São José, 1959.

Dixon, Paul B. *Retired Dreams: "Dom Casmurro," Myth and Modernity.* West Lafayette: Purdue UP, 1989.

Ellis, Keith. "Technique and Ambiguity in *Dom Casmurro*." *Hispania* 45 (1962): 436–40.

Erasmus, Desiderius. *The Praise of Folly.* Trans. Hoyt H. Hudson. Princeton: Princeton UP, 1941.

Faoro, Raimundo. *A pirâmide e o trapézio.* São Paulo: Nacional, 1974.

Frede, Michael. "The Sceptic's Two Kinds of Assent." *Philosophy in History.* Ed. R. Rorty, J. B. Schneewind, and Q. Skinner. Cambridge: Cambridge UP, 1984. 255–78.

Gill, Anne-Marie. "Dom Casmurro and Lolita: Machado among the Metafictionists." *Luso-Brazilian Review* 24 (1987): 17–26.

Gledson, John. *The Deceptive Realism of Machado de Assis: A Dissenting Interpretation of "Dom Casmurro."* Liverpool Monographs in Hispanic Studies. Liverpool: Cairns,1984.

———. "The Last Betrayal of Machado de Assis: *Memorial de Aires.*" *Portuguese Studies* 1 (1985): 121–50.

Kinnear, J. C. "Machado de Assis: To Believe or Not to Believe?" *Modern Language Review* 71 (1976): 54–65.

La Rochefoucauld, François, duc de. *Maxims.* Trans. Leonard Tancock. London and New York: Penguin, 1958.

Long, A. A., and David Sedley. *The Hellenistic Philosophers.* Cambridge: Cambridge UP, 1987.

Machado de Assis, Joaquim Maria. *Contos esparsos.* Org. R. Magalhães Júnior. Rio de Janeiro: Edições de Ouro, 1966.

———. *Contos esquecidos.* Org. R. Magalhães Júnior. Rio de Janeiro: Edições de Ouro, 1966.

———. *Contos recolhidos.* Org. R. Magalhães Júnior. Rio de Janeiro: Edições de Ouro, 1966.

———. *Counselor Ayres' Memorial.* Trans. Helen Caldwell. Berkeley and Los Angeles: U of California P, 1972.

———. *The Devil's Church and Other Stories.* Trans. Jack Schmitt and Lorie Ishimatsu. Austin: U of Texas P, 1977; Manchester: Carcanet, 1985.

———. *Dom Casmurro.* Trans. Helen Caldwell. Berkeley and Los Angeles: U of California P, 1966.

———. *Epitaph of a Small Winner.* Trans. William L. Grossman. New York: Noonday, 1952.

———. *Esau and Jacob.* Trans. Helen Caldwell. Berkeley and Los Angeles: U of California P, 1965.

————. *The Hand and the Glove*. Trans. Albert I. Bagby, Jr. Lexington: UP of Kentucky, 1970.

————. *Iaiá Garcia*. Trans. Albert I. Bagby, Jr. Lexington: UP of Kentucky, 1977.

————. *Obra completa*. Org. Afrânio Coutinho. 3 vols. Rio de Janeiro: Editora José Aguilar, 1962.

————. *Obras completas*. 31 vols. Rio de Janeiro and São Paulo: W. M. Jackson, 1937–58.

Maia Neto, José R. "Machado de Assis: Scepticism and Literature." *Latin American Literary Review* 18 (1990): 26–35.

Massa, Jean-Michel. "La bibliothèque de Machado de Assis." *Revista do Livro* 21–22 (1961): 195–238.

Meyer, Augusto. *Machado de Assis*. Rio de Janeiro: Simões, 1952.

Montaigne, Michel de. *The Complete Works of Montaigne*. Trans. Donald M. Frame. Stanford: Stanford UP, 1958.

Nunes, Maria L. *The Craft of an Absolute Winner: Characterization and Narratology in the Novels of Machado de Assis*. Westport, CT, and London: Greenwood, 1983.

————. "Time and Allegory in Machado de Assis' *Esau and Jacob*." *Latin American Literary Review* 11 (1982): 27–38.

Nussbaum, Martha. "Sceptic Purgatives: Therapeutic Arguments in Ancient Scepticism." *Journal of the History of Philosophy* 29 (1991): 521–57.

O'Loughlin, Michael. *The Garlands of Repose—the Literary Celebration of Civic and Retired Leisure: The Traditions of Homer and Virgil, Horace and Montaigne*. Chicago and London: U of Chicago P, 1978.

Paim, Antônio. *História das idéias filosóficas no Brasil*. São Paulo: Convívio, 1987.

Pascal, Blaise. *Pensées*. Trans. A. J. Krailsheimer. Lafuma ed. London and New York: Penguin, 1988.

Pereira, Oswaldo P. "Sobre o que aparece." *Revista Latinoamericana de Filosofía* 17 (1991): 195–229.

Popkin, Richard H. *The History of Scepticism from Erasmus to Spinoza*. Berkeley and Los Angeles: U of California P, 1979.

————. "Scepticism, Old and New." *The Third Force in Seventeenth Century Philosophy*. Leiden: E. J. Brill, 1992. 236–45.

Pratt, Mary L. *Toward a Speech Act Theory of Literary Discourse*. Bloomington and London: Indiana UP, 1977.

Schwarz, Roberto. *Um mestre na periferia do capitalismo: Machado de Assis*. São Paulo: Duas Cidades, 1990.

Sedley, David. "The Motivation of Greek Scepticism." *The Sceptical Tradition*. Ed. M. Burnyeat. Berkeley, Los Angeles, and London: U of California P, 1983. 9–81.

Sextus Empiricus. *Against the Mathematicians*. Trans. R. G. Bury. Loeb Classical Library. London: Heinemann; Cambridge: Harvard UP, 1933–49.

———. *Outlines of Pyrrhonism*. Trans. R. G. Bury. Loeb Classical Library. London: Heinemann; Cambridge: Harvard UP, 1933–49.

Striker, Gisella. "Ataraxia: Happiness as Tranquility." *The Monist* 73 (1990): 97–110.

Index